The
Siege
of
Gibraltar

# The
# Siege
# of
# Gibraltar
## 1779-1783

## T. H. McGuffie

Dufour Editions
Philadelphia 1965

LIBRARY OF CONGRESS CATALOG CARD NUMBER: 64–25508

*First published 1965*
© T. H. MᶜGUFFIE, 1965


MADE AND PRINTED IN GREAT BRITAIN FOR
DUFOUR EDITIONS

'. . . these are deeds which should not pass away,
And names that must not wither, though the earth
Forgets her empires with a just decay. . . .'

*Byron, 'Childe Harold's Pilgrimage'*
*(Canto the third, LXVII)*

# Contents

# List of Illustrations

## The Plates

## Maps and Plans

The drawing on the title-page is taken from the crest of the Suffolk Regiment
(12th Regiment of Foot). The motto of the Rock, ' *Montis Insignia Calpe* ',
which appears beneath the Castle and Key of Gibraltar, has been omitted.

# Acknowledgment

Generous help has been given by many people and institutions in the writing of this book. As always when the Public Record Office has to be consulted, the co-operation and quick efficiency of the staff there must draw grateful thanks. The Director and Chief Librarian of the Royal United Service Institution, Brigadier John Stephenson, with his staff, has been of immense help, along with the Librarian of the War Office, Mr D. W. King, and his staff. Many regimental museum curators, especially Lieutenant-Colonel D. V. W. Wakeley of the Dorset Military Museum and Captain A. J. Wilson of the Royal Highland Fusiliers, Brigadier R. G. Thurburn of the Army Museum Ogilby Trust and Mr E. F. E. Ryan of the Gibraltar Garrison Library have also been of assistance, along with many fellow members of the Society for Army Historical Research. Particular thanks are due to Captain R. G. Hollies-Smith of the Parker Gallery for advice and help in suggesting and supplying illustrations.

T. H. McGUFFIE

The Author and Publishers wish to thank the following for the illustrations appearing in this book: the Cincinnati Art Museum for fig 16; the National Gallery for fig 1; the National Maritime Museum for figs 3, 13, 15, 23 and 25; the National Portrait Gallery for figs 12 and 22; the Parker Gallery for figs 2, 4, 10, 11, 17, 18, 21, 24 and 26; the Public Record Office for figs 6, 19 and 20.

Figs 5, 8, 9 and 14 and the tailpieces on pages 102, 138 and 167 are reproduced from John Spilsbury, *A Journal of the Siege of Gibraltar*, and fig 7 from John Drinkwater, *A History of the Late Siege of Gibraltar*.

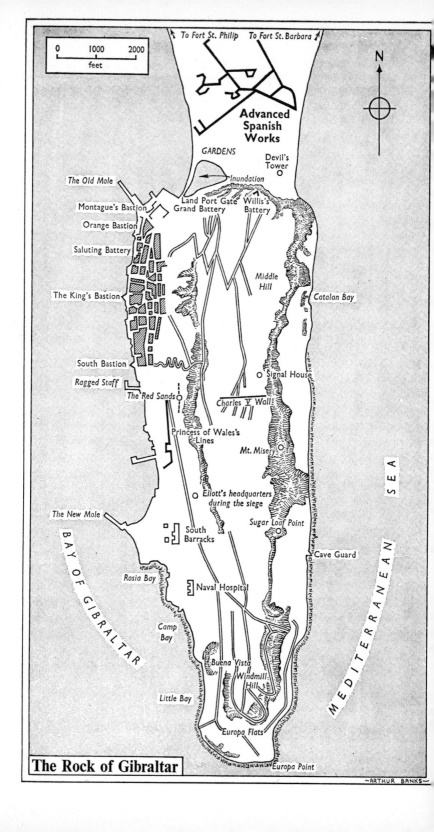

The Rock of Gibraltar

# I

---

# *The Rock*

The Rock of Gibraltar is a bold and mountainous promontory projecting due southwards from the Spanish province of Andalusia. It is
nearly three miles long from north to south and some three-quarters of a
mile in breadth; a flat, sandy isthmus, a mile long but only half a mile
wide, and never more than ten feet above sea level, joins it on the
northern side to the low hills and rocky crags of the mainland. The
most southerly part, Europa Point, is of flat water-worn rocks; but the
Rock itself is an immense shelf of limestone, sandstone and marble,
tipped out of the sea and tilted at such an angle that the eastern front,
facing the broad Mediterranean, like that to the north, is of impressive
sheerness and height. The loftiest point of the long and jagged crest
rises almost to 1,400 feet above sea level. The base of this irregular cliff,
frowning over the eastern seas, is embedded in shining banks of sand,
the accumulation of the ages, heaped against the rocky face. The
northern front, looked at from the isthmus, rises abruptly from the sand
with great magnificence, climbing upwards to a narrow apex, its steep
slopes and precipices commanding the restricted approaches from the
landward side. The whole gives the impression of absolute domination
over its approaches, looming threateningly over all who draw near it,
whether on land from the north or by sea from the east.

On the west, where the lower edge of this complicated slab of geology
slides into the sea, the town of Gibraltar has been built. Part of it
climbs up the lower slopes beside the water, but the tortured nature of
the crags, torn with fissures and pot-holes, confines all building into a
long narrow strip along the shore. The houses face over the Bay of
Algeciras to the town of that name, five miles away across the water,
twice that distance by land round the curve of this sheltered stretch,
with its anchorages shielded from all but the most exceptional gales.
However, wild winds and savage storms in the days of sailing ships

were just as frequent in these seas as they are today, and were infinitely more difficult to meet successfully. Nowadays docks and moles provide good cover, projecting so far outwards that the vessels have almost as much space in which to anchor or moor as that covered by the Rock itself, while a long airstrip, projecting westwards into the sea towards Algeciras from the isthmus close under the North Face, further extends the facilities of the base. In the time of the Great Siege with which this book is concerned there were two short moles: only the Old Mole at the north-western corner of the town's defences and the New Mole over a mile away to the south broke the natural outlines of this enormous heap. But even today, with all its modern accretions and arabesques of slipways, wharves, docks, detached moles, artificial berths and airfield built out on the rocky foreshore and shallow waters of its western edge, the Rock still preserves its startling appearance. Formidable in aspect, it looks what it is: a natural stronghold. From sea or land or air, it stands in isolation. Joined to Europe by an insignificant thread, Gibraltar is an incomparable fortress.

As a citadel, Gibraltar has two great handicaps: its only fresh water supply is from its rainfall; and the nature of its surface is so torn and rocky that but a very small proportion of a garrison's foodstuffs can be raised on its own soil. There are no springs of pure fresh water, but the Spaniards, its first possessors, early constructed an aqueduct and fountain to contain rainwater, and as the town grew so did the number of tanks and cisterns attached to newly-built houses. The rainy season lasts usually from September or October until April or May. December and January are the most generally violent and wet months, with heavy rain, high winds and storms of thunder and vivid lightning. From the signal points and outlooks on the various summits of the Rock snow can be seen lying for long winter months on the mountain tops of Granada to the north or on the summits of the Great Atlas range over 200 miles away in northern Africa. Snow falls but rarely in Gibraltar itself and ice is seldom seen. Although rainfall in Gibraltar fluctuates violently between 19 and over 65 inches a year, the average of 35 inches usually supplies all that is needed. Water is often short, and more than half of the population in the eighteenth century had to buy any fresh water they used; but it never failed to reach the minimum needs, when added to the brackish supplies obtainable from wells. In the summer months, however, when the temperature in the sun can reach over 150° and there is no rainfall, water became often so scarce or expensive that the resulting uncleanliness of persons and the filth of their surroundings made life vulnerable to outbreaks of yellow fever and typhus. Mortality among children in Gibraltar was often extremely high, even in peace-time. The prevalence of an easterly wind, known as the Levanter, needs particular notice. Damp, hot and sticky, it is often accompanied by a dense, lowering mass of cloud which clings to the summit of the Rock, precipitates a clammy and unpleasant moisture and makes people bad-tempered and irritable. Mists and fogs also occur, which obscure visibility so much that, although the distance from Gibraltar to the coasts of Africa is less than that between Dover and Cap Gris-Nez, one is as useless as the other for a year-long maintenance of close watch. Without friendly ships patrolling at sea, in war-time an alert or lucky enemy may always manage to slip through unseen.

Far more serious than difficulties over fresh water are those con-cerned with growing food. Only a few acres (79 in 1862) of the total area of two-and-a-quarter square miles of the colony are cultivable. Steep rocky slopes, dry and unfruitful soil, bare rock faces, gullies, precipices and the burning unclouded summer sunshine make regular crop-raising impossible on any scale. There were few trees or shrubs, except palmettos, to be seen. Only on the neutral ground of the isthmus could garden vegetables be sown with any hope of success. Whenever advanced works of the Spanish attackers forced the British occupiers of Gibraltar to relinquish these profitable gardens, many new plots to the south of the town were enclosed and cleared. Soil was collected and carefully distributed and in the winter months roots and garden-stuff became available for those of the reduced population who either grew them or could afford to buy them. But often privation reached the point of starvation, when close blockade reduced supplies of meat, flour and fruits, all usually imported from Spain or Africa. Fish, it is true, were abundant in the nearby waters. Hake, cod, mullet and mackerel were taken in vast numbers when the weather and the enemy permitted. But hunger was always the most threatening menace in war-time, provided disease could be kept within limits.

The saying 'All history is geography' is particularly applicable to Gibraltar, where the geographical background and physical facts are vital. Gibraltar itself, as a natural phenomenon, is dramatic. Situated at the mouth of that cradle of Western civilisation, the Mediterranean Sea, it has been well known to mariners for centuries. On maps and charts, it looks as though it stands sentinel over some of the world's most vital trade-routes; or as an obstacle or impediment. Attached physically to Spain, its occupation by an alien power is provoking to national pride. All Spanish governments had longed for its recovery in the days after the invading Arabs occupied it in A.D. 712 and named it after their leader, Tarif Ebn Zarca, as 'the mountain of Tarif': 'Gibel-Tarif', quickly corrupted to 'Gibraltar'. Its loss to the British in 1704 was even more galling. Over 1,100 miles distant from Great Britain, separated from home ports by long stretches of the Atlantic presumably dominated by the vast hostile fleets of France and Spain, the fortunes of this outpost were watched breathlessly by all Europe in the long years of its Great Siege which lasted from June 1779 until the spring of 1783. Even those Whigs who wished the Americans success in their breakaway from the British Crown found their feelings engaged on behalf of their fellow countrymen who held Gibraltar with such spirit and energy for so long against the full strength of two great empires. The 13 colonies might go, and good luck to them. But to keep Gibraltar, even though its preservation might conceivably have been one of the causes of the loss of Yorktown and the relinquishment of all attempt to subdue America, was a sufficient salve for honour.

The preservation of Gibraltar for Great Britain during the War of American Independence was a mighty feat of arms. The aim of this book is to tell the story in terms of what we know today and to revive once more the memories of those men, at both ends of the isthmus, whether British or French or Spanish or their allies, who fought so long and so bravely to achieve ends which they thought worthwhile and noble.

In July 1704 a large fleet of English and Dutch warships with transports containing troops commanded by the Prince of Hesse-Darmstadt, all under Admiral Sir George Rooke, arrived off Gibraltar. They had just completed a pointless cruise in the Mediterranean, where they had failed to bring the French to action or to perform any effective action in support of the Austrian Archduke Charles, the allied candidate for the throne of Spain. Rooke held a council of war, where it was decided to make a sudden attempt on Gibraltar, then held by forces supporting the rival French claimant, the Bourbon Philip, Duke of Anjou and grandson of Louis XIV. A brisk bombardment from the sea, the landing of 1,800 troops on the isthmus and a spirited landing from ships' boats secured part of the New Mole. After a very brave defence of three days, the Spanish Governor, Don Diego Salinas, capitulated on 24 July 1704; he and his garrison were granted the honours of war, which they well deserved. The highest estimate of the defenders put their numbers at 150, an immensely strong force of warships and men had been launched at them, and they had inflicted over 320 casualties.

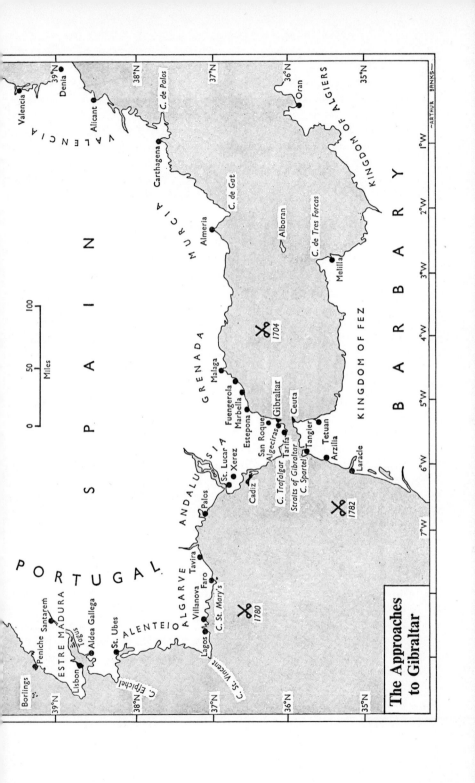

The Approaches
to Gibraltar

Although the official surrender was made to Charles' forces, Rooke ordered the Imperial Standard which had been hoisted to be pulled down and the Royal Standard of Great Britain to be raised in its place. The town was occupied in the name of Queen Anne, and 1,800 English seamen were landed to secure it, with the Prince of Hesse as governor.

It was a remarkable achievement, this swift overwhelming of an immensely strong fortress. Without doubt the Spanish Government was to blame. Sheer neglect and inefficiency gave Rooke an opportunity which was taken swiftly and with great good fortune. He received little credit for it. Perhaps he deserved none, for he was not a conspicuously vigorous or successful admiral. In the hard and bloody battle he fought shortly after capturing Gibraltar, off Malaga on 13 August 1704, he had one of the largest fleets in action ever commanded by an English Admiral: over 50 ships against a rather similar number of Frenchmen. But the result was indecisive, and on neither side was any ship taken. Rooke sailed his battered vessels back to Gibraltar; which then for the first time and so shortly after its capture proved its value as a base and refuge. He stayed there for eight days, refitting his ships and landing men and provisions for the defence of the town, before leaving for England.

The Spanish Government reacted immediately to this unexpected loss and moved at once to recover Gibraltar. Operations on the frontiers of Portugal were abandoned, and the troops marched off southwards. Some 9,000 Spaniards and 3,000 Frenchmen were assembled, supported by a strong French squadron of a dozen ships-of-the-line and seven frigates. On 9 October 1704 the enemy began digging trenches; they opened fire, from a three-gun battery, on the 15th. For the Spanish this was acting with the speed of light.

Although the inhabitants of Gibraltar at the capitulation had been given the opportunity of remaining in their homes, provided they would take an oath of allegiance to the Archduke Charles, most of them deserted the town. According to the Spanish authorities, the British attacks had been marked by pillage, the violation of women and the burning of churches. Many of these refugees stayed in San Roque, seven miles away on the Spanish mainland. The new garrison, now consisting of about 3,000 men under the Prince of Hesse, occupied the deserted town, repaired the damage caused by their own bombardment, built some new bastions along the sea-front to the west, installed 20 guns to defend the Land Port Gate at the northern end and formed an inundation which confined the approaches to this front to a narrow strip between the waters of the bay and this fresh and impassable obstacle.

At the end of October 1704, 500 Spanish volunteers crept round the eastern side of the Rock and scaled it. There they surprised and massacred or captured the guard at Middle Hill. However, they were isolated and unsupported and were finally overwhelmed, with the loss of 160 killed or driven over the precipices to their deaths. In January 1705 some desultory attacks were made at various points which had been weakened by bombardment from the batteries raised opposite the Land Port Gate. But, although there were critical moments when food and medicines were short and disease rife and the total healthy strength of the garrison down to 1,300, reinforcements and food always arrived by sea in time to save them. Storm, rain and disease also scourged the besiegers. Whenever they put in any strong attacks across the open spaces of the isthmus their casualties were heavy. Even when a celebrated French Marshal, Tessé, arrived to conduct the siege he found sea transport uncertain, land supplies inadequate, Spanish roads impassable, and the British indefatigable in keeping their defences manned and in the quick repair of any damage. Sickness was everywhere and any attempt at large-scale assault impossible. The siege was raised in April 1705 after 70,000 shot and 8,000 shell had been thrown against the land fortifications of Gibraltar. Some thousands of soldiers had perished, most of them by disease, caused by harsh weather and scarcity of provisions. The men had been left destitute, unpaid and despairing, their magazines empty and the cannon worn out with incessant firing. British losses came to about 400 men.

When peace came at Utrecht, in 1713, although Bourbon Philip retained the Throne of Spain, Gibraltar was yielded absolutely to Great Britain. His Catholic Majesty handed over all claims to 'the full and entire propriety of the Town and Castle of Gibraltar together with the Port, fortifications and forts belonging thereto. And he gives up the said propriety to be held and enjoyed absolutely with all manner of right for ever without any exception or impediment whatsoever.' It was making the best of a bad job.

The capture of Gibraltar in 1704 and the recognition of this fact by the Spaniards in 1713 did not mean either that Great Britain was absolutely determined to keep it or that Spain was reconciled to its loss. At various times, in 1715, in 1720 and in 1721 negotiations took place (sometimes initiated by Great Britain) in which the possible return of Gibraltar to the Spanish crown was seriously discussed.

During 1726 it was rumoured that a secret treaty between the King of Spain and the Emperor promised Gibraltar's restoration, if necessary by force. Diplomatic denials were not believed, and the British Parliament voted men and money to strengthen the national defences. In February 1727 a Spanish army 12,000 strong assembled near San Roque and batteries were built on the western beach within half cannon-shot of the Land Port Gate. A polite enquiry as to their purpose by the British Lieutenant-Governor, General Clayton, brought an arrogant reply from the Spanish Commander, Count las Torres. Firing began and a new siege opened.

Gibraltar by this time was a very different place from that defended over 20 years earlier by the Prince of Hesse. Several well-gunned works had been built on the North Face of the Rock; notably that called Willis's batteries. Lines had been extended and strengthened and the inundation made an even more formidable obstacle to any assault planned to take place due south along the narrow sands of the isthmus. The town itself was beginning to acquire the odd yet strong 'London look' which is still so remarkable a feature. The drinking shops bore such titles as *The Queen's Head, The Tower of London,* or *Ye Old Coal-Hole.* There were other evidences, now thankfully gone: a pillory, a 'whirligig' for nagging women, public floggings. There were also newspapers. Trade had flourished, for Gibraltar served as an entrepôt for British cloth and attracted both supplies of Spanish merino wool and of oil used in cloth manufacture. Though still on a small scale, the ports of Tangier and Tetuan in North Africa, of Leghorn in Italy, of Genoa, Malaga and Cadiz, of Mogador, were being used by traders either based on Gibraltar or using the harbour as a halting place. The new inhabitants of this expanding town owed no allegiance to Spain. Their interests were those of the British, even though they themselves might be Genoese, Moors or Jews (though the presence of these last two groups had been specifically forbidden in the Treaty of Utrecht).

The siege of 1727 proved a less serious affair than that of 1704–5. It was all over by June, when an armistice was signed. At no time did the Spaniards try to interrupt Gibraltar's sea communications and British warships bringing in supplies used to cruise up and down off the seaward ends of the Spanish lines, enfilading their trenches and batteries until new defensive works were made. British troops rose from 1,500 to 5,500 (including the 1st Regiment of Foot Guards). There was a great deal of heavy gunfire across the isthmus, resulting in the bursting of no fewer than 70 cannon and 30 mortars on the British side. Many of these guns were comparatively small. Willis's mounted six-pounders and other works threw three-pounder balls. After a fortnight's heavy bombardment in May, when 92 Spanish guns and 72 mortars were in constant play and 700 shot were thrown against the northern defences every hour, the Spanish weapons also deteriorated. Many iron ordnance burst and brass guns drooped at the muzzle. But a plain, straightforward bombardment on one limited section of the defences, unsupported by assault or even threats by land or sea, was perfectly useless. And when the Governor, Lord Portmore, had perfected his own arrangements to bombard the enemy's lines, he blew the Spanish batteries and trenches to pieces in a few hours. During the course of these 17 weeks of bombardment, the garrison fired away nearly 53,000 rounds, most of them 12-pounders or smaller. British casualties totalled under 400 when the fighting stopped; and of the 69 dead many had perished through the bursting of their own cannon. The only new move by the Spanish was a useless attempt to dig a mine in the North Face, using the limestone crevices and coves below Willis's as an aid; the English knew all about it and used to harass the sentries with musketry fire; but it was never a serious threat. The number of Spanish casualties was unknown, but was probably about 3,000, including those dead of sickness (much the largest figure).

Between 1727 and 1779 Britain and Spain were at war on several occasions, but Gibraltar was never seriously threatened. In fact the chief danger to British occupation was diplomatic. Gibraltar was a useful pawn in any negotiations between the two countries. After the loss of Minorca to the French in 1756, William Pitt the elder indulged in some equivocal exchanges on the future of Gibraltar. By this time the fortifications of the Rock had been widely extended. The two sieges had taught the British many lessons, as had their own lucky capture of the place. The old Spanish religious buildings had been turned to new strange uses: the nunnery of Santa Clara was converted into a barracks, one convent into a storehouse, another into the home of the senior naval officer in Gibraltar. The Franciscan convent, which was finely placed above the town, with a wide view over the Bay of Algeciras, became the official residence of the British Governor. There were about 3,000 civilian dwellers in the town. A third of them were Jewish, engaged in dealing, as shop-keepers or money-lenders; they had their own synagogue and openly practised their religion. Those Genoese who were not traders and shop-keepers fished or followed an industrious life as gardeners and horticulturists. Pitt knew all this. He must have been aware that Gibraltar, whatever it might have been in the past and no matter how much it seemed to belong by nature to the owners of the Spanish mainland, by 1757 was an anglicised British colony in a sense which could never be applied to the settlements on the African mainland or in India.

Yet Pitt in August 1757 definitely authorised Sir Benjamin Keene, British Ambassador in Madrid, to make a forthright offer of Gibraltar to Spain in exchange for an alliance between the two countries and the subsequent restoration to Great Britain of Minorca. Owing, however, to the intense desire of King Ferdinand to remain neutral in the struggle, the transaction came to nothing. In later years, Pitt was to come forward as one of the most active advocates of keeping Gibraltar. When war broke out between Great Britain and Spain, in January 1762, the fighting had barely another twelve months to run, and all proved immensely successful and profitable to British arms. Havana was returned to Spain. But Minorca was restored to Great Britain and nothing further was heard about Gibraltar being handed back to the Spanish.

To the Spanish royal family the hope of one day regaining Gibraltar remained a firm and determined wish. King Ferdinand was succeeded in 1759 by King Charles III of Spain. He and his advisers, Grimaldi and the Count d'Aranda, reformed the Spanish army and navy, introduced new tactical and disciplinary systems in their forces, and gathered large revenues aimed at financing a successful war. With Great Britain hard put to it by the summer of 1779 to make head against the Americans and French, it seemed to the Spaniards that this was the one supreme moment at which to recover their lost possession.

# 2

# *The Fortification of Gibraltar*

On 29 May 1777 Lieutenant-General George Augustus Eliott sat down in his office at his headquarters in Gibraltar and wrote to the Secretary of State for the Southern Department announcing his safe arrival on the 25th, 'in the evening', to take command of what he termed 'this important fortress'. The soundest seeming apple may be useless if it has disease or a maggot at its heart. In most matters of military importance the quality of the immediate leadership is vital. It will therefore be well to see what kind of man was this new Governor of Gibraltar.

George Augustus Eliott was born on Christmas Day, 1717. When he arrived at Gibraltar he was thus in his sixtieth year; certainly not a young man, and certainly past the age at which new and glorious military distinction is usually achieved. He was the seventh son of the third baronet of Stobs in Roxburghshire, the middle county of the three Scottish Border shires which confront the English northern marches of Cumberland and Northumberland. Like many fellow-countrymen of good family, young Eliott received his early education as a boy in Holland, at the University of Leyden. A younger son, he had to earn his own living; and, as with many impoverished Scots, he became a soldier. By special permission he was allowed to study at the French military academy of La Fère in Picardy, which, founded by Vauban in the seventeenth century, was supposed to provide the best military education of the age. When still only 17 years old (they started early in those days and were not ridden by age and academic regulations) Eliott saw service as a volunteer in the campaigns of 1735 and 1736. He was intelligent and ambitious. One route to high commissioned rank open to hard-working young officers lay through the technical services, then in their infancy. The Royal Artillery was not founded until 1716, the year before Eliott's birth; the Royal Engineers were not to exist under that name until 1856, but in 1717 military engineers had become a section of the Ordnance Office. They were educated, since education was absolutely necessary, at Woolwich, where Eliott took a course of instruction as a field engineer. Not until 1757, however, were engineer officers directly appointed by receiving their commissions as such from the king. In young Eliott's day it was the practice for field engineers to hold a normal, respectable commission in a regular cavalry or infantry regiment; and as one of his father's brothers, James Eliott, commanded a body known as the 2nd Horse Grenadier Guards, he became a cornet in that regiment in 1739. With this regiment, after serving as adjutant and progressing by purchase to the rank of captain, Eliott saw the battles of Dettingen (where he was wounded) and Fontenoy. In 1748, just before the end of the war, Eliott married a Devonshire heiress, Anne, daughter of the last Sir Francis Drake of Buckland Abbey. He rose, also by purchase, to the rank of lieutenant-colonel in 1754. In his campaigning, Eliott had attracted the attention and personal liking of that dour and strange man, George II, who made him his aide-de-camp in 1756. By this time Eliott was sufficiently firmly fixed in security in the regular army to relinquish his standing as a military engineer and proceed along purely orthodox lines. Besides his wide experience and specialised knowledge he was a fluent speaker of French and German.

On 10 March 1759 Eliott was selected to raise a new regiment of horse to be trained as light cavalry. This unit, the first of its kind in the British army, later became the 15th Light Dragoons and then the 15th Hussars. Eliott trained and commanded this regiment personally in the field, which was not always the case with full colonels. Their activities brought them one of the first battle honours ever granted to a British regiment. At Emsdorff they captured five battalions of French infantry, complete with their 16 colours and nine guns, and were permitted to carry the name of this victory embroidered on their colour.

Eliott himself was promoted major-general in June 1759 and commanded the whole of the cavalry in an attack on the French coast in 1761. Next year he had the good fortune to be selected as second-in-command of the expedition to Cuba, which resulted in the capture of Havana. This brought him great riches, for the prize-money totalled over three-quarters of a million. Eliott's share was over £25,000 in a single instalment; his chief, Lord Albemarle, acquired over £122,000. Prize-money was one military reward of virtue often overlooked by later historians, but never by the potential recipients. One result of

Eliott's settled military and financial position was that he bought himself an estate, a very handsome house called Heathfield, in Sussex.

After peace came in 1763, Eliott was not idle, but held no appointment of note until late in 1774 shortly after he had lost his wife. He was appointed commander-in-chief in Ireland. This, however, was not to his liking, for he found so many petty interferences with his own authority that before he had unpacked his baggage he had written home and asked to be recalled. This was granted. His next official appointment was the command of Gibraltar.

Although Eliott got on well with George II, he was not apparently a man with any personal charm. As a young man, while still a captain in the Horse Grenadier Guards, one acquaintance remembered him described by a fellow-officer as 'singular and austere in his manner', though an able officer; 'sour' and 'intractable' were other adjectives applied to him. He was capable of generous praise and an occasional courteous gesture. When his regiment of light dragoons was reviewed in Hyde Park after the Seven Years War, the standards they had captured at Emsdorff were presented to the king. George asked what mark of his favour he could bestow worthy of the regiment's deserts, and Eliott replied that they all would be proud if they could be termed a 'Royal' regiment, and went on to declare that such a distinction would be a sufficient reward for himself also. There were many occasions during the Great Siege, too, when a gift for straightforward dealing caused his actions to shine with exquisite courtesy.

Abstemious Eliott certainly was. His only drink was water. He never touched wine or spirits, or animal food; he ate a purely vegetable diet. An early riser and late in going to bed, he never slept more than four hours at a time. A stern but just disciplinarian, he was a man indifferent to the niceties of military parade and etiquette. During the course of the Great Siege, and afterwards, he was often spoken of with deep respect, even veneration, as far as his military qualities were concerned; but rarely with warmth or affection. Rather like Arthur Wellesley, Eliott inspired confidence, with little cordiality or personal devotion. In person he was tall, upright, well built, robust and solid but not graceful of figure. His features were somewhat heavy, impassive, close-mouthed; a man without any of the sparkling (and often meretricious) attributes of 'the born leader of men'. But of his unflagging devotion to duty and the task in hand there was never any question.

Such was the 59-year-old widower and regular soldier who in the summer of 1777 began to take a long careful look at the condition of Gibraltar.

The actual state of the defences of Gibraltar had caused concern some years before Eliott's arrival there. British people and governments on the whole despised the ability of Spanish leadership and regarded this particular foe with even more arrogance than they displayed towards France. Even before the close of the Seven Years War the lines and bastions which had withstood the assaults of 1727 had been allowed to decay. Very few guns were mounted. The parapets in many places were crumbling to dust and the ditches at the north angle, near the approach between the sea and the inundation, were choked with rubbish. Magazines and provision stores were nearly empty and the neglected ammunition was scanty. The main powder magazine was on a hill half a mile above the town, in full view from the sea and exposed to fire from hostile vessels. A commission was assembled by the Master General of the Ordnance at Westminster in 1769 to report upon these matters. It was held that any attack on the place across the isthmus, like those of 1705 and 1727, was certain to fail. The chief danger came from the sea, either from direct attack (which might be driven off if Gibraltar's fortifications were adequate) or from blockade and subsequent starvation (to be met by stores of food and ammunition). The usual garrison of the place consisted of some four or five foot regiments, almost always well under their official strength, totalling up to 4,000 men, but perhaps as low as 2,300; this was quite a high proportion of the British standing army in peace-time, which in 1764 totalled 45,000 in all, including the royal guards, all horse, foot and artillery, whether stationed in Great Britain, Ireland or the colonies. As the collapse of Minorca had shown in 1756, the stationing of weak garrisons in strong and tempting isolated fortresses was an invitation to an enterprising foe.

To be Governor of Gibraltar during the eighteenth century had its compensations from the financial point of view, but the usual tenure was short. After the Prince of Hesse-Darmstadt's initial governorship a dozen others filled the years until 1730. Then came two tenures lasting 19 years between them; another rapid succession of five from 1749 to 1755; and a further run of nine short governorships until Eliott's appointment. The official pay of the Governor of Gibraltar was, in 1742, £730 a year. But this was a trifle compared with the cash which various practices of long standing brought into his pocket. Peculation was rife and corruption and mismanagement of the works, constantly on foot in the fortress, brought in various cuts, rake-offs and regular payments which in 1729 were reckoned at £20,000 a year. One of the principal sources of income of the Governor was from the many grog shops wherein the garrison, bored and idle in peace-time, found their main solace.

To Eliott the attraction of pecuniary gain was not particularly powerful. Though he was never averse to getting money and was to prove tenacious in pursuing what he thought were legitimate cash rewards, he already was well-to-do. Nor were the peccadilloes of British soldiers unknown to this professional of over 40 years' experience. To him on arrival what mattered were men, supplies and material defences.

Eliott found in the place a most able officer of engineers. This was William Green, an Irishman who had been educated at the Royal Military Academy, Woolwich, first as a gunner and then as a military engineer. Like Eliott himself he had served competently in various campaigns in Europe and North America; and, shortly after being wounded on the Plains of Abraham at the taking of Quebec in 1759, had been promoted to lieutenant-colonel and appointed senior engineer at Gibraltar. He had given evidence before the 1769 commission, and the new fortifications which Eliott found there in 1777 had been built to Green's designs.

William Green has one special claim on the memories of all military engineers in the British army. Before 1772 the engineering workmen at Gibraltar, though under the command of soldiers, had been recruited from civilian mechanics. They were hired by the hour, were not amenable to discipline and were free to leave the Rock or their labours whenever they wished. Green had found that some of his most reliable workmen came from the various types of semi-skilled or skilled mechanics to be found occasionally in the ranks of the regiments stationed at Gibraltar. Artillerymen particularly were useful. Green therefore proposed that a corps of military artificers should be formed, and put the proposition before the Governor, who recommended the scheme to the Secretary of State. A warrant, dated 6 March 1772, authorised this force, known then as the 'Soldier-Artificer Company'. In later years they became 'Military Artificers' (1788), 'Royal Military Artificers' (1812) and Royal Sappers and Miners' (1813). In 1856 the men were amalgamated with their commissioned officers under the designation of 'Royal Engineers', one of the most active, intelligent and necessary of all corps.

William Green, lieutenant-colonel, became the first captain of the first company of 'soldier-artificers', recruited and formed at Gibraltar. He then proceeded to build several new works, the first of which was the King's Bastion. This formidable defence point, which was to be of immense value in the approaching siege, was built on the shore-line a few hundred yards south of the New Mole, before the middle of the then existing town and half-way between the Land Port Gate and the pier and wharf named the Ragged Staff. The foundation stone was laid in 1773 by Lieutenant-General Boyd, Deputy Governor of Gibraltar (another man of whom more will be heard). The King's Bastion commanded the whole stretch of foreshore between the New and Old Mole heads. It mounted 12 32-pounders and four 10-inch howitzers in front, with ten more guns and howitzers on its flanks; it also provided shelter in casemates for 800 men, with kitchens and ovens for cooking, so that this garrison could live in its own shelters and be self-sufficient under attack for as long as its supplies and stores lasted. It was completed under pressure, work going on from the morning gun to that of the evening on every day of the week, including Sundays. Handsomely made of cut stone, the King's Bastion made an impressive addition to the defence of Gibraltar.

Eliott consulted closely with both Green and Boyd, and then sent Green back to England to urge still further strengthening of the town. This was agreed to. The Soldier-Artificers were augmented and new regiments were sent to the Rock. These replaced some of the Hanoverian troops who had long been there and increased the available numbers; though they were still far short of the total of 8,000 men, which Eliott thought necessary and asked for in October 1777.

Meanwhile the new works went steadily ahead, while reports kept accumulating about Spanish fleet and troop movements, all indicating that some great project was afoot. In March 1778 Eliott wrote home to his Secretary of State (then Viscount Weymouth) mentioning that, while he had beef, pork, pease and butter for a bare five months, his flour, including biscuit and oatmeal, would only last three months. At the same time 19 Spanish line-of-battle ships were ready for sea at Cadiz, nine more were expected from Ferrol and other ports, and ten French vessels under d'Estaing were sailing for Cadiz from Toulon. In Seville arms and cannon were being gathered. Eliott believed that all these were ultimately destined for use against Gibraltar.

By the summer of 1779 the British defences were in a much improved condition. Around the Land Port Gate loomed the Grand Battery. On the precipitous face of the North Front stood Willis's. Various bastions, as well as the old Moorish castle, commanded the inundation and the narrow ways leading from the flat and sandy neutral ground of the isthmus. Along the town front facing westwards rose not only the embrasures and solid walls of the King's Bastion but several other lesser

1  *Lieutenant-General George Augustus Eliott*

*From the portrait by Sir Joshua Reynolds*

2 *Lieutenant-General Eliott on the King's Bastion, with his aide-de-camp and assistant engineer Lieutenant G. F. Koehler*

but powerful works. Montague's Bastion swept the length of the Old Mole and commanded the waters on each side of it; then, south of this and between it and the King's Bastion, came Orange Bastion and the Saluting Battery. Near the Ragged Staff rose the South Bastion, considerably higher than the works mentioned, with a wall cutting off the town by joining the seashore to an inaccessible precipice on the Rock itself. A line-wall strengthened by a small bastion of eight guns ran south along the beach to the New Mole, where a fort mounting 26 guns was constructed, with a circular battery for heavy metal on the New Mole Head itself. Round the Ragged Staff, where supplies for the garrison were usually landed, there were various local defences designed to halt any sudden assault: a drawbridge, a covered way, a small stone fort holding two guns. As the total distance between the most seaward points of the Old and New Moles was a mile and a half, all these defences covered one another and swept the whole anchorage. Behind this line-wall, on the rising ground ran a second line of defence, the Princess of Wales's lines, containing several strong batteries commanding the sea. At various points were water tanks, the principal collection being near the Ragged Staff wharf.

South of the New Mole lay three small bays: Rosia Bay, Camp Bay and Little Bay. The usual peace-time anchorages for both naval and civilian shipping were between or at the Old and New Moles; but this stretch of water was exposed to battery-fire from the Spanish territory to the northwards, and during the siege it was in these bays that any British shipping at Gibraltar usually moored. Landing from the sea was rather difficult, the coastline being rocky and steep in many stretches. Fortified lines and batteries commanded the foreshore, close along the beach at those places were boats could land, retired where the hilly and broken nature of the ground rose above the shore. Buena Vista, between Camp and Little Bays, is so called because of the magnificent prospects across the Bay of Algeciras towards Spain and over the straits to Barbary and the spectacular mainland of Northern Africa. Here, although the rocky coastline was hard of access from the sea, a line-wall gave shelter to the defenders and cannon were placed at intervals in case of attack by boats. Batteries on the heights gave command not only over wide areas of sea but on the waters south of the New Mole. Windmill Hill, looming over this lower southern part of the Rock, was also fortified, both to the west and the east; and as the peninsula tapers at this point, the walls and batteries on this eminence were within musket shot of the beaches, 200–300 yards away. Windmill Hill, moreover, rises sheerly and roughly from its base and a narrow winding pass giving access to the summit prevented any sudden assault standing much chance of success against vigilant defenders, even if an initial landing took place. The southern extremity of Gibraltar, the broken flats at the foot of Windmill Hill extending to Europa Point, were armed with more batteries and stretches of line-wall standing guard over the steep, narrow and rocky foreshore.

The long, narrow and jagged crest of the Rock, running south from the strong works at Willis's, was marked by several strong points and observation posts. These were maintained at the old Moorish Castle; Middle Hill (which lies close to the north end of the defences, overlooking the steep long drop to Catalan Bay on the Mediterranean shore); at a work called 'Charles V's Wall'; and in two others nearby and overlooking the Mediterranean at the Signal House and the Moorish Wall. Thence, continuing southwards and linking with the defences of Windmill Hill, came stations at Mount Misery and Sugar Loaf Point, the highest peak of the crest. Below these guard and look-out posts the precipitous eastern face of the Rock fell through formidable and almost unsurmountable broken masses of stone, slides of scree and slopes of sand to the long inaccessible coast. At one isolated spot, almost directly below Sugar Loaf Point, where a small beach and cave exist, the garrison manned a post named the Cave Guard.

Concealment of one's own defences during this period was not usually desirable. On the contrary, the more obviously formidable the position was, the more did it deter an enemy. Thus as the works grew so did the terrifying nature of their appearance. As a traveller drew southwards towards the Land Port Gate and Grand Battery, he saw the narrow, sheltered and impressive Gate itself, built in heavy and finely dressed stone and approached by a road raised on arches. A wide ditch fenced in by steel-pointed palisades was backed by a sheer stone wall topped by embrasures filled with the mouths of cannon. On one side lay the inundation, on the other the sea. The beaches were blocked by more palisades, stretching down into the waters, with sentry boxes mounting guard, and backed in the distance by the Old Mole, complete with more embrasures, observation posts and tall and menacing batteries. Above the Land Port Gate itself rose the steep walls and many gun-mouths of the Grand Battery, the high rocks and long lines of Willis's, 600 feet above sea level, and other defences encrusted on the steep northern face to a height of over 900 feet. On the topmost crest, and at intervals all along the ridge of the Rock, rose tall towers, flying flags, marking where the look-outs were stationed. From the sea, the town itself and its high plain walls glared outwards, crowned with cannon, broken by various walls and batteries linking the two moles, interrupted by the larger projections of King's Bastion and South Bastion. To any hostile craft sailing round towards Europa Point, the sight of more batteries, more walls, encampments, the huge three-storey blocks of barracks and hospitals, the evidence of careful preparation stretching from the very edge of the sea to the commanding heights above, brought no comfort. From the east the uncompromising precipices looked down, remote and hostile, topped by more towers and flags.

All these works, whether battered by the enemy or not, were steadily augmented during the siege; by the end they mounted over 452 cannon (most of them 18-pounders or larger), 70 mortars and 28 howitzers; over 100 other guns were in reserve. The total number of serviceable pieces of artillery came to 663. Ten years earlier there had been in all 412 piece of ordnance; in 1727 the Spanish attacks had been met by only 126 guns.

In clear weather these new batteries could cover accurately and with heavy fire and round-shot all the approaches to Gibraltar from the sea, from whichever direction, up to a mile or more distant; the mortars provided a plunging shell of great size (most were 13-inch) for close cover and the howitzers contributed a similar protection for intermediate distances. Even in peace-time it was common form to keep all guns constantly loaded, with five rounds of complete ammunition (shot, charge and wads) for every gun ready in the magazines of each battery; for those next the sea an extra 30 round-shot and five double-headed shot (for use against men, masts or rigging) were prepared and immediately available. Only on the King's Birthday (4 June after 1760) was every gun regularly unshotted, to be fired with powder only in honour of the day.

After the Spanish experiences of 1705 and 1727 when assault from the north directly along the isthmus was attempted, it was generally thought that the strengthened batteries at the Land Port Gate and at Willis's would render any further such attacks foolhardy. There were, however, other dangers to be run and encountered, and Eliott, Boyd and Green recognised and conscientiously did their best to meet them. There was nothing casual, inefficient, unintelligent or unprofessional in their attitude to their charge. This was not always the case in the eighteenth century: at Gibraltar itself in 1704, at Minorca in 1708 (when the British captured it) and in 1756 (when it was lost; and it was to go again in February, 1782), and at many other natural strong points in the world, determined attackers had taken their chances against the odds and gained the victory; as for example at Quebec in 1759. The wisdom of hindsight and the knowledge that Gibraltar was to come through her long ordeal with honour and triumph should not obscure the skill and vigour with which its defenders prepared themselves to meet the threat.

# 3

# *The Opening of the Great Siege*

The world-wide struggle now generally termed the War of American Independence began when shots were exchanged between American militia-men and British regular soldiers in the early morning of 19 April 1775 on the village green at Lexington, near Boston, Massachusetts. It became a desperate contest, for with so able a leader as George Washington against them, supported by a truly revolutionary spirit, the British had little hope of winning quickly. In October 1777 a British force some 3,500 strong, under General Burgoyne, found itself surrounded and starving at Saratoga on the River Hudson; Burgoyne surrendered his army, the remnants of a body originally twice as large, to the American Commander, Major-General Horatio Gates.

Saratoga was the first important major defeat which British land forces sustained in the eighteenth century. It not only gave heart to the Americans, who had on 4 July 1776 signed a Declaration of Independence in Philadelphia, but brought them allies with whose help their ultimate freedom became assured.

In March 1763 the Treaty of Paris had brought to an end the Seven Years War, during which both the French and Spanish had been humiliated by the British on land and sea. Canada, Cape Breton and Louisiana east of the Mississippi, many West Indian islands and trading stations in Africa had been ceded to Great Britain, and French ideas of an Indian empire had been forcibly terminated. Spain also had suffered. The British restored Havana and other conquests; but Florida was handed over to Britain, and Spanish claims on the new world of America, made in the arrogant days of the Conquistadores, were shown up again as hollow and pretentious.

British difficulties in North America gave to the French their opportunity for revenge. At the beginning of General Burgoyne's advance from Canada he had captured from the Americans the strong fort at Ticonderoga. Viscount Stormont, British Ambassador in Paris, informed Charles Gravier, Comte de Vergennes, the French Foreign Minister, of this in September 1777; he at the same time demanded that the French should treat the colonists as rebels and outlaws and that French ports should be closed to them. The French procrastinated; and when early in December they heard from the American commissioners in France of Burgoyne's surrender they hastened to make friends with this new ally. On 6 December 1777 Vergennes in the King's apartment and in his presence wrote a note recognising the United States as a sovereign state; and Louis XVI himself signed and dated it, so eager was he to make profit out of this stroke of good fortune.

In February 1778 the French signed an open treaty of friendship (as well as a secret treaty of defensive alliance) with the Americans. This was the equivalent of declaring war against Great Britain and Stormont was recalled. In a diplomatic daze, for war was not openly declared, France in the summer of 1778 began to indulge in war-like actions against the British all over the globe. A French fleet of 12 ships-of-the-line and five frigates, under Count d'Estaing, with 4,000 troops, sailed on 13 April 1778 for the American coast from Toulon, with orders to begin hostilities when 40 leagues west of Gibraltar. A British frigate watched this fleet on its passage through the Straits of Gibraltar, and accompanied it far enough westwards to be sure it was destined for America; but not until 5 June was this news brought certainly to London. Open hostilities at sea began on 17 June, when Admiral Keppel with a large British fleet met two frigates and a couple of smaller craft in the English Channel and ordered a general chase; two of the French vessels were taken without much trouble, but a very fierce single-ship action took place between another, the *Belle Poule*, and H.M.S. *Arethusa*, the Frenchman escaping to her own coast. Charges of treachery were levelled at Admiral Keppel, because the two nations were not officially at war. But the point was purely academic, and from June 1778 onwards until the conclusion of peace in 1783, the French were the open allies of America and the enemies of England. The King of France subsequently declared that the fight on 17 June 1778 marked the date of the war's beginning.

Saratoga and the threat of intervention by the French caused a wave of patriotism in Great Britain. Many Britons, including people like Edmund Burke in the Commons, had felt that the American claims to self-determination and to 'no taxation without representation' (surely one of the most awkward-sounding slogans ever raised) were valid. Now most British people felt that a national war was afoot. Men and money were forthcoming. In Manchester a new regiment of foot was locally recruited by private subscription, the first of a reinforcement of some 15,000 men similarly raised in Great Britain. Between Tuesday, 9 December 1777 and March 1778 over 1,000 men and 30 officers were recruited, uniformed, staffed, armed, provided with band and colours and approved. This force, part of the regular army of Great Britain, was named the 72nd Regiment of Foot, 'The Royal Manchester Volunteers'. They were marched away from Manchester in April 1778, a local body, raised and officered predominantly by Manchester people in Manchester itself. Their first and only station outside Britain was Gibraltar, where they were by far the strongest unit amongst the six British and three Hanoverian regiments present throughout the Great Siege. During the year 1778, however, Gibraltar was not seriously engaged, except (as always) as a base for British ships, a gathering point for information and a strong point in time of trouble.

It was against the background of these events that Gibraltar became involved directly in the war during the month of June 1779. By that time the war in America had lasted well over four years. Washington's iron determination had kept the Congress Army in being at Valley Forge through the starving winter of 1777–8. Boston and Philadelphia were abandoned by them and many mercenaries hired from German princes and British forces had been concentrated in New York and Rhode Island; while other British troops moved into the Southern states, where loyalist sympathisers were supposed to exist in a larger proportion than the event proved. French troops were by then supporting the Americans on land, and French squadrons bringing supplies and reinforcements and threatening or impeding the free passage of British vessels of war and of commerce across the Atlantic. America was still far from being lost to the British crown, but no prospect of early success was in sight.

At this critical moment Spain intervened. On 12 April 1779 a secret alliance, the convention of Aranjuez, was signed between France and Spain. Spanish aid to the American colonists was certainly inspired, not by approval of their political ideas, but by hatred of Great Britain. The chief Spanish aim was to recover Gibraltar, and the French promised to fight on until this was achieved. For their part, the French aimed to take Newfoundland, to recover Senegal and Dominica and to re-establish French influence and dominion in India.

The open rupture came on 16 June 1779 when the Spanish Ambassador in London waited on the Secretary of State with a long list of complaints against the British. In effect this was a declaration of war and brought against Great Britain a combination of enemies more powerful than she had ever faced in the past. Spanish warships, part of a fleet large in numbers and in individual size of vessels, began to cruise towards the English Channel, where in the summer the largest enemy fleet since the days of the Spanish Armada was to sail unchecked in sight of the English south coast. Luckily for Great Britain these ships were almost completely leaderless, ravaged by fever, ill-found, ill-managed and unsound.

The horrid truth became clear that the English had no friends any-where in the world. The position was in fact to get worse, for in 1780 the northern powers of the Baltic were to form the 'League of the Armed Neutrality', the principal aim of which was to resist the British habit of stopping neutral ships on the high seas in order to search them for contraband. When Holland joined this combination in December 1780, Great Britain declared war against the United Provinces. But by that time things were generally so bad that another enemy more or less seemed a trifle. Even in India circumstances were adverse. At the worst moment of the war, in June 1780, the Mohammedan adventurer Hyder Ali marched out of Bangalore with the most powerful native army ever seen in the south of India, the avowed ally of the French, to fight some of the most desperate (and in some cases disastrous) battles ever fought against the British in the east. At the same time a brilliant French sea-man, Vice-Admiral de Suffren, was conducting some remarkable naval operations against the British fleets in Indian waters.

The siege of Gibraltar occurred during these long years when it was plain that no help could reach any part of Great Britain or her posses-sions by outside means. Only Britain could save Britain.

King George III was born on 4 June. This 'King's Birthday' has be-come an annual event in certain quarters even today. Whatever the actual birthday of the sovereign may be, in the civil service and at Eton, to name only two examples, the 'Fourth of June' is celebrated in various ways. On that date in 1779 Eliott gave a grand party on the Rock. A gun was fired in salute for every year the King was old; on this occasion 41. A feu-de-joie was then fired by the troops in the garri-son, a splendid spectacle of disciplined drill, marked by the flashes, flames and clouds of gunsmoke running from one end of the red-coated lines to the other as the regiments shot off their muskets in turn. A Gala and Ball and a grand dinner were given at Eliott's official resi-dence, where the inside courtyard and colonnade were illuminated. The dinner was attended not only by the senior British officers and their wives, but by the Spanish Governor of San Roque, Don Joaquin Mendoza and his lady, with many other Spanish officers. This exchange of courtesies was common enough, but this time was rather special. The large armaments of Gibraltar were freely displayed, and no secret made of the garrison's instant state of readiness.

During the days which followed, news reached Eliott that Mendoza had been promoted to Lieutenant-General in the Spanish army. Once again it was common courtesy for a British officer to congratulate his near neighbour on this honour. Once more Eliott and his senior officers put on their best uniforms; they all rode out, colonels and lieutenant-colonels and majors, attended by their aides-de-camp, over the isthmus and made their way to San Roque, with Eliott at their head. At San Roque, however, it was quickly noted that Mendoza appeared embarrassed and not glad to meet them. No refreshments were offered to the British officers beyond a cup of chocolate brought to the British Governor himself. The visit was short. Eliott and his companions were displeased at their reception and returned to Gibraltar. There they were met by the British Consul in Barbary, Mr Logie, who had just arrived from Tangier in a Swedish frigate.

Logie had news for Eliott which explained Mendoza's behaviour, strange for a fellow-soldier and for a representative of a hospitable nation. A few days earlier a Swedish trading vessel had met a French fleet of 28 sail-of-the-line off Cape Finisterre, and had learnt from its commander, Comte d'Orvilliers, that they were waiting for a Spanish squadron from Cadiz to join them. Although the British officers still found it hard to believe that war was close, it can have been no great surprise to Eliott himself when, on 21 June 1779, no mail arrived from San Roque and the British post, sent out as usual from the garrison for carriage forward, was refused. Eliott then received a personal letter from the Spanish Commander, saying that he had orders to shut up Gibraltar. It was couched in the most courteous terms and concluded with a prayer that God would 'preserve your life for many years'. British officers riding out for their morning exercise of pleasure through the Spanish lines onto the mainland were stopped by sentries and ordered back.

As already mentioned, the open rupture between the Governments had occurred on 16 June, in London. But such news took time to travel. It was afterwards learned that although Mendoza knew unofficially about the impending outbreak of war at the moment of Eliott's congratulatory visit, only accidents of travel, which had delayed the courier bringing the official order to shut up Gibraltar, prevented the despatches arriving during the British officers' presence in San Roque.

Eliott at once gave orders to reinforce all guards, and to ensure that outlying picquets carried loaded muskets. He held his first council of war of the siege and some measures of defence were put immediately in hand. The civilians of Gibraltar, Jews and Genoese, were ordered to begin levelling the sand-dunes on the isthmus before the North Face; and they were told that only those who had property or would help to defend it could remain in the town. Mr Logie returned to Tangier, where he was to set in train preparations for getting regular supplies of provisions into Gibraltar and to make arrangements for forwarding letters and packets from the besieged town to England.

The Commander of the naval forces at Gibraltar was Rear-Admiral Robert Duff, with a 60-gun ship, H.M.S. *Panther*, three frigates (though only one, *Enterprise*, was actually in harbour, the others being off on a cruise) and a sloop-of-war in his little squadron. He shifted his vessels from their usual anchorage near the Ragged Staff to the southward, off the New Mole.

British officers and their families had been accustomed to live in San Roque itself and other small villages a few miles inland. These were all sent back into the garrison, even children with smallpox not being allowed to remain until they recovered. Many of the families had to leave most of their possessions behind them and were hustled into Gibraltar in what the British felt was a thoroughly ungentleman-like manner. Two officers, Colonel Ross and Captain Vignoles of the 39th Foot, were making a holiday tour of Spain when war was declared. They were rounded up and sent to Cadiz with their baggage. Thence they reached Faro on the Portuguese coast and after over a month managed to rejoin their comrades and their regiments in Gibraltar, linking up with a third officer in the same predicament and making their final stage in a small rowing-boat.

Work on the batteries went briskly on. The barriers at the Land Port Gate were kept shut, one guard was stationed in advance of the main face of the Rock at the Devil's Tower (on the isthmus and detached from the rest of the defences), and an artillery officer was stationed at Willis's with particular orders to watch both this outlying picquet and the movements of the Spaniards. Empty hogsheads were filled with earth and chained together in rows along the tops of walls, to increase their height and absorb any shots. After a fortnight the picquets ceased to carry loaded muskets, because the Spanish, although active enough behind their own lines, did not annoy the defenders of Gibraltar. At times the working parties of Gibraltar civilians, up to 300 strong, were busy levelling the sand-dunes within 50 yards of the Spanish sentries, who never made any attempt to prevent them.

On 5 July 1779, a possibly warlike move was made: a Spanish squadron of two 74s, five frigates and other vessels came in sight and lay-to, motionless but unanchored off the western side of the Rock. Three small British privateers stood in from the west; and when a schooner, flying Portuguese colours but accompanying the Spanish fleet, drew across to reconnoitre them, Europa batteries opened fire upon her, the first hostile shot fired by the British during the siege. These batteries again fired later on the same day, after dusk; this time on one of their own ships, H.M.S. *Enterprise*, which had crept through the evening's squadron and brought into Gibraltar Consul Logie from Tangier; the *Enterprise* had refrained from giving the agreed night-signals for a friendly vessel, wishing to avoid discovery by the Spanish. Luckily no harm was done.

One reason for Logie's return was to support Eliott in a dispute with the British Admiral. Duff, an elderly and not very active man, had re-fused to allow his stores to be used for repairing one of the Emperor's ships at Gibraltar. He was sufficiently stimulated to send on 6 July *Panther* and *Enterprise* to sea to get in amongst a fleet of small vessels sailing from Malaga with stores for the Spanish squadron. One British ship's boat, approaching too close to a settee (a small sailing vessel with long lateen yards), provoked a shot from the Spanish fort at Santa Barbara, at the Mediterranean end of their lines. Duff himself went off to Windmill Hill to see what was happening. Later a few small Spanish coastal craft were seized and brought into Gibraltar, the first prizes taken. As on the same day a letter from England had been received with official notice that hostilities had commenced between Great Britain and Spain, it could be taken that from this point all shootings, killings and captures were legal on both sides.

The war, however, took a long time to warm up in the neighbour-hood of Gibraltar. Both sides continued to work hard. The Spaniards unloaded stores, horses and men on their end of the isthmus; their fleet lay off the town, so that sea communication was halted. The place was under close blockade by 18 July 1779.

Eliott thereupon took two significant steps. He rationed all fresh meat and he ordered his soldiers to stop powdering their hair. It was the usual practice to use white flour for this purpose, and Eliott could see that even this small quantity might be needed in the future. Horses, too, came under the Governor's ban. Only those civilian horse owners who

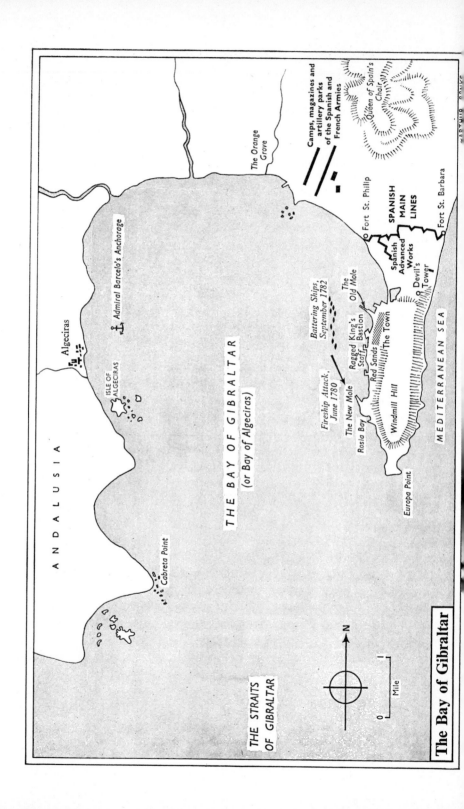

ANDALUSIA

Cabreta Point

Algeciras

ISLE OF
ALGECIRAS

Admiral Barcelo's Anchorage

The Orange
Grove

Camps, magazines and
artillery parks
of the Spanish and
French Armies

Queen of Spain's
Chair

Fort St. Phillip

SPANISH
MAIN
LINES

Spanish
Advanced
Works

Devil's
Tower

Fort St. Barbara

THE STRAITS
OF GIBRALTAR

THE BAY OF GIBRALTAR
(or Bay of Algeciras)

Battering Ships,
September 1782

Fireship Attack,
June 1780

The New Mole

The
Old Mole

Ragged King's
Staff

Bastion

Rosia Bay

Red Sands

The Town

Windmill Hill

Europa Point

MEDITERRANEAN SEA

N

0                    1
Mile

**The Bay of Gibraltar**

could prove that they possessed 1,000 lb. of feed for each horse were allowed to keep them. Field and staff officers, even, were ordered to drive out or kill any horses for which they had not absolute need. Eliott, because of this order, had one of his own horses shot. Civilian mules could be kept only under the same conditions, and all stray dogs were killed.

Other measures were taken: each regiment had to draw up a list of their best marksmen; firearms were inspected and made perfect for service; rations for all men were made equal. Eliott made a large addition to his own staff, appointing four aides-de-camp for himself and two for Boyd. He made a major-general, with an A.D.C., of the senior Hanoverian officer, de la Motte; a quartermaster-general; an adjutant-general; a town-major, with an assistant town-major; and a director for the hospital. These appointments were local. When they were in due course reported to the Commander-in-Chief at home, Lord Amherst doubtfully acquiesced. He queried the necessity for having a quarter-master-general and an adjutant-general as well as a town-major and pointed out that Lord Portmore, Governor during the siege in 1727, had employed no generals or appointed any special staff except aides-de-camp; but left the actual arrangements to the 'Governor command-ing on the spot'. These appointments were in fact to cause continuous queries and correspondence, since each staff officer claimed extra pay for his new duties.

Eliott also reinforced the artillerymen by beginning to train 180 infantry to use the guns. In spite of the hundreds of cannon in position there were only 485 gunners available, including 15 drummers and 25 officers. Some stations were kept permanently manned, but the habit was to move the men round from one threatened post to another. The newcomers were paid at a higher rate than that of privates of the line, so the service was popular. Later came the strain of almost constant duty, the irregularity of working hours, and, as the Spaniards increased their efforts, the continuous alarms with the occasional spell of exceptionally heavy bombardment in exposed places. At times, no matter what the danger, the artillery officers (who by Eliott's orders were in charge of their own affairs and free from any interference by officers of any other branch) had to give orders for fire to be slackened, to allow the gunners to snatch a few hours sleep. The Royal Artillery in Gibraltar, consisting of five companies (out of a national total of 32) came under three com-manding officers during the siege: Colonel Godwin, who left, worn-out but promoted, in 1780; Colonel Tovey, who died under the strain; and Major Lewis, who later was severely wounded and invalided.

At this time of the beginning of their trial, the tireless and lively Logie had a dramatic escape. While returning to Tangier on a Moorish galley, his voyage was interrupted by a Spanish vessel. Logie hid Eliott's despatches and codes, which he was carrying, in a loaf of bread; he had changed into Arab dress and during a search of the galley successfully hid himself under a pile of sails. He was to prove a great help to the British in Gibraltar, doing his best under often hard circumstances to provide information and provender.

The increase in tension brought a welcome dispersion of many of the civilian population of Gibraltar. Various vessels or small craft, very often fired at by Spanish shore guns, brought bullocks, sheep, fowls, rice, currants, onions, fruit, eggs, flour or other welcome supplies to the town. Each, in the summer of 1779, left crammed with refugees and their families. Other Jews and Genoese laid in all the supplies they could. Many moved out of the town itself into the more open and remote stretches of ground on the south of the Rock. Standing orders in the garrison before the outbreak of war had commanded every inhabitant to have in store sufficient provisions for six months. But many, through poverty or neglect, had not made themselves secure; yet because all they possessed in the world were the chattels in their houses they remained in or near Gibraltar itself, trusting to luck for future food and hoping that any destruction might pass them by. Eliott himself reckoned there were 3,000–4,000 souls in Gibraltar, over and above the garrison; about half of them were useless, being too old or infirm or women and children, and few could lay in stocks of provisions. Fortunately both civilians and garrison remained healthy and in good spirits in these early months.

Near the military camps below Windmill Hill towards Europa Point the troops also prepared huts and put up tents, in case the town itself should come under fire and be made uninhabitable. Guns were ranged, magazines stocked with powder. Palisades were strengthened and lengthened. Extra embrasures were formed to command new defensive prospects. The naval people built a new battery, arming it with some of the lower-deck heavy guns of *Panther*. The marksmen were formed into two squads and underwent daily practice. Regiments practised grenade-throwing. During August some experiments were made with red-hot shot from the guns; other new measures included the shooting of 'carcases', filled with combustible materials intended to set on fire any wooden structure which they hit, such as a ship's boat or a warship or the wooden components of a gun-battery. One special gun, called the 'Rock-gun', was hauled into place by enthusiastic volunteers at the highest possible point of the North Face, looking out over the isthmus; later a road was constructed to it, but its first appearance was made after it had been dragged up precipitous slopes and over gullies by sheer man-power. This Rock-gun was later to prove very galling to the Spaniards and was to attract much hostile fire; it was dismounted and replaced several times during the siege. In honour of Green, with whom Eliott had daily consultations, this battery was named 'Green's Lodge'.

The Spaniards for their part were equally busy. By road and sea their lines were reinforced with men and materials. They landed guns and mortars, and set up a large laboratory in their camp, for the preparation of shells, fuses and powder. Fascines were put up to form mortar and gun-batteries. Magazines were built among their defences. New regiments, some of cavalry, arrived and new camps were built to accommodate them.

By the end of August the intention of the enemy had become plain: they intended to starve the garrison out. Only 40 head of cattle remained in Gibraltar, so that fresh meat quickly became scarce. All shipping was interrupted. A bold attempt was even made by some Spanish boats to seize a small British-owned craft which was anchored off the Old Mole; but when the garrison fired a gun at them the Spaniards retired. From then onwards all shipping used only the New Mole. The general shortage of domestic supplies in Gibraltar brought an end even to the small amount of entertaining which the officers of the garrison had maintained for the first months of the blockade.

The question now was: what was to be done? Eliott had by his representations during 1777 persuaded the government to increase his stores. A large quantity of provisions had arrived in April 1779, and during the following month 'very good supplies' had come in from Morocco. The British regiments in Gibraltar had been augmented to the establishment of troops in Great Britain. Boyd while in London had ordered 400 extra sets of hospital bedding (bed, pillow, bolster, pair of blankets, pair of sheets, coverlet), as well as medicines and surgical instruments. Eliott's constant reiterations of need had brought results. But these results had brought drawbacks. He had under his command some 5,382 men: three rather weak Hanoverian regiments, each about 450 strong; five British regiments, of which the new 72nd Foot numbered well over 1,000, the others 600 or so apiece; and his artillery and engineers. These men consumed large quantities of food daily. So it was natural enough that, as the diarist John Drinkwater, of the Royal

Manchester Volunteers, said, when 'affairs began to wear a more serious aspect . . . the operations of the enemy now began to engage our serious attention'.

Eliott held a council of war, and on Sunday 12 September 1779 the British opened the first large-scale bombardment of the siege at half past six in the morning, using the cannon on the North Face. One account says that the first shot at the Spanish lines was fired by an artillery officer, Captain Lloyd, from the New Battery, 900 feet up. According to another story, a lady, Mrs Skinner, wife of an officer in the Soldier Artificer Company, fired a gun at Eliott's command, while a military band, stationed nearby in readiness, struck up 'Britons strike home'. The Devil's Tower guard had been withdrawn before the shooting, and from this day on the British were confined behind their linear defences. All day long the steady firing continued. Towards evening it slackened, but thenceforth and for years Gibraltar had at most times of day (and very often at night) cannon or mortars in action. The wreaths of smoke, the flashes and flames of discharges, the roaring and thundering from the Rock went on unceasingly. To the innumerable vessels of many nations passing through the straits, this constant rumbling and the sight of British flags flying along the ridge marked a defence so long lasting that it became a regular feature of life.

The Spaniards did not retaliate. As the opening shells burst on the isthmus, the workmen gathering for their morning labours ran back to the Spanish lines, the cavalry which had come out to protect them galloped off for their camp and the covered waggons which were bringing forward new supplies went hurriedly to the rear without unloading. The British artillery practice, it seems, was poor: not much damage was done to the Spanish works and as the day wore on guns were discharged only when movement was noticed.

In Gibraltar itself the town became almost deserted, except for soldiers and gunners. The civilians were sure that the Spaniards would reply by opening fire from those batteries already in position in their lines, or from Fort St Philip, opposite the Land Gate and Old Mole, and with a clear view and field of fire on the houses of the town. Eliott and his advisers apparently thought so too, for he began to dismantle steeples, towers and such conspicuous landmarks as the cupola of the convent and the town clock, which might serve as aiming marks and range indicators. To stop round-shot ricocheting and to prevent bursting shells being made even more effective, teams of 80 men were formed to draw ploughs along the street pavements, softening the ground. Officers of the garrison who had their wives and families with them moved out of their town billets, burying their silver-plate in bomb-proof shelters and taking refuge in huts at the southern end of the peninsula.

# 4

# *Blockade and Relief*

Eliott had foreseen the possibility of a close blockade before the open rupture occurred. He had continually pressed for food of all kinds, powder, cannon (he found over 60 unserviceable) and fuel. Cooking and warmth on the Rock consumed and needed large stocks. Coal was the most economical, effective and least bulky means, but it all had to be shipped from Newcastle. In heavy storms welcome supplies of drift-wood (and sometimes wreckage) were washed up along the shores, but this was too uncertain to rely upon. Money also was required, par-ticularly for paying the active and venturesome blockade runners who managed to slip through the Spanish small craft which cruised almost continuously in the Bay of Algeciras.

These blockade runners were as a rule not English vessels, though occasionally a British privateer or two got in. Most came from the Mediterranean or from North Africa. A Venetian vessel, for example, brought to England some of Eliott's despatches about his first bom-bardments; she took 23 days on passage to Falmouth, calling at Lisbon en route. The Moors at this time were well disposed, though the Spanish were opening negotiations which led to a change of attitude. In 1781 they succeeded in leasing Tangier and Tetuan from the Sultan of Morocco for £7,500,000, and the tone of behaviour of the Muslim authorities altered for the worse. But for the time being Eliott's ex-changes were conducted on the elevated if slow planes of eastern courtesy. Letters opened with praises to God and were signed by 'the slaves and servants' of the Arab leaders.

When writing home Eliott put the vital parts of his despatches in code. He often sent several copies of each, using different methods of carriage. Just as almost all of his messages home reached the British authorities (only one seems to have miscarried out of the scores he wrote), so the letters and instructions from London appear to have arrived at Gibraltar without much trouble. Eliott heard in December 1779 that a fleet and convoy under the command of Admiral Rodney was soon to be on its way to Gibraltar and Minorca with men and stores; he was warned that, though Gibraltar was to be the first port of call, he was only to take what was essential for his needs, because Minorca was not to be neglected.

In the meantime the natural boredom of garrison life, just as wearisome in war-time as in peace, led to some lively internal quarrels. Admiral Duff was not at any time a particularly lively man: it was over 20 years since in Quiberon Bay he had won renown by his promptness and daring during the early part of Hawke's famous victory in storm and darkness. His alleged inaction at various moments led to soldiers and seamen looking out from their ramparts and seeing ships attempting to reach Gibraltar intercepted and captured by the Spanish. The blockading fleet consisted of at least two 74-gun ships-of-the-line, with two of three frigates, a number of felucca-rigged craft (which mounted up to 32 guns apiece), several galleys (the traditional warship of the Mediterranean, driven by condemned men and convicts) and as many as 20 armed boats. Part was usually in the bay, part at Ceuta and others prowled around the shore. The Spanish strength in seamen alone was reckoned at well over 6,000, a number larger than the whole garrison, soldiers and sailors, of Gibraltar.

Duff's lack of vigour was highlighted during November 1779, first by a failure, then by a daring action by an English privateer. A 20-gun British privateer, the *Peace of Plenty*, had sailed from Leghorn, called at Minorca and gone on to Gibraltar; she was seen and chased by several Spanish zebecs and galleys when close to the Rock, and was driven ashore on the isthmus under the guns of Santa Barbara fort. The crew (except for one man) was saved, but the Spanish set fire to the wreck. Apart from some ships' boats, which went to her aid, she received no help from the Navy.

A week later another British vessel, the 20-gun *Buck* of Folkestone, appeared in the bay. The English garrison saw her arrival signalled from the Spanish watch towers; the Spanish commander, Admiral Barcelo, himself put to sea, with two ships-of-the-line, a frigate, a zebec and some galleys. The *Buck*, a cutter and very well handled, drew the Spaniards over to the Barbary shore, sailed across the bows of Barcelo's ships, slipped between them and anchored safely off Gibraltar, having caused Barcelo to lose station and to be forced into the Mediterranean, leaving the Bay in British hands. *Buck*'s captain, a man called Fagg, declared he did not know Gibraltar was blockaded. Far from bringing supplies, he himself was in need of biscuits. His only damage was a shot through his ship's boat. On this occasion Duff went as far as to drop topsails in H.M.S. *Panther*, but he made no move.

Food was now beginning to run short for all except those who were on military rations. One officer, Captain Spilsbury of the 12th Regiment (another diarist, who enlivened his writings with amateur but lively and detailed sketches) recorded being charged seven shillings for a 'dinner of salt beef and a little bit of fish and pudding', during October. The position worsened rapidly. Prices increased, profiteers flourished and people starved. When ships sailed from Gibraltar they usually carried away refugees and useless mouths, some of them military wives and families. In those days the British regiments in particular were regarded as the soldiers' homes for life, men and officers together forming what was often called a 'family'. The married soldiers would live in the large barrack-rooms with only blankets hung about their beds for privacy; the wives washed for the men (though sergeants' wives were usually forbidden to do this) and their children enlivened a dull existence. In late October 150 of these women sailed for Malaga.

Eliott once more showed his close contact with the realities of the situation and his firm control over events. When the principal civilian baker in Gibraltar, a Mr Holliday, refused to go on making bread, on the pretext that he had no wood for his fires, Eliott at once seized 49 of his stock of 57 sacks of flour. At this time flour was selling at a shilling a pound, nearly £15 a barrel, and the temptation to make money out of hunger was very great. Bread was sold through grated doorways, under armed guard, so large were the crowds which pressed round those shops which still openly sold loaves. Fighting and quarrelling took place in the streets. Fish was scarce and dear; the few surviving bullocks, pastured on the scrub round the base of Windmill Hill, were using up the fodder there and were down to skin and bone. The Governor tried to encourage as many as were interested to take up little gardens, for vegetables were extraordinarily scarce. When attempts were made to work once again the gardens on the isthmus itself the Spaniards opened fire with their heavy cannon and drove the men off. At night they raided and destroyed these plots and took away the fishing nets and lines which some garrison Genoese had left staked out from the beaches. This was considered very mean behaviour. Eliott then allowed both soldiers and civilians to use any land available on the lower slopes of the Rock itself. His own indifference to food did not endear him to his fellow officers, who acidly recorded not only that he had ceased to serve either hock or claret at his own table (for guests only, because he never touched either),

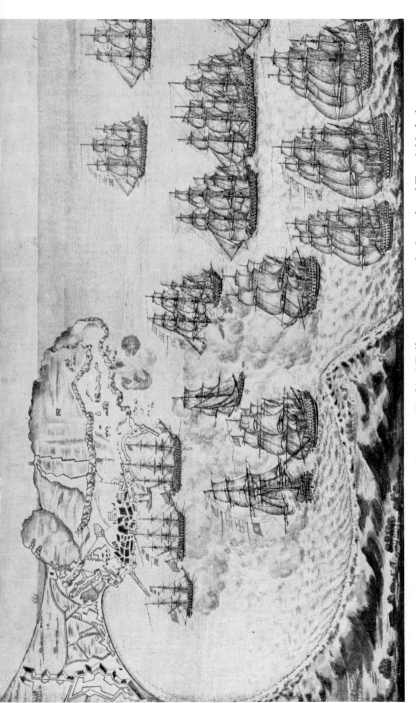

3 *Captain George Fagg, in the cutter 'Buck' of Folkestone, running the Spanish and French blockade*

*From a pen-and-ink drawing by J. Rob*

4   *Admiral Sir George Rodney defeating the Spanish fleet, under Don Juan de Langara, at Cape St Vincent, 16 January 1780*

*From an engraving by James Fittler after Thomas Luny*

5   *Part of Rodney's fleet, with two of his prizes from the Battle of Cape St Vincent, anchored off the New Mole*

*From an eye-witness sketch by John Spilsbury*

but that he had lived for eight days on four ounces of rice a day. Drinkwater, thoughtfully noting this, wrote down that while this might do for the Governor himself, it would be 'far from sufficient for a working man kept continually employed, and in a climate where the heat necessarily demands very refreshing nourishment to support nature under fatigue'. Even when a Moorish vessel managed to land a few cattle, these had been aboard for so long and were so weak and emaciated that several died on the beach as soon as they were landed. However, they were eagerly bought, cut up and cooked. Fuel, too, was short, and Eliott apportioned what was left of the coal among the regiments. Christmas was a poor time for rejoicing, though small parties were held by the senior officers.

These general shortages caused unrest and confusion in the town. Robbery in the streets became frequent, houses were broken into and billets plundered while their occupants were absent on duty. Sentries were placed and the town regularly patrolled. One soldier, caught robbing a wine-shop and court-martialled for the crime, was publicly hanged. He was the first man executed during Eliott's term of office. Tempers and patience were wearing out. One piece of depressing news arrived: Captain Fagg and his *Buck* had sailed for Minorca, after re-fitting, just before Christmas. Quite a parade had been made of his departure, because the whole garrison had been encouraged by the spirited manner of his arrival; Eliott had gone aboard and presented money to the crew just before she sailed. Unfortunately Fagg fell in with a French frigate; a fight took place, and after a few broadsides the *Buck* was severely damaged and captured; she sank before she could be towed into port.

Throughout the siege there was a two-way traffic in deserters. Men from the regiments were always liable to disappear. Sometimes they reached the Spanish lines; sometimes they were re-taken before they got very far; occasionally they fell over the precipices and their mutilated and broken bodies were recovered long afterwards. All regiments were affected in this way, from the brisk youngsters from Manchester to the Hanoverians and the hard-bitten veterans of the older corps. The only exceptions were the seamen (who were formed into a small Marine regiment) and the Soldier-Artificer Company, who lost no one from this cause.

Spaniards and other members of the besieging force also deserted. Quite a sizeable number of Walloon Guards broke away into Gibraltar, often by daylight. The British frequently watched these fugitives chased by dragoons, who caught or cut down several as they tried to dodge across the neutral ground. Such events were usually followed by another even more melancholy spectacle: the Spanish regiments were paraded and the recaptured deserters were publicly hanged before them on a high gallows, the bodies being left suspended until nightfall. From the news more fortunate deserters brought to the garrison, the Spaniards were having difficulties of their own, from fever, shortage of food and the flooding of trenches from the winter rains. The Spanish were busily fortifying and arming with guns and mortars not only the batteries which were placed directly against Gibraltar, but new works guarding their two flanks and looking out to sea. Since the British had long ago ceased to entertain any hope that Duff would perform any aggressive action against the besiegers, the sight of these defensive preparations highly encouraged the besieged garrison. Rumours about a possible relief by Admiral Rodney had been leaked, and the British hoped against hope that he would not be long in arriving.

Although one or two small craft managed to creep through the blockade, they brought little to help: a few goats, fowls and eggs. The most valuable cargo was 6,000 bushels of barley, found in a Neapolitan vessel driven within range of the British guns and forced to come in. But shortage to the point of starvation was the order of the day. Only the generosity of regimental comrades, putting their small rations together, kept alive many soldiers' wives and children. Even so, one such woman died through want. Thistles, dandelions, wild leeks, the various scanty growths among the barren gullies of the Rock, were carefully gathered and stewed up into broth. Dogs were killed off. Officers' wives eked out their meagre supplies. The wife of the chief engineer, Mrs Green, was another diarist of the siege. Her charming and artless account waited until 130 years after her death before publication; in it she described how at this critical moment of the siege she mixed the 'King's flour' (the official ration) with what was left of her own (which was 'exceeding white and good') and made bread enough to have eight friends in to dinner and to feast on 'a very good leg of pork', for which she had paid 30s.

In the early days of 1780 the situation became progressively worse. The soldiers' rations were reduced, half a pound of salt beef, a quarter pound of salt pork and a pint of pease being taken off each man's weekly portion. Moreover, the Spanish, who had refrained in a rather surprising way from any large-scale retaliatory firing in reply to the daily cannonading from the British guns at Willis's and at Green's Lodge, began to show some signs of action. On 11 January 1780 they fired four shots directly at the town. One struck the Old Mole, a second hit a sentry box by the Land Port Gate, the others hit houses and plunged along the streets. A mule was lamed and a woman in the street was wounded in the heel by a splinter. During this brief attack a British burial party was disturbed at its work while a clergyman was saying the service. Most British people regarded these shots (and others which followed on succeeding days) as means to establish the range; they also thought it in bad taste to choose such a moment. The inhabitants, many of whom had returned to their homes from their makeshift huts on Europa flats for shelter from the winter winds and rains, took flight once more. The soldiers of the garrison, however, bore both their own privations and the threat of bombardment with extraordinary cheerfulness.

Then on 15 January 1780, after over seven months of close blockade, definite good news arrived. An English brig flying the British flag approached from the west, and, though fired on by some small enemy vessels, got safely in to the New Mole. She brought news that a large convoy was approaching, and that relief was in sight. Once more the Jews and Genoese, or what was left of them, crowded back into the town. Frantic with joy, they joined the garrison in rousing cheers. The wine-shops were reopened and over bottle and glass there were happy celebrations.

Although a few days were still to go slowly by before Rodney and his fleet arrived in full force, the rejoicings of 15 January were not to prove premature. Rumours about a great battle at sea circulated. But first a brig laden with flour arrived; then it was noticed that, although Spanish signal flags flew to show that ships were in sight, Barcelo and his squadron and even his small craft remained close under the land at Algeciras and seemed to be making a boom across the harbour there, to secure his safety. Duff gave orders for the *Childers* sloop of war to stand by to go out to protect any more single vessels from the British convoy which might come in sight. Then on the evening of 16 January another brig arrived, *The Good Design*, bringing flour (which immediately dropped from 2s. to 6d. a pound)—and news of a battle in which Rodney had not only beaten a Spanish fleet and captured some warships, but was approaching Gibraltar with a large convoy bearing stores, food and reinforcements. The walls of the fortress were lined with men carrying spy-glasses like muskets, all levelled at the western entrance to the bay. The weather was hazy, with storms of lightning; vessels were seen being forced past the Rock on the strong current. But the news was true. First a frigate, H.M.S. *Apollo*, got in; then other warships, then a Spanish vessel, the *Phoenix*, an 80-gun line-of-battle ship recently captured. More and more ships arrived; then the remaining ships of the convoy and its escort. Among them was Rodney himself, in H.M.S. *Sandwich*, one of the largest and most redoubtable British warships of the day; there was as well the *Royal George*, an even larger vessel of 100 guns.

Admiral Sir George Rodney was a year or so younger than Eliott, and just at the beginning of a spell of command and a series of successes which were greatly to influence the outcome of the whole war. A professional seaman of vast experience, he had first gone to sea when he was a boy of fourteen. Captain of his own ship when only 23 years old, commanding frigates and line-of-battle ships in the years between 1742 and 1763, he returned to England after the end of the Seven Years War as vice-admiral, and had been made a baronet for his services. He was extravagant in his personal taste, a man of fashion, and reckless with his money, squandering much on various parliamentary elections, through which, though successful, he became more and more deeply in debt. In 1775 he retired to Paris to escape his creditors, and was able to leave that city in 1778 only when a friend, the French Maréchal de Biron, paid his debts and sent him back to England, in time to take part in the war between their two countries. He and the First Lord of the Admiralty, Lord Sandwich, detested one another. Rodney blamed Sandwich for falsely withholding arrears of pay which would have cleared his debts. But Rodney was too skilful a seaman to be ignored, even by Sandwich, and a personal friend of the young king. Thus it was to Rodney that a new, large and important command was given in the autumn of 1779.

As in many wars before and since, British trade had to continue, fighting or no fighting. Ships sailing alone easily fell captive to enemy commerce raiders, which during the American war were particularly active and successful. It therefore became the practice for great convoys to gather at English ports along the Channel coast. Thence, under strong escort, they went to sea together, giving mutual protection in dangerous waters. Rodney was appointed to command the Leeward Islands station in the West Indies in October 1779. He took out with him a direct addition to that fleet of only four or five ships-of-the-line; but a very much larger force of naval reinforcements for other stations was placed under his command, and an immense convoy of hundreds of trading vessels destined for Portugal, Gibraltar, Minorca and the West Indies was gathered at Plymouth. After the delays inevitable when so many sailing ships were involved, Rodney left the Channel at the end of December, having under his command no fewer than 22 large warships,

14 frigates and other smaller vessels, and a convoy of various store-ships, victuallers, ordnance vessels, troopships and merchantmen.

On 7 January 1780 the West India ships and their escort parted company. The departing vessels saluted Rodney with 15 guns, and the Admiral replied with 11. Next morning 22 Spanish sail were seen and chased; all of them, including a 64-gun ship and six other warships, were captured. A British crew was put aboard the 64 and it was sent off at once for the relief of Gibraltar, taking a dozen captured provision ships which had originally been intended for the Spanish fleet at Cadiz. Passing vessels informed Rodney that a larger Spanish squadron was at sea, cruising off Cape St Vincent. In the afternoon of 16 January (during which time the first store-ships were arriving at Gibraltar, giving confused accounts of the earlier action) the British fleet sighted the Spanish, who included 11 ships-of-the-line and two 26-gun frigates. Rodney gave the signal for battle, the Spanish accepted the challenge and at a few minutes after 4 p.m. the battle began. One Spanish 70-gun ship, the *Santo Domingo*, blew up with all on board and another struck her colours as darkness was setting in. A night battle followed, which continued until 2 a.m. the following morning, when six of the Spanish line were taken. One of the Spaniards was later recaptured by her crew and reached Cadiz; another drove ashore and was lost. But four remained as prizes, including the 80-gun *Phoenix*, on board of which was the Spanish Admiral, Don Juan de Langara, who was wounded. The Spanish defeat was blamed by their French allies on the bad sailing of their vessels and the imperfect seamanship of their crews, with the result that de Langara's ships were caught at very great distances from each other, and were incapable of supporting one another. However, Rodney himself thought that the Spanish craft, looked at from the point of view of design and potential performance, were much superior to his own. Rodney's own ship, H.M.S. *Sandwich*, to quote her captain's log, 'Ran alongside the Monarch at ½ past 1 a.m. and poured in a Broadside, great guns and small arms, to which she struck, without any resistance. Strong gales and squally. At daylight four of our ships and two prizes in sight.'

This victory, fought partly at night (it was christened Rodney's 'moonlight battle') on a lee shore (which meant that any badly crippled ship would be driven onto the Spanish coast), and during a storm which rose to the volume of a tempest, with a great sea, was a daring action in itself. Coming when it did, so shortly after his previous success, and quickly followed by the relief of Gibraltar, it had many triumphal qualities. At the time no fewer than 20 Spanish and four French battleships were lying in Cadiz Bay. But they had made no move to support Langara and made none later, even when Rodney was refitting and repairing at Gibraltar. To the British in that fortress, the sight of Rodney's victorious fleet, the spectacle of captured Spanish vessels at anchor, flying their Spanish colours below the British flag, and the steady unloading of supplies at their own wharves and moles, all this was cause for ecstasy.

Rodney himself, in H.M.S. *Sandwich*, anchored off Gibraltar on 26 January. He had been delayed in his arrival by adverse winds and the necessity for making up that part of his convey destined for Minorca, but though he sent on the store-ships under escort to that place, Eliott retained at Gibraltar the second battalion of the 73rd Regiment of Foot, originally destined for Port Mahon. Explaining his reasons for this in a despatch to the Earl of Hillsborough (who at this time held the seals of office as the Secretary of State 'for the Southern Department', which dealt among many other matters with the affairs of Gibraltar) Eliott stated that he had 4,330 rank and file fit for duty, and of that number 2,250 were needed for service every day in the various guards, batteries, sentry-posts and strong points of the Rock.

The second battalion of the 73rd, like the 72nd Foot from Manchester, had been specifically raised for the American War. Most of the men of the regiment and many of their officers came from the remote parts of Cromarty and Ross-shire; their muster-rolls are crammed with Mackenzies, Macleods, Frasers and Mackintoshes. The first battalion had sailed in January 1779 with the raiser of the regiment, Colonel John Lord Macleod, to the East Indies. The second, under his brother, Lt.-Col. the Hon. George Mackenzie, had been embarked in transports for Gibraltar in Rodney's convoy; but after the capture of the Spanish convoy and escorts in the Bay of Biscay they had been redistributed among the ships of war (whose crews had been reduced by the necessity of manning the prizes) as marines. The largest group, 154 strong, were placed aboard the flagship, H.M.S. *Sandwich*, the others down to parts of companies as low as 29 men in number, in the other warships and frigates. There these new soldiers, most of them Gaelic-speaking, had fought in Rodney's 'moonlight battle', thus receiving their baptism of fire in wild and strange circumstances, pulling and hauling amidst the clamour and uproar of a sea battle at night in a rising storm. They lost four men killed aboard H.M.S. *Defence*, a fair proportion of the total British dead in the encounter, which totalled 32.

A welcome addition to the garrison, they were also picturesque in appearance. They wore the red coat worn by all British infantrymen but this was of Highland cut and worn with Highland accessories: a cocked bonnet with a plume and a belted plaid of tartan. They were accompanied by their band of bagpipes. The cramped quarters, foetid air and low rations of siege life caused an early outbreak of sickness in the ranks; they were to lose 58 men from disease (as against 44 killed or died of wounds and 37 seriously disabled) and had seldom fewer than 100 in hospital through dysentery or other diseases. But they were a fine, youthful and vigorous body of men, who quickly took their part alongside the comrades they found in Gibraltar.

Aboard Rodney's fleet was His Royal Highness Prince William Henry, third son of George III, at this time in his fifteenth year and serving in H.M.S. *Prince George*: he was rated as a midshipman during the relief of Gibraltar. It was natural that a great deal of attention should be paid to him, and he frequently went ashore, visiting the Governor and sightseeing around the fortress. Another distinguished visitor, though a less willing one, was the Spanish Admiral, de Langara, who was carried ashore in a sedan chair still incapacitated from his wounds. He was given the naval honours due to his rank at every guard he passed and was well lodged in the town. He was said to be very bitter about the French, blaming his own disaster on their inactivity. On a later occasion, when he was somewhat recovered, he went the rounds of formal visits ashore and afloat. It is recorded that he was astonished, while aboard the *Prince George*, to find Prince William Henry actually doing duty in the capacity of an officer of low degree, announcing that de Langara's boat was ready when he wished to return to shore. The Spaniard was not used to seeing 'the humblest stations' of a royal navy 'supported by princes of the blood'. But William Henry was a proper seaman, spending the rest of the war afloat and going to sea again (as a highly opinionated and extraordinarily unpopular young captain) between 1785 and 1789. Later, as Duke of Clarence and King William IV, he was to occupy still more exalted positions. At Gibraltar he was just beginning his Royal Navy connections, of which he was always very proud, and which were to bring him the title of 'the Sailor King'. When he returned to England, he brought his father the flag of de Langara and a plan of Gibraltar which he had drawn himself. Chief Engineer Green had personally conducted the prince around the fortress, so that he had had the best possible guide and instructor.

According to his own account, another distinguished visitor who arrived at Gibraltar was the celebrated character Baron Munchausen. Naturally enough, he voyaged in Rodney's own flagship, to see his 'old friend', General Eliott. And equally naturally, he enlivened his stay by dressing like a Popish priest and insinuating himself into the Spanish lines, where his activities caused a great explosion and did immense damage. Just as inevitably, this explosion is not mentioned by any of the contemporary diarists, nor is it recorded in Eliott's despatches.

Rodney's departure was delayed until 13 February 1780 while the unloading of stores of all kinds took place. Eliott reported that he now had bread and flour for 607 days, pork for 487 days, beef for 291 days, butter for 183 days, pease for 164 days, salt fish for 160 days and oatmeal for 104 days. He was, however, short of wines and spirits (50 days) and oil (25 days) and had no more than 300 chaldrons (a measure of $25\frac{1}{2}$ cwt or 36 heaped bushels much used in those days) of coal. He had received a most useful amount of cash money; but he needed not only nearly 900 men to bring his regiments up to strength, but clothing for them. The 72nd Foot he described as 'almost naked', and the newly arrived 73rd were also short. Wine and strong liquors were replenished by seizing this part of the cargoes of such vessels as carried them, paid for by drafts on the Treasury. Many of the British supply vessels in Rodney's convoys had brought mixed cargoes, in the hope of making large profits in Gibraltar. One of them carried beef, pork, butter, flour, pease, oatmeal, raisins, biscuits, coals, iron hoops and candles; she was appropriately named *The United Grocers* and her freight found a ready market. Such goods were usually sold publicly to any who could afford to buy. Government stores went straight into Eliott's warehouses; and the Governor also purchased from Rodney the contents of some of his prizes.

Captured Spanish warships provided some of the heavy guns and powder needed, and Rodney had brought large supplies, but even more was required. With the intelligent care which marked so many of the besieged's actions during the siege, tests were made of this captured powder, which was found inferior to the British. While the fleet was in, there were many cheerful parties among the officers, both ashore in the as yet undamaged houses of the town and in the hospitable wardrooms of the fleet.

Not everyone, however, was happy. Eliott ordered that those soldiers' wives and children who did not have 12 months' provisions in store were to leave with the fleet; each person remaining had to possess either 250 lb. of flour of 360 lb. of biscuit. By this regulation 'many useless hands', as Drinkwater called them, were sent out of the garrison.

Besides the masses of government stores, there were packets and boxes for such private individuals as were lucky enough to have well-to-do friends or relatives in England. The Greens, for example, received a box which had been aboard for six months; they also obtained from private sources three sheep, a cask of butter and two hampers of sugar (though these last proved wet and verminous).

When Rodney was about to sail, Admiral Duff also prepared to go. He had maintained his reputation for indifference by not bothering to go aboard *Panther* even when the fleet first began to arrive at Gibraltar. A naval officer paying the customary courtesy call had been astonished to find him not there at such a moment. He was, as Mrs Green said, 'a quiet man'. His final departure for home was marked by no ceremony and 'he seemed a good deal discomposed and discontented'. He was not employed on active service again, and was in fact one of the very few participants in the siege on the British side who did not gain honour from it.

The weather during much of the fleet's stay was bad, with rain and heavy winds. During storms, shots were sometimes exchanged between British vessels beating about under duress and any Spanish battery to which they approached too closely; but on the whole the Spaniards were remarkably quiet. Their chief activity was the pursuit of several little groups of hopeful deserters from the Walloons. Cavalry and foot came chasing over the isthmus, cutting down and bayoneting some, beating others with the butts of their firelocks or slashing them with sword-cuts. The survivors, if captured, were hanged in public, as usual. Any who got into the garrison gave accounts of flooded trenches and great discomfort in the Spanish lines. The presence of the large British fleet stopped many of their supplies from arriving, for in any country with bad roads (which was the case with most European countries of the age and most certainly true of Spain) coastwise shipping was essential transport; and the Spaniards suffered from shortage of food and stores.

Another result of this quiescence was that, in addition to the stores of the convoy, supplies began once more to come in across the straits: lemons and oranges (most valuable against the scurvy, as had been quite recently discovered), bullocks and other items arrived in port.

Parleys were held between the two sides, and many Spanish prisoners, including the sick and wounded, were returned home. Several Spanish officers were also released on parole, for in those days it was usually accepted that a promise made not to take any further part in the war would be honoured. Among those who left in this way was de Langara. Eliott sent him over the isthmus to the Spanish lines in his own carriage. It is said that the impression made on the enemy Admiral and his countrymen by their treatment during captivity was deeply lasting and, as a result, English prisoners taken afterwards were looked after much better.

The weather improved just before the fleet sailed on 13 February, when Rodney made signal to weigh. About midday the fleet was under sail and going off, and by evening they were out of sight. Their passage could be marked for several hours more by the actions of the Spanish, who fired alarm guns and a great number of rockets from their watch towers along the coast, as the British fleet sailed off to the westward. Rodney, besides the delays due to the disembarkation of stores, had waited for the return from Minorca of the store-ships for that place and their escort of warships. These, three ships-of-the-line and frigates, were among the fastest in the British fleet, having their bottoms covered with sheets of copper. These coppered vessels were largely free from the prodigious masses of barnacles and other clustering forms of marine growth which accumulated quickly on wooden-hulled vessels. Not all British ships of 1780 were so fitted, though the advantages of the system were by then well known. It had been the coppered vessels, sailing faster than the others, which had outstripped and delayed de Langara's squadron. The whole fleet was destined to play a most important part in the war. Rodney fought the French, under de Guichen, near Martinique in April 1780 and again in May of the same year, preventing them from any attempt to regain St Lucia; and in April 1782 he was to defeat decisively a large French fleet under Admiral de Grasse off the isles called Les Saintes, between Guadeloupe and Dominica. It was largely this victory which enabled the British to get reasonable terms of peace and end the whole disastrous war in not too disgraceful a manner. Rodney's relief of Gibraltar in January 1780 was the first decisive act of a decisive series of fleet movements and successes.

# 5

## *The Blockade Resumed*

With Rodney's departure the first major phase of the great siege was over. There were five principal ways in which Gibraltar had been captured in the past: direct attack by land and sea; through hunger; through disease; through treachery; and through prolonged and heavy bombardment. Direct attack had failed when tried by the Spanish in 1704-5 and again in 1727. There was obviously no easy way for it to succeed against such a man as Eliott with the force he had at his disposal. Nor was there any hope of obtaining the fortress by treachery. One of the more alarming stories of the 1727 siege had concerned two Moors within the walls who had plotted to admit the Spaniards; they were discovered, seized, killed and flayed, their skins being nailed on the main gates. Both being very large men, their remains had been impressive and had attracted much attention from visitors, who were in the habit of cutting off sections to take home as grisly souvenirs. Under Eliott's vigilance, with a strong garrison of British and Hanoverian soldiers and a civilian population reduced in size and composed of Jews and Genoese, any such ruse was unlikely to prove profitable. Disease and plague might always be hoped for, of course, in the crowded, squalid and cramped conditions inside Gibraltar; but it could hardly be induced. From June 1779 the Spaniards had made a sincere and commendable attempt to starve out the garrison. They had very nearly succeeded, as they must have known from their own observations, the reports of the Spaniards who had been exchanged as prisoners, the accounts of the few British deserters who had managed to reach them and of the seamen who had run the blockade both ways and returned home to Barbary with tales of high profits, great demand and severe shortages.

The Spaniards determined to continue with a close blockade and to endeavour to reduce Gibraltar by hardship and hunger. By 28 February a Spanish squadron of four line-of-battle ships, two frigates and other craft, still under Admiral Barcelo, was once again operating in the bay.

On the British side, confidence had been greatly increased by Rodney's relief. The practical assurance that Gibraltar had not been forgotten by the people at home in England was most encouraging. Stores and magazines had been replenished. The 73rd Foot was another new corps, like the 72nd. It was a Scottish regiment, a second battalion raised by Lord MacLeod, and up to a strength of 944 rank and file, 30 officers, six staff officers, 50 sergeants and 22 drummers: a substantial reinforcement, in fact. It was true that they had been intended for Minorca, which was down in strength to a mere 1,400 fit men; Eliott took the 73rd in spite of being warned that the safety of Minorca might be jeopardised if he did so. In the upshot Minorca was in fact lost. It capitulated in February 1782, two years after receiving Rodney's new stores and some men; at the conclusion of six months of close siege, constant bombardment, and (at the end) of a widespread attack of scurvy, 600 men crawled out to surrender, the remnants of two British and two Hanoverian regiments. Whether the presence of the 73rd Foot would have made much difference is doubtful. But it is a further indication of Eliott's resolute and independent character that he had no hesitation in retaining this numerous corps in Gibraltar. They were at first stationed in the casemates of the King's Bastion.

Eliott had another reinforcement besides the 73rd. Manning the Spanish prizes and an outbreak of the sickness always present at sea on long voyages put such a strain upon the crews of Rodney's fleet that he had left behind him, more or less perforce, H.M.S. *Edgar*, a 74-gun ship, under Commodore Eliott; so that with the *Panther* (60 guns), the frigates *Enterprise* and *Porcupine*, and the sloops *Gibraltar* and *Fortune*, quite a respectable little squadron lay in the sheltered anchorages around the New Mole. Eliott believed that a large man-of-war, with its heavy batteries, was essential for the proper defence of Gibraltar. He had asked for one earlier; after *Edgar*, with a crew recovered from sickness, sailed to the west on 20 April, leaving the remaining ships undermanned, he was to press for another. These big ships were of impressive size; they provided stable firing-platforms; their batteries of 32-pounders and 24-pounders on lower and upper gun-decks threw a tremendous weight of metal. Moreover, they were in 1780 being armed with a new weapon: the carronade, a short heavy smasher (invented, as it happened, by a General, Robert Melville), of great value in close-quarter work.

Eliott, in spite of his replenished stores, was not lavish in expending his new resources. Before the end of February, and while his sheds and warehouses were still bulging with food, he tried an experiment: instead of meat he distributed salt fish, with some rice and peas; no butter was issued, but the men were paid cash in its stead, so that they could buy what they pleased; this was 'at a very low rate', according to Spilsbury, and led to much discontent and grumbling. To Eliott, with his undemanding stomach, it must have seemed sensible enough; and the salt fish, a cargo brought in by a Newfoundland ship, he no doubt welcomed. But Drinkwater, who was no critic of the Governor, described it as 'indifferent in its kind', and blamed it for encouraging an outbreak of scurvy which began about this time to distress the garrison. The 73rd, after its long sojourn aboard ship, had landed in rather a sickly condition. And as there was at the same time a good deal of what was called 'spotted fever' among the seamen in the port, the Spanish hope that perhaps disease would come to their aid looked in a fair way to become justified. Not until this supply of pernicious salt fish was exhausted, by September, and supplies of salt beef once again more freely distributed, was the upward trend of disease halted.

During March the soldiers of the garrison were put upon definite rations, fixed for officers and men. Apart from bread, each soldier was to receive, in the first and third weeks of a four-week period, the following quantities: 1 lb. pork, $2\frac{1}{2}$ lb. fish, 2 pints peas, 1 lb. rice, $1\frac{1}{2}$ lb. oatmeal, 5 oz. butter, $\frac{1}{2}$ lb. wheat, $\frac{1}{4}$ lb. raisins; in the second and fourth weeks, $1\frac{1}{2}$ lb. beef, 2 lb. fish, 1 lb. rice, $1\frac{1}{2}$ lb. oatmeal, 5 oz. butter, $1\frac{1}{2}$ lb. wheat, $\frac{1}{4}$ lb. raisins. This made a dull menu, but not more conspicuously so than that usually enjoyed by private soldiers in the British army of the period.

The whole treatment of soldiers, in pay and dress and housing as well as in food, was comparable with that accorded to ordinary day-labourers in England. Just as a farm worker or journeyman would be expected to provide his own clothing, so the soldier had to pay out of his meagre daily pay for the replacements of the regulation uniform with which the colonel of his regiment supplied him when his recruitment was approved. The farmer supplied his workmen with ploughs and harrows; the government produced the muskets and bayonets which the soldier needed. The farm worker lived in his master's house or was given a subsistence allowance; the soldier had his place in a regular fortress at home or abroad. As barracks were few and far between in England in the eighteenth century (before an immense expansion in the wars against the French Republic), at home troops on the march or in areas where regular military establishments did not exist were usually billeted in inns.

None of these places had particularly interesting means of cooking food, nor anything especially exotic to cook. The ordinary labourer lived chiefly on bread, cheese and beer, with fresh meat in summer as occasion served, varied with bacon, and salt beef or pork in the autumn, winter and spring. Cromwell's army had fought and marched on a similar diet; bread and Cheshire cheese had been their mainstay. As far as soldiers fared a century later they did little better. Their beef was invariably boiled. Potatoes were then hardly used at all anywhere as a main vegetable. Broth, bread and biscuit at Gibraltar was not supplemented by cheese, which could not be stored and kept in quantity. And owing to the chronic lack of garden space and the impossibility of using the ground on the isthmus to produce such vegetables as cabbages and turnips and beans the garrison's food was dull in the extreme. It was, however, sufficiently nourishing to sustain men in good health and strength, provided that disease on a large scale did not appear. Provision of lemons and oranges, easily enough obtained during normal times in the Mediterranean, though not grown in sufficient quantity on the Rock itself, served to keep away scurvy, the dreaded disease which struck particularly at men aboard ship on long ocean voyages and at beleaguered garrisons deprived of fresh fruit and vegetables.

The Spanish seamen taken prisoner in Rodney's action were a sickly lot, and Eliott was glad to get rid of them by exchange. In his own hospitals the Governor provided a rather more liberal diet than that for troops in barracks and casemates. Each patient received each week the following allowance: 2 lb. beef, 2 lb. fish, 1 lb. rice, 1 lb. flour, 3 pints oatmeal, $1\frac{1}{2}$ lb. raisins, 5 oz. butter. Officers' rations were very similar; they had their quantities issued monthly instead of weekly, had no raisins and a double ration of butter (40 oz. per month). But many had private resources. The Greens for example killed a small cow during March 1780 and obtained 400 lb. of fresh beef. Much of this they gave away; Boyd, the Deputy Governor, had one joint from them; and while the supply lasted they gave a party to their friends. After this, the Greens still had two cows and a small heifer left, as well as their sheep.

March, April and May were on the whole uneventful months. Very few ships came in. Desertion both ways occurred. During March three of the 72nd disappeared in the course of the evening; they were discovered next day asleep in a cave near the crest of Sugar Loaf Point, with their working clothes beside them torn into strips and tied together to form a rope, with which they had hoped to descend the precipitous eastern face to the sea. One of these men, after court-martial, was publicly executed, the first official death for this offence in Eliott's term of office; capital crimes were common enough, but the death penalty was rarely enforced, severe in outlook though the Governor was.

During March also the garrison was interested to notice a spectacular celebration by their enemies. The Spanish squadron off Algeciras had on Rodney's departure abandoned the formidable boom behind which they had sheltered and were anchored in the bay. On the 19th they dressed their masts and yards with innumerable colours and in the afternoon fired off a triple salvo. The troops in the camps were all under arms and three times delivered a feu-de-joie; and so did their batteries both in the lines and at Algeciras, firing a salute of 12 guns each, three times. These were unshotted and purely in celebration. The British, deeply interested, guessed this was in honour of the birth of a prince; and this proved true.

An even more attractive occurrence, because faintly scandalous, took place in Gibraltar itself on the last day of the month. It was Eliott's practice to review each foot regiment in turn, when all officers and men were paraded. Though this was an excellent custom, in the case of the 39th Foot there were complications, for both the colonel of the regiment (who was no less than the Lieutenant-Governor of Gibraltar, Robert Boyd) and the lieutenant-colonel, Charles Ross, were present during the siege. In the ordinary way, the lieutenant-colonel of an infantry regiment was the senior executive officer. To be 'colonel of a regiment' was an honour, which could prove highly lucrative; some colonels were deeply concerned with their own corps, but as a rule they left the actual day-to-day administration to the lieutenant-colonel. Between Boyd and Ross it appears there existed a deep personal antipathy, which they made little attempt to conceal. As always in the restricted circles of a military society, and particularly in the cramped conditions of Gibraltar, this mutual dislike was a source of wry amusement and much malicious comment by their subordinates. Whenever the 39th Foot paraded for inspection, no one could be certain who would appear to take command and report the regiment to Eliott. Sometimes it was the major, William Kellett; now and again Charles Ross (who held the rank of 'colonel in the army', but was lieutenant-colonel of the 39th); and occasionally it was Robert Boyd (colonel of the 39th, and holding the rank of lieutenant-general in the army as well as being Lieutenant-Governor of Gibraltar). On this occasion there was an open quarrel in full view of the paraded regiment and of those spectators who turned up to see this entertaining spectacle. Later there was to be an even more spectacular affair; but this one whetted the appetites of the sensation-hungry spectators.

Sickness, especially smallpox, gained a hold during the spring; and, as smallpox does, this horrifying disease killed many of those it attacked, particularly children. The climate of Gibraltar appears more dangerous for children than for adults. Almost a century later, and at a time when the whole of the Mediterranean world was settled and in deep peace, one historian of Gibraltar, Captain Sayer, a magistrate and of long residence, said that not only were still-born births frequent, but that up to a third of the children born there died before they were three years old. During the siege, with little exercise, no fresh meat, no fruit and general short commons, children were very vulnerable.

In an effort to make more fresh food available for the population, Eliott gave orders that those officers who had enclosed and cultivated patches of ground must send all the produce they did not use themselves to the public market. There those with money were free to buy it. There was, neither at Gibraltar nor elsewhere, any notion in those days of providing equal shares for all. Those who had no supplies of their own, no garden, or no money to purchase food, had to go without. As Rodney's ships had not brought great large stocks and as the blockade was severe, there was still a good deal of genuine hardship among the civilians and among soldiers' families. All the lettuce and other greenstuff which could be grown within the fortress was insufficient to keep the total population in good health. Along with the smallpox, scurvy began to flourish.

It was during this lull in the active fighting between the two sides at the Rock that there developed an extraordinary secret exchange between the governments of Great Britain and Spain. One of the principal objects of Spanish participation in the war was the recovery of Gibraltar. At this point the British were hard pressed. A British seaman, Commodore George Johnstone, a man of considerable political influence, then commanded the squadron on the Lisbon station. He had late in 1779 let fall some hints to politicians in Portugal that an alliance might be made between the two nations, based on the cession of Gibraltar to Spain. Negotiations were opened, with Mr Richard Cumberland, private secretary to the British minister for the American colonies, acting for his master, Lord George Germaine; his opposite number was an Irish priest called Hussey, who had been chaplain to the Spanish Embassy in London; he was then living in England, temporarily acting as a priest on behalf of Spanish prisoners in British hands. Various unofficial exchanges took place between Germaine and

Madrid. Hussey took Germaine's proposals to the Spanish capital, where he showed them to Count Florida Blanca, the Foreign Minister. According to Cumberland, who left an account of this strange transaction, there were several exchanges; Hussey passed freely between Madrid and London. It appears that the proposal was that Spain was to recover Gibraltar, the fortifications of which she was to purchase for at least £2,000,000, with extra sums to cover all stores and artillery; that Great Britain in return was to receive not only the island of Puerto Rico, but other ports and a harbour and fortress near Oran; and that Spain and Britain were to sign a separate peace. France was to be abandoned by her family ally. These ideas were discussed at cabinet level in England. Naturally there was much heated opposition. But Hussey himself certainly thought that the British might cede Gibraltar.

These activities, begun about the time Rodney was preparing to leave the Channel at the end of 1779, dragged on through the months until the following August, when Cumberland, who had himself gone to Madrid to talk things over with Florida Blanca, returned home. The attitudes of the Spanish government changed violently during this period. At first Rodney's relief seemed to make improbable the prospect of taking Gibraltar by force, so that any possibility of obtaining it by negotiation was welcome. Then came exaggerated reports of the undoubtedly violent 'No Popery' riots in June 1780, led by the half-witted Lord George Gordon, which paralysed London for a week and burnt Newgate Gaol and many other buildings; the Spanish believed these might be the beginning of a universal insurrection which would destroy British power. And when d'Estaing, with a powerful French squadron, reached Cadiz, and while plans to unite the northern powers into a confederacy against Britain were maturing, optimism once more returned, and the Spanish Government determined again to renew the direct assault. Gibraltar was to become the trophy of Spanish valour, not the reward of diplomatic jugglery.

Just how seriously all this was meant by the British cannot nowadays be judged. Like the negotiations which the elder Pitt had conducted during the dark days of 1757, all these proceedings were most discreetly conducted. If they had ever been publicly announced, there would have been an immense political and public outcry. Germaine (previously known as Lord George Sackville), one of the principal architects of the disaster at Saratoga in 1777, had a long record of disgraceful behaviour behind him. It had begun with an open display of disobedience, if not plain cowardice, at the battle of Minden in August 1759, which had resulted in his being stripped of all military honours and declared 'unfit to serve his Majesty in any military capacity whatsoever'. Every commander who served with him, from Prince Ferdinand in Germany to Burgoyne, Howe and Clinton in America, demanded an enquiry and was involved in open quarrels. Always highly critical of others, a bully to his subordinates, sarcastic, dull and impervious to hostile comment, he obtained high cabinet rank by unscrupulous jobbing. Germaine was to be very largely responsible for the final disaster at Yorktown in America in October 1781; and when he was finally dismissed and 'promoted' out of harm's way to the House of Lords, he took his seat only after violent opposition and frenzied protests by members jealous of its honour. With such a man in a position of power, almost anything was possible. It is an odd coincidence that it had been a well-fought duel with the same George Johnstone who began these negotiations which many years before had restored his reputation for courage.

Certainly no conception that such negotiations were on foot can have reached Eliott; or if he had any clue he ignored the possible consequences. He continued calmly and methodically to send his despatches home. Regular reports were given on the state of the enemy's batteries and trenches, about the movements of Spanish regiments and fleets and about the merchant vessels or warships under various flags which passed through the straits in either direction. He also recorded the preparation by the Spaniards in their harbours of several fire-ships.

The month of June 1780 began with another celebration of the King's Birthday on the 4th. Eliott, abstemious and unimpressed with ceremonial as he undoubtedly was, believed in the maintenance of routine. The more obviously unflurried he and the garrison were, the better for the morale of his own men, the more daunting it was for the Spaniards observing the imperturbable behaviour of their British enemies. The regulation 42 guns were fired, and Eliott gave a dinner in the garden of his official residence to all military officers of field rank and over, his own staff and the principal naval officers.

But the Spaniards had not been as quiet as many of the British observers believed. Eliott himself had already noted that fire-ships were being prepared, but when on the night of 6–7 June 1780 the attack was actually launched, it came as a complete surprise.

About an hour after midnight, on a very dark and cloudy night, with a moderate wind from the west-north-west, a ship was discovered standing in towards the New Mole. Here the remaining British vessels were anchored; they had drawn as close to the shore as they could, after the departure of H.M.S. *Edgar* and the *Hyena* on 20 April, with their crews recovered from sickness. The *Enterprise* hailed the stranger and received an answer, 'Fresh beef from Barbary'. The *Enterprise* hailed again and then opened fire, making an agreed alarm signal of three guns. The first ship immediately burst out in a blaze of fire, as did a second and a third close behind her. So close was the leading Spaniard that several fireworks and inflammable substances were actually thrown aboard the *Enterprise*, which cut her cable on her captain's orders and drove closer into the shore. Other Spanish vessels followed, until nine tall 'moving mountains of fire', as Mrs Green described them, were drifting down towards the anchored British vessels. All the drums began to beat on ship and shore and the whole garrison rushed to arms. The British squadron and the nearby batteries opened fire and the scene became partly visible through rolling clouds of smoke and flame, from the fire-ships themselves, with their tall masts and sails burning or enveloped in fire and from the flashes of Gibraltar's cannon. The Spanish crews had at once abandoned their burning vessels and made off towards Admiral Barcelo's squadron, which had put to sea in the hope of catching any British ships forced out from the shelter of the New Mole and the neighbouring bays. The British seamen also knew their drill. Officers and men manned their ships' boats, grappled the fire-ships slowly drifting down upon them and towed them out of harm's way, in spite of great heat and the danger of explosion from the powder barrels which it was the usual practice to store between decks for a final burst of destruction. On this occasion, however, the Spaniards had made no such arrangement. Nor, oddly enough, was there any bombardment from the Spanish batteries in the lines, now nearly a year in preparation, over against the North Face of the Rock. Expecting a torrent of cannon-balls from this and other directions, terrified crowds of inhabitants, with their wives and children, roused from their beds in the dark hours, were shrieking and wailing in the streets; which, like the giant face of the long mountain and the high bastions and battery walls of the defences, were lit like daylight.

None of the fire-ships inflicted any damage—though it was touch and go for some time. Two of them drove out to sea. One, burning fiercely, came past the *Panther* anchored in Rosia Bay, and the rest were beached towards Europa Point. There they all burnt very fiercely until about 7 a.m., when it began to rain. Even so, two of the largest burned all day. The biggest had been a ship of 700 tons, originally a 50-gun vessel. A few well-directed bar-shot, of great hitting power, from a 32-pounder at the New Mole Head helped to turn her round and send her out again into the current, which swept her safely away southward. As the dull morning broke, all was quiet; and the garrison rejoiced to see Barcelo's squadron with its cloud of small craft put back to Algeciras.

This attempt by fire-ships very nearly succeeded in its object, as Eliott admitted in code when describing the events of the night to London. The wind had been favourable and the night well chosen. The largest enemy ship had passed within 150 yards of New Mole Head, where several naval vessels and about 20 transports and store-ships and prizes were moored. All had been in great danger, as were the store-houses along the quays and their contents. Four fire-ships had come very close to H.M.S. *Panther*; one so close as to melt the pitch caulking the seams on her sides. Luckily the wind had dropped at the critical moment. And, as Eliott said, the wrecks all made an 'excellent supply of firewood'. He once again asked for a line-of-battle ship to be sent to support his little squadron. Another matter which worried him was the state of the main powder magazine of the fortress, placed in full view from the sea; he thought they might have been in danger if the waterfront had been in flames and the Spaniards had followed their attack with a bombardment.

One odd feature of the night's alarms was that in the midst of the excitement a boat arrived from Tangier. Laden with fowls and leather, she sailed in without any difficulty, evading the Spanish vessels cruising off the Rock, and very luckily not even being fired on by the garrison. During the next day or two other ships successfully ran the blockade, bringing sheep, wine, oil, lemons and other valuable cargoes. These small successes were extremely galling to the Spaniards, particularly to Admiral Barcelo.

Barcelo seems to have been inspired with a deep hatred for the British. The attitude of many other enemy leaders, both Spanish and French, towards the capture of Gibraltar in particular and the war in general seems to have been tepid. They did their duty, but only just. Against Barcelo the British had many complaints. During the exchanges of prisoners during and after Rodney's arrival, it had needed repeated demands from Eliott before British naval prisoners were sent into Gibraltar. Barcelo never indulged in the compliments which even Eliott accepted as part of normal warfare. His blockade before January 1780 had been effective, and the fire-ship attempt was well planned and came near to success. Had the fire-ships got among the British ships-of-war and supply vessels, many would certainly have been destroyed. Fire at sea is the most dangerous of all hazards, the most terrifying to behold, the most difficult to overcome, the most complete in its effects. A huge blaze at the New Mole and along the waterfront might have led to a bombardment from the sea, the destruction of many stores and the capture of any vessels which in the confusion might be forced to put out to sea. The psychological results of such a success on both British and Spaniards would have been very great.

As it was, the attempt on the night of 7 June 1780 redounded to the credit of the garrison. Eliott and his men had now withstood both famine and fire. After a year Gibraltar seemed stronger than ever.

Once again the close blockade was resumed. At the end of June Barcelo sent over four of his vessels, headed by a 70-gun ship, which cruised within gun shot of the Rock and opened fire on the *Panther* and *Enterprise*. No great damage was done, except that an accident in *Enterprise* led to a powder explosion which sent nine seamen into the naval hospital, and injured others. Mrs Green remarked in her diary that the Spaniards had begun to behave 'in a very impertinent way'. Three nights later they extended their impudence to the point of sending in gunboats and bombarding the *Panther* in Rosia Bay, opening on the shore defence when they replied. As it was very dark and other fire-ships had been reported at Algeciras, once more the drums beat, the big guns roared, the women and children were roused and the regiments in the south stood to arms for a couple of hours. *Panther* was hit three times, once in the hull.

The Spanish gunboats, which were to play an increasing part in the enemy's plans, were fast, strongly built, flat-bottomed galleys, quickly and rather roughly constructed. They carried a small mast, slanting forward, which bore a lateen yard and sail. In their bows each carried a heavy single 26-pounder or 36-pounder gun. About 70 feet long and 20 feet in the beam, these gunboats were excellent at their particular task of harassing the British and attacking both shipping and fortifications.

As one result of these measures, *Panther* sailed early in July, when a snoring breeze sprang suddenly up from the east. She had aboard over 100 British seamen returned from Spanish captivity and made for England. Eliott strengthened his southern batteries and camps to support his diminished little squadron, for reports had come in of a strong Spanish and French fleet concentration at Cadiz.

Eliott's information, which he always promptly passed on in code to England, was often very detailed. He gave names of enemy vessels in various ports, with their number of guns, as well as their condition of readiness and the stores they were loading. He also recorded the types and numbers of mortars, howitzers and cannon being mounted in the Spanish forts at each end of their lines on the isthmus, and the constant strengthening and extension of the trenches and batteries themselves; all their troops movements, parades, marchings, reinforcements and changes of station were also described, both of horse and foot. Occasionally there was especially bad news to tell. The Cadiz fleet was not yet to be used against Gibraltar itself; but in July 1780 they captured the outward-bound convoys sent from Great Britain to both the East and the West Indies. The harbour of Cadiz became crammed with these prizes.

One of the despatches from Britain which Eliott received during the summer should have served to set his mind at rest concerning the exposed state of his chief powder stores. The ordnance people at Greenwich, reporting to Lord Amherst, said that these two large magazines at Rosia could not be bettered: they were bomb-proof, with solid roofs of tiles laid on masonry and without any timber, while all doors and shutters were sheathed in copper. Eliott must have known this, but perhaps it gave him some satisfaction to learn of the complete confidence shown at home about these vitally important buildings. Certainly, although there were occasional explosions in expense stores of gunpowder in some of the exposed British batteries, and though during the siege several heavy detonations at various times occurred in the Spanish siege works, both of laboratories and magazines, Gibraltar's main stocks of powder remained intact; nor at any time did the Spanish (who must have been well aware of the exact nature of the defences of Rosia's magazines) think it worth while to lay on any particularly heavy bombardment.

Meanwhile in Gibraltar itself sickness grew. By August 500 had died of smallpox. Only 50 were soldiers, but the army families were hard hit, as well as the wretched inhabitants. Among the children deaths from smallpox rose to 18–20 a week. The weather was hot and oppressive. Fuel again became very short, as the wrecked fire-ships were used up. As much as nine dollars (31s. 6d.) was paid for a single rib pulled from their ruined hulls. Hot and close, clammy weather with dense mists and the thermometer at 92° not only made life oppressive but through mould and decay helped to ruin many stores of food, both public and private. Prices rose. Fifty guineas was paid for a cow 'and a pint of milk a day until she went dry'.

All the time the British bombardment of the Spanish lines went slowly on; save when parleys were held under a flag of truce, as happened when exchanges of prisoners and sick were arranged or executed. The Spanish bore this affliction with astonishing patience. A deserter had described how during the fire-ship attack in June the Spaniards in their

6 *Plan of the additional batteries installed on the North Front*
*From an engineer's drawing sent back to London during the siege*

7 (above)   *The Spanish lines, as seen from
the north flèche*

*From an engraving after an eye-witness
sketch*

8 (left)   *Part of a caissoned British battery*

*Both from sketches by John Spilsbury*

9 (bottom)   *British artillery during the siege*

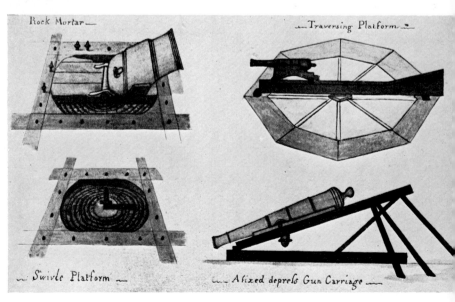

Rock Mortar

Traversing Platform

Swivle Platform

A fixed depress Gun Carriage

batteries had stood ready to fire; he himself, an assistant gunner, and his comrades had their cannon loaded and their matches lighted; they had waited only for the command to fire upon the town; but the fire-ships had missed the Mole and their wait had been in vain.

This meek acceptance of the intermittent cannon-fire from the British works was a matter of policy. It was not because the onslaught caused little danger or damages or few losses. On the contrary, the siege of Gibraltar was marked by many instances of great ingenuity on the part of the British artillery. One of the most effective discoveries was made by Captain John Mercier, an infantry officer in the 39th Foot.

The usual types of shot used in the middle eighteenth century were solid iron spherical balls. These had great battering power, but if they missed the target their effect was often negligible. Some variations were available. Chain-shot consisted of two halves of a round case joined by an iron chain; when discharged they broke the rope which bound them, whereupon they whirled through the air, doing great damage to masts, spars and rigging in shipping or among men unlucky enough to be in their path. Bar-shot were a stiffer version of the same theme. Shells, on the other hand, were spherical cases filled with explosive and fitted with a fuse; when fired from a gun or (more usually) a mortar they blew into fragments when the fuse, in its passage through the air, burnt down to the charge. By 1750 fuses were made of beechwood and cut to lengths according to the requisite time of burning. For short ranges, however, such as those most commonly used on the North Front of Gibraltar, these had to be curtailed to such an extent that either the flash failed to ignite the bursting charge and no explosion occurred, or the fuse caused a premature explosion in the bore of the gun. These 'prematures' are always a cause of great danger to gun crews, and their effect on morale was shattering. To obviate this risk special fuses, filled with a quick-burning composition, were adopted. At the time when the great siege began, the British forces were using three fuses, burning at the rates of 4, $4\frac{1}{2}$ or 5 seconds an inch.

The main Spanish lines were about a mile distant across the isthmus from the batteries around the Land Port Gate, Willis's and the Rock-gun. Many of the British guns were high above sea level, built upon the Rock itself (though it should be noted that not until the last few months of the long struggle was a gallery made inside the mountain). When Eliott began the bombardment on 12 September 1779 great difficulty was at first found not only in finding the range but in doing any appreciable damage. The range was such that only cannon could be relied upon to reach the Spaniards with solid round-shot; but, until the enemy's works drew near the face of the Rock, the British mortars had difficulty in throwing their shells so far. Solid shot plunged harmlessly into the sand of the enemy's works, and anything other than a direct hit was wasted effort; in ordinary conditions balls bounced along the ground after the first strike until they struck something solid or their impetus ran out. Several shells burst immediately on leaving the mouth of the mortar. Even when a shell hit one of the enemy's trenches, it generally sank so deeply into the sand that the explosion was muffled and the damage negligible. At such short ranges it was maddening to be unable to do greater harm.

These disappointments, naturally upsetting to military men intent on good performance, to a large extent ceased when Captain Mercier proposed what proved to be a very successful experiment. He worked out a system of 'calculated' fuses, based on exact ranges, well known to the British. Five-and-a-half-inch mortar shells were then fired from 24-pounder guns on the North Face. The results from a technical point of view were admirable. It became possible to judge times and distances so closely that shells could be made to burst in the air over the heads of Spanish working parties. Moreover, less powder was required to hurl the shell than the round-shot; and the longer barrel of the gun enabled greater accuracy to be achieved in aiming this man-killer. The fragmentation of the casing put the Spaniards in considerable hazard. As Drinkwater said, 'the enemy was more seriously molested'. When the final count was made, it was found that over half the total number of rounds fired during the siege by the garrison were shells: 129,000 out of 200,600.

At the time Mercier's suggestion was regarded as a makeshift, suitable only for the special conditions of Gibraltar. Not for another 20 years was a development of his idea formally adopted by the Royal Artillery, when Henry Shrapnel's spherical case shot was approved. Shrapnel had been greatly taken, as a young officer, by the successful practices at Gibraltar, and worked steadily away at perfecting this deadly projectile; to which, in 1852, his name was officially given.

Less general use could be made of another artillery invention connected with Gibraltar during this period. In 1771 a Lieutenant Healy of the Royal Artillery, while stationed at Gibraltar, had thought of using the solid rock itself to house both charge and projectile. Holes were scooped out at the proper angle, three feet across and four feet deep, shaped like a wine-glass and crammed with gunpowder, topped with a wooden stopper and masses of small stones; a hollow copper tube ran down through the stones and the wood to the powder. After ignition, the powder in the tube took five minutes to burn down to the charge. In the initial experiments, all went well and the stones were successfully fired away. As Gibraltar was at peace at the time, this stone mortar was aimed out to sea. During the siege itself, it is not clear whether Healy's invention (he himself does not appear among the lists of those officers present between 1779 and 1783) was ever used. The trouble no doubt was in arranging for the enemy to present himself in exactly the right place and remain there for at least five minutes.

The rate of fire from the fortress varied greatly. From the opening in September 1779 until the arrival of the relieving fleet and convoy in the following January, over 2,000 shot and 1,700 shells were discharged. Then followed the doldrums of the renewed blockade, with very little activity in any months except July and August; only six cannon-shot were recorded in the whole of April, with another six during September. These figures, it should be noted, relate only to the garrison. The various naval engagements are not included. The picture was to change drastically in October 1780; and again in April 1781 when the Spanish at length opened fire. But for most of the summer of 1780 a dull, tedious inactivity is to be recorded, varied by small naval actions, shortages of food, disease, rumours and gossip.

Towards the end of August there was a delectable and scandalous affair concerning the two officers of the 39th Regiment whose hostility to one another had already caused comment. One morning when the regiment paraded, both General Boyd and Colonel Ross appeared. Ross lost his temper and openly quarrelled with Boyd, calling him 'a storekeeper' and the 39th 'the storekeeper's regiment'. Boyd put Ross under arrest; and reported the matter to the Governor. Colonel Green of the Engineers was made President of the court-martial which tried the case.

The odd thing was that Boyd had indeed been a storekeeper, for he is first noticed in official lists as the civilian storekeeper of ordnance at Port Mahon, Minorca, in 1740. He had remained there during the siege and surrender of 1756, when he had made a gallant but unsuccessful attempt in an open boat to reach Admiral Byng with despatches from General Blakeney, the old veteran who was to receive so much un-deserved praise for his defence. Boyd later gave evidence for the Crown against the unfortunate Byng. In return he was commissioned into the army as lieutenant-colonel. Then, in the strange way in which people of unremarkable background but considerable ability often did make their mark in the eighteenth century (Field-Marshal Ligonier and Captain James Cook are two other instances), Robert Boyd moved through the army lists until he became Colonel of the 39th Foot in 1766 and Lieu-tenant-Governor of Gibraltar two years later. He it was who laid the first stone of the King's Bastion in 1773; and, when it was completed, he had addressed the troops concerned and declared he would wish to see it resist the combined efforts of France and Spain; an event he was to live to experience.

As far as the court-martial went, there was no doubt about Ross being grossly at fault. He had referred sarcastically in public to 'Bob' Boyd and quite clearly had attempted to depreciate the colonel before the eyes of his own regiment. Ross admitted everything; and the sentence of the court was that he should be suspended for 12 months and rendered incapable of ever serving again in the 39th Foot. But Ross was a capable man, like Boyd; and Eliott used his prerogative as Governor and drastically altered both parts of the sentence. Nine months were taken off the suspension and the latter part was mitigated. The 39th was very uncomfortable about the whole affair, and there was a good deal of resentment among many senior officers against Eliott's interference. The truth seems to be that a deep personal antipathy between two able men came to a head in the cramped conditions of their monotonous existence. Both Boyd and Ross had done well before this open quarrel, and both were to distinguish themselves still further during the siege.

As at the same time there was not only a duel between two young officers (no one was hurt, but one of them had a waistcoat button and part of his shirt shot away) but a death through sickness of a senior officer, life on the Rock had its own peculiar interests, quite apart from the actions of the enemy.

The death of Colonel Charles Mawhood on 29 August 1780 came as no surprise. Colonel of the 72nd, the Manchester regiment, he had been ill for some time, suffering in great pain from 'the stone'. He was buried in style and with full military honours, while *Enterprise* fired minute guns throughout the ceremony. The dead officer's effects were publicly auctioned, as was the general practice when a soldier died on active service. Eliott took all his maps, and he and Boyd had the first choice of all Mawhood's books. The rest of Mawhood's belongings fetched amazing prices, partly no doubt because of the general short-ages (though this was not unusual, as the money collected went to the widows and families). Mawhood had been one of the three full colonels of regiments present in Gibraltar during the siege, the others being William Picton of the 12th Foot (who had come at great personal risk to join his regiment) and Robert Boyd of the 39th (as already noted). The other British regiments were commanded by their lieutenant-colonels, the more usual practice. Eliott made use of Mawhood's loss to transfer Ross from the 39th to the 72nd, thus neatly solving a difficult problem with despatch and acumen.

One of Eliott's personal customs did not endear him to some of his senior commanders. This was the stern way he looked upon private indulgences in food at a time of increasing privation in the garrison. He detested the practice of some of the better-off and more influential officers in ordering from Barbary private supplies, and made regulations that everything brought in from the outside world was to be sold in public. This extended even to gifts for himself. When some presents of food arrived for Eliott from General Murray in Minorca (not at that moment quite so hard pressed as Gibraltar) these went to the general market. Mrs Green recorded this with displeasure, for she thought that what might be all very well for a single man of abstemious habits need not necessarily be equally so for married officers with children. And, when it became known that Eliott had in fact accepted some grapes and a melon for himself, she noted not only the details but the embarrassment he had shown when thanking the officer who had made the present. The least slip of this iron man gave a certain pleasure to those who found their own lives unpleasantly (and, as they thought, needlessly) affected by his austerities. Another indication of the irritation which Eliott's single-mindedness could cause is a comment by Spilsbury: after recording that a captain in the 56th had been put under arrest for failing to report the desertion of two men, he complained, 'He expects all garrison orders to be obeyed, whether in the guard orders or not, which not only required a good memory, but is also in a manner contrary to the garrison orders, which say that the Town Mayor shall see all orders relating to the guard wrote in their book of orders.'

The narrowness of life in the fortress, however, did not stop Colonel Green from holding his usual annual meeting on 13 September (the anniversary of the battle on the Plains of Abraham in 1759 which had resulted in the capture of Quebec) of 'The American Gentlemen', in honour of General Wolfe. Green, who was naturally proud of his connection with this remarkable man, was president of this Society. Twenty-one members attended, and a pleasant time was had by all, siege or no siege.

These top-level events, however, dealing with squabbles among their superiors, supper-parties and gossip, meant very little to the bulk of the garrison. Ordinary British private soldiers have always had a strongly detached attitude towards their officers, whose peculiarities of behaviour (often very singular and remarkable) leave them unmoved, so long as they themselves receive what they consider normal fair treatment. If the conditions of time and peace meant the acceptance of what appears today excessively harsh punishment, plain fare and appalling living conditions, these were generally placidly accepted. Flogging was part of military routine in the British army, and was to remain so for a century longer. It had once been recorded in Gibraltar itself that one man, a drummer in the 20th Foot, had in 14 years there been given no fewer than 30,000 lashes, 4,000 of them in a single year. According to an officer, the man at the end of this period (in 1728, after the siege) appeared 'hearty and well'. Regimental flogging, though rarely on this scale, was accepted. So was hanging, in certain circumstances. A soldier given 300 lashes for desertion received them on the Grand Parade during September 1780. Another was given 500 for sleeping on his post. Inaction, boredom and shortage of food seemed to make attempted desertion attractive to some British soldiers; they were willing to run the risk of being shot at by their former comrades, of being dashed to pieces at the foot of precipices or of being hunted down, starving and waterless, in their caves of refuge; but their numbers were never very great, and in all the long years of siege only 43 losses were registered; though this did not include those who were seized before reaching the Spanish lines, either across the isthmus, or, for some few, trying to swim out at night to the Spanish blockading vessels.

# 6

## *The Second Relief*

The Spaniards succeeded in striking a heavy blow at the end of August 1780, though it was the kind of stroke only the results of which were noticed by most of the garrison. The Emperor of Morocco, persuaded by Spanish gold and arguments that Gibraltar must fall and Great Britain lose the war, announced that he would give no more protection to any powers engaged in the struggle. In practice this meant nothing to the French and Spaniards, who had the free use of all waters around the Straits of Gibraltar. But as the Emperor also declared in form that the contending nations were at liberty to carry on hostilities against one another either in his ports or along his shores, one result was that several British vessels in Morocco waters, laden with stores for Gibraltar and waiting for a favourable wind or moment to stretch across to the Rock, were immediately seized by the Spaniards.

This action was followed by others, more directly hostile. British subjects were ordered to leave Morocco. The British Consul, Mr Logie, was attacked in the streets, as were many hapless traders and refugees, British subjects only by accident, who were living in and around Tangier and Tetuan. The old days of violence and atrocity by the true believers against the infidels returned; women and children owing allegiance to the British were brutally treated and families driven from their homes. Not only was a valuable source of supplies sealed off but also a highly organised information service was interrupted. Logie, an indefatigable worker, escaped; but his secret channels of intelligence were largely closed.

Food in the garrison became even more scarce than before. Baking stopped. Biscuits were delivered to the regiments, instead of soft bread, from the beginning of October. Scurvy increased. At sea the Spanish paraded before the helpless garrison many of the blockade runners they had captured, with ensigns reversed. And on land they began to develop their works and to show more animation than usual.

Eliott reported home that the Spanish had built in their lines nearly 200 stone buildings, large and small. They put up, in one dark night, a breastwork over 56 feet long and 10 feet thick, within half a mile of the British lines, as well as breaking down and setting on fire the huts which some of the British soldiers and civilians had constructed in the quiet months which were now ending. Even more daringly, they had come undiscovered as far as the palisades built in front of the British guard-houses or stretching down into the margin of the sea and had attempted to burn them with fireworks and combustibles. But the first flames aroused the British, firing from the fortress's muskets and cannon began, the blazes were put out by the guards and many of the Spanish bundles of 'fire machines' were carried into the town. When daylight came, it was noticed that the Spanish batteries and earthworks were fully manned and the garrison confidently expected a bombardment to begin. Many of the inhabitants once again took alarm and fled to their huddled quarters on the southern part of the Rock. But little happened. Willis's for a few nights threw light balls towards the enemy, with an occasional shot. One recorder, noting this outbreak of violence, said that, when shells were fired at a Spanish sentry mounted on the new earthwork, 'the man shewed tokens of defiance, and turned his backside to us'. Drinkwater had previously declared that 'the enemy's operations on the land side had been for many months so unimportant as scarcely to merit our attention'. Times were changing. Another night attempt to set the palisades alight failed, and the little vegetable patches on the isthmus, once again replanted, were once more abandoned by their hopeful gardeners and trampled flat or looted by the Spaniards.

The only bright spot in the garrison's life was that the last of the detested salt fish was served out. From Eliott's point of view, much more important was the happy capture of a vessel from a Danish convoy, which the navy boarded from ships' boats when she drifted close to the Rock in a fog. She proved to be laden with lemons and oranges from Malaga. This invaluable cargo was at once purchased by the Governor and distributed to the soldiers. Scurvy, which had been filling the hospitals and crippling even men who had a few months before been hale and active, was halted. In a few days the sick were back in service. Their old sores and wounds, even broken bones which once perfectly healed had separated again after the onset of this horrible and little-understood disease, were made well. Fresh fruit and newly expressed juices were most efficacious, as twentieth-century readers well versed in knowledge of vitamins will appreciate. But Eliott, sooner than see the rest of this wonderfully lucky cargo go to waste, had the lemons squeezed out before they could rot, mixed the liquid with brandy at the rate of 60 gallons of juice to five or ten gallons of brandy, and preserved it in barrels. The sick had been given from one to three fresh lemons a day, depending on their degree of disease, until recovered. It was found that the preserved liquor, though not so speedy in its well-doing as the fresh fruit, usually succeeded in curing scurvy if long continued. When the siege was over, several casks of this reserve supply remained in store; opened, they were still in good condition. The seizure of this single ship's cargo, captured when it was, was almost as valuable as any other single action during the whole long trial of the great siege.

Further to strengthen their grip over the food supplies of Gibraltar, the Spaniards deployed their gunboats against the fishing boats which regularly put out under the shadow of the Rock. These small craft quickly retired on the appearance of the swift double-banked galleys. The Spaniards repeated this practice daily until fish became scarce ashore. As Drinkwater said, 'we did not much approve of this conduct'. Attempts to reopen cultivation on the isthmus garden plots were foiled by an enemy now vigilant and determined. New and lower ration scales were brought in. The garrison became restive, though Eliott himself thought they bore their trials 'cheerfully'. Money became almost useless, so little food was there to be had. Mrs Green, when offered 12 guineas for one of her remaining sheep and £60 for a cow, refused the butcher. Her hardships, however (which included having her house shaken by shot going overhead every time the British fired on the new Spanish works), did not stop her regular attendance at a weekly whist party given by an artilleryman friend, Captain Lloyd.

A new nuisance now appeared. The Spanish gunboats, spurred on by their success in driving the British fishermen from the sea, came softly in towards the town and moles on every quiet or dark night and opened fire on the *Enterprise* and the other vessels at anchor and on the town itself. November 1780 was remarkably calm and dry, giving plenty of scope for this new harassing method. A boom was constructed, of masts joined by cables and held in position by anchors. It was a heavy work, but gave some protection in the waters it enclosed near the New Mole; though Eliott, writing home, had some doubt as to whether it would withstand the very heavy seas which occasionally and with great violence rolled in from the west.

On every side the Spanish determination to press the siege more closely was observed. Their new works on the isthmus were continuously strengthened. Magazines and support trenches were constructed. Fire was opened on mule-trains and strings of carts bringing up baulks of timber and building supplies. Eliott had 10,000 shell cases cast for his 32-pounders, each with a cavity only large enough to contain the least quantity of powder sufficient to burst them.

In order to prevent the enemy from prying too closely into conditions of defence and nourishment within the garrison, from the latter part of October 1780 onwards arrangements were made for all parleys between the opposing sides to take place in boats at sea. Movement across the isthmus was forbidden.

One or two blockade-running vessels got in, some from Minorca, now the nearest friendly spot, and that over 600 miles away across the hostile Mediterranean. One of these visitors, an English armed ship of a kind known as a polacre, the *Young Sabine*, raised the garrison's spirits, as had the *Buck* during the previous year, by fighting a spirited engagement with the Spaniards on 12 November 1780. Several small craft and three gunboats attacked her, coming close enough to attempt to board. The English vessel, however, of 200 tons and possessing eight 6-pounder guns, with a crew of only 18 hands (another account says nine), including boys, repelled the close-quarter assaults by musketry and reached port safely. She had taken 18 days from London and had been hit by no fewer than 29 shot in her rigging. Her captain, a resolute bold Irishman named McLorg, was well rewarded, for his ship's cargo, mostly of food, sold for prodigious prices: she carried cheese, ham, flour, sugar, butter and potatoes (which brought 1*s*. 3*d*. a pound); as she also had porter, newspapers and letters, and carried news of a projected convoy, the *Young Sabine* was a very popular ship as she lay under the guns of Gibraltar. Her rum fetched 10*s*. a gallon, porter £6 10*s*. 0*d*. a hogshead, herrings £4 a barrel, flour £3 12*s*. 0*d*. a barrel, coals 14 guineas a chaldron, candles 1*s*. 4*d*. a pound. She sailed for Minorca in January 1781 and apparently got clear away.

Supplies of leather which occasionally arrived in blockade runners were always welcome. Military activities are traditionally hard on the legs and feet and soldiers' boots notoriously heavy and solid. The conditions of life on the Rock kept the garrison vigorously occupied, and as early as the May of 1780 many of the men and several officers had been reduced to wearing shoes made of canvas, with soles of spun yarn.

The weather during December was extremely bad. Torrents of water flowed down the gullies of the Rock, carrying away parts of the works and breaking the leg of a gunner caught in a flood at Willis's. Mrs

Green recorded sorrowfully that a violent hailstorm had destroyed almost all the beans, peas and young salad stuff she had been carefully tending in the garden of her house at Mount Pleasant. However, she got a quarter of mutton from Boyd, who had killed a sheep. Christmas Day was fine, and a large ship arrived from Liverpool, with 300 casks of flour, and other stores, so she and her husband passed a tolerable holiday. And on New Year's Day the Greens, with a small dinner-party and no other celebrations, entered the third calendar year of the siege, along with the rest of the garrison and the remaining miserable and depressed inhabitants of the place. Since the main church was being used as a store for dry provisions, services were held in the shelter of the King's Bastion.

Another event a few days later gave rise to more speculations about Colonel Ross's future; for he, 'thinking himself colonel of the 72nd' (to use Mrs Green's words), gave a dinner-party to all the officers of the regiment. Ross, indiscreet as usual, had reason to rejoice; but to do so in this fashion was unwise. Secure in the knowledge of Eliott's personal interest in his affairs, Ross often gave cause for gossip.

During the early days of January 1781 it became known that one of the deserters from the Spanish lines had been arrested as a spy. He had come in late in the previous September, dressed as a peasant, but declaring himself as a native of Strasbourg and a sergeant in the Spanish army. A very handsome, clever man, he spoke English well, having, so he said, lived for four years in England. He was placed out of harm's way at Windmill Hill, but fell under suspicion when he was found in the soldiers' barracks of the 58th Regiment there, talking to the men. When seized, several suspicious papers were found on him; one was supposed to be to a Colonel Nugent, of the Irish corps in the Spanish service, acknowledging certain sums of money; according to Drinkwater, this spy recommended the Europa Flats as the best place for an assault. Though how this was to be done in the face of extensive line and battery defences, supported by many military camps, and sheltered behind rocky and dangerous approaches, was not explained. With one of the strange and almost inexplicable twists of eighteenth-century justice, this man, though kept under close guard, was not brought to trial, and some time later was returned, during one of the frequent flags of truce, to the Spaniards. Other deserters, coming in later, left no doubt that he had indeed been a spy, and that he had been liberally rewarded when he arrived with his budget of news.

As far as British intelligence from the outside world was concerned, practically all the news was bad. The support of the Moroccans for the

enemy became more than ever evident. Logie and all the British subjects in Tangier and Tetuan arrived under a flag of truce in Gibraltar;
they were glad enough to be with their own folk; but they had been
forced to leave behind all their belongings and brought no effective help
to the garrison. They reported that the Emperor of Morocco was now
calling the Spaniards 'his best friends'. Obviously there was no hope of
succour or supply from that quarter. Spanish mortar boats were seen
undergoing trials off Algeciras. These vessels were an adaptation of their
gun launches. Instead of having a gun mounted in the bows, the mortars
were fixed in a solid bed of timber in the middle of the boat, masts and
yards being so placed that they could be braced athwartships to give
free passage to the shells despatched high into the air. In spite of rains
and storms and almost constant bombardment, the enemy's trenches,
batteries and emplacements, all well protected by sand, crept over the
isthmus towards the North Face. Eliott kept London well informed on
these matters, sending home beautifully drawn plans on which the new
hostile works were shown in detail, on a scale of 200 feet to the inch.
London, in return, after telling the Governor that to make the 400
fathoms of chain which he needed for a boom would take six months
'and not sooner', recommended that the British should build some
launches of their own to operate against the Spanish vessels, since
ships' boats were not suitable. The boom problem Eliott had solved for
himself. The recommendation about the building of launches he was to
act upon, with good results.

Besides Eliott's despatches, letters from his Lieutenant-Governor,
Robert Boyd, occasionally arrived in London and were filed away.
These were often curiously ingratiating, talking of his 'present state of
insignificancy', or saying that he was of 'too little consequence to take
up the time of a Secretary of State'; he gave news of Spanish ship movements; and remarking on increased prices of different articles in February 1781 gave some examples: a pair of ducks cost 18s. 9d. (against 1s.
11½d.); a nutmeg 1s. 6¾d. (1d.); a bottle of porter 2s. 1d. (3½d.); a
quarter cask of sherry £12 10s. 0d. (£7 16s. 3d.); of more essential
supplies, a hen egg cost 5¾d., and a pound of butter 2s. 4d., against ½d.
and 6¼d., respectively. Boyd commented: 'Do hang this up by the
Oxford Almanac in your office.' But the garrison had no news of any
help coming.

Boredom grew, with grim results. The master of the *St Fermin*
killed himself by drink. Men deserted from the 56th and the 73rd; even
two of the Germans went, from Hardenberg's regiment. One deserter
from the 56th was a sergeant; he bolted while in command of a post

under the North Face, going away slowly towards the Devil's Tower, and halting occasionally, even while his own guard fired at him, as if undetermined whether to proceed or not. He left a wife and two children behind him and had always previously been thought of good character. Money troubles were the cause of his desertion. He had been paymaster to his company and had run a mess for officers, but got into debt. Eliott thought that there had been too much liberty on the picquets when these desertions took place. He circulated 'a very severe note', which was not openly published, to the officers of regiments dealing with their neglect of duty.

Other indications of a falling morale are to be found. There are frequent comments in contemporary diaries about men being punished for drunkenness. On 28 March two soldiers of the 56th were hanged for burglary and robbery. Officers, too, were in trouble. Three officers of the 72nd were brought to justice for refusing to pay their debts to a couple of Jews and for beating them up. It appears that the Jews had bought food for these young men for cash, but had not received it. When they protested they were knocked about, and one officer fired a pistol at them; the pistol was loaded only with powder, but the abuse was flagrant. It cost these officers 50 guineas to get out of this scrape.

Eliott tried to combat idleness and despair by giving money rewards for men spotting and reporting any new enemy activity. Various new artillery expedients were practised. Holes were bored in the living rock and used as mortars, in the manner used previously by the artilleryman, Healy. One gun was tried at elevations of 2, 4 and 6 degrees, first lashed so as not to recoil; and again unlashed, when the shots went the farthest. The higher the elevation, the fewer were the subsequent ricochets. These experiments aroused some interest; and even more important, created a diversion. 'Quadrants, Spirit-levels and instruments of various forms and machinery adorn the batteries, for the more exact and certain method of killing', wrote Ancell of the 58th; 'I suppose in a few weeks more practice, they will be so expert in levelling a gun that should a Spaniard raise his head about the épaulement, it will be immediately severed from his shoulders.' The gunners certainly did their best. In the first three months of 1781 they shot off over 1,700 rounds at the steadily developing sand-shrouded works on the isthmus.

A series of field-days was also held. First each regiment was reviewed in the normal manner. The stiff rows of redcoats, with halberded sergeants and sword-bearing officers interspersed among them, their field-officers mounted, were inspected by the Governor. Then they marched away to their alarm posts, and indulged in several volleys of parapet firing. The preparations and the release of tension gained by some pretence of action no doubt was of benefit to the men; but all that Eliott could think of did not prevent the officers of each regiment from presenting, through their commanding officers, a general memorial of complaint, a kind of round robin, to the Governor. Such an expression of feeling, from lower ranks to those above them, was almost equivalent to mutiny in the British army. Only their idleness and the unpleasant conditions of their everyday life can have brought English regimental officers to such a pass.

These officers, however, had very genuine sources of grievance. There were, of course, the increased prices of all necessities. British officers normally had to supply and pay for their own food. At a time when a subaltern's daily pay might be swallowed by the cost of his dinner alone, most of them depended on private incomes or parental allowances. The siege had naturally caused these charges to rise; while at the same time the general uncertainties of their conditions brought about violent fluctuations in the rate of exchange between the pound sterling and the Gibraltar dollar, which was used for cash transactions. Expenses for clothing and general supplies had also gone up. Moreover, and this was a most important point, the chances of promotion had almost entirely vanished. The expanding war had offered all manner of opportunity for ambitious officers to rise in the service, always provided they were not prevented from participating by being shut away in a distant and confined place like Gibraltar. New regiments were raised at home, of horse and foot; second battalions were added to several of those already existing; each gave employment to 30 or so additional officers, of whom the lieutenants and captains usually came from those already serving; but officers in Gibraltar could not exchange or buy higher rank or gain it by raising men for these new corps, like their friends at home. Even their light losses in action were a grievance. Commissions for all ranks up to lieutenant-colonel were usually obtained by purchase money. But in war-time promotions abroad and in battle were freely gained by officers of the regiment actually on the spot who moved upwards to fill vacancies caused by death. In the field it was a matter of keen interest to the senior captain as to what happened to the major; should death snatch him away promotion to the vacancy almost automatically followed. Subalterns and junior officers used to drink toasts to 'a long and bloody war'. To gain a step meant not only honour but a cash bonus. Yet all this was denied to those cooped up in the threatened but, it seemed, immortal walls of the Rock.

This first mentioned memorial was followed by a second. Each was profoundly respectful, each was duly delivered to the Governor. Neither received any acknowledgment or reply. Eliott was not a man to encourage either innovation or insubordination, however slight, in matters of military etiquette; but he reported their arrival and contents to the home authorities.

By mid-February 1781 real hardship was being felt. Once more the bakers left off work, both for want of flour and of fuel. Firewood was selling by the pound, and was still scarce. Damaged biscuits, onions, even tough meat from elderly oxen, all commanded high prices; crumbled biscuit dust sold for 1s. a pound; salt, half of it dirt, the sweepings of ship's bottoms and storehouses, cost 8d. a pound; English farthing candles were sixpence apiece. The few supplies which were slipped in from Minorca were almost all of luxuries, since that island also was running short of essential foodstuffs. Wine and brandy were not much use to people on the very edge of starvation. Eliott reduced rations; bread and biscuit shrank to a pound a day, beef and pork to one pound each a week; though, if they could pay for it, the soldiers were permitted to buy an extra weekly pound of beef. Yet, Eliott reported, the garrison was healthy. By March these short allowances had to be reduced still further. A soldier received only $5\frac{1}{4}$ lb. of bread a week; his 13 oz. of salt beef and 18 oz. of pork were both of them stinking when he got them, his miserable $2\frac{1}{2}$ oz. of butter 'little better than rancid congealed oil'. The Greens staved off their own hunger in some measure by slaughtering their heifer. It yielded only '200 weight' of meat, being a mere year and eight months old. In recompense for Boyd's earlier generosity, they sent him a sirloin. The officers' whist parties were still maintained, but life was becoming anything but normal.

Because food was short, Captain Patrick Leslie suggested that *Enterprise* and *St Fermin* might be sent away to Port Mahon with all the invalids. Eliott agreed, since things were very bad and the arrival of a convoy uncertain. But he decided that the impending departure should not be any way divulged or advertised, particularly to the traders of Gibraltar. Some alarm had been felt by the discovery of a long-boat from the frigate H.M.S. *Brilliant*, empty save for oars and a sailor's jacket, adrift off Cape Palos; she actually arrived safely at Port Mahon; but any reduction of naval strength at Gibraltar might well have appeared like desertion. Morale had as far as possible to be maintained even if hope was running out. Eliott wrote to General Murray in Minorca, confided that 'a very little time will reduce us to the utmost straits', and begged that the naval officer commanding the squadron then off the island should come down to Gibraltar with all his force. He wanted this officer (one Captain Curtis, who was later to play a noble part in Gibraltar itself) to use his warships to escort a convoy to the Rock, and to load aboard his own vessels as much of Murray's own stores as he could spare. He also suggested that the ordnance store-ship at Port Mahon should give free passage to any supplies from private sources which could be obtained, so that as much as possible should be sent. Eliott said that as there were at that time (27 March 1781) only three bad sailing frigates and a few zebecs and gunboats about the Rock, this expedition might be ventured without much risk. Events of the next fortnight were to make many of these suggestions unnecessary. At the end of March *Enterprise* sailed for Minorca, accompanied by the sloop *Fortune*; the *St Fermin* failed to clear the New Mole, and remained behind. She finally got away early in April, one moonlight night; but was pursued by Spanish zebecs and taken, with the last of the garrison's invalids aboard.

Gibraltar's plight had not been overlooked in Great Britain. Colliers were being steadily collected, as well as supplies of rum 'of the strongest kind', medicines, and *sauerkraut* (a recommended remedy of the time for scurvy), as Lord Hillsborough told Eliott early in January. In fact, on reduced rations Gibraltar had sufficient supplies to exist until April or May; but the moment he heard that a convoy was being assembled, Eliott sent home an immense list of requirements, ranging from wheat, rye and barley (in grain, meal or flour) and going down to charcoal, pitch, tar and rosin.

It was largely the Spanish obsession with the assault on Gibraltar which permitted its relief. The French wisely kept their European fleets concentrated at Brest, where they were well placed to conduct two important campaigns: one in support of the Americans; the other against the immense British convoys which regularly sailed for the West Indies, for the American ports in British hands and for the East Indies. But the Spaniards were reluctant to leave Cadiz. A resounding enemy success in August 1780, when only eight ships escaped out of a British convoy of 63 sail (and 16 of the captured vessels were carrying troops and supplies), had shown how vital the role of a large allied fleet might be. During the year 1781 French squadrons under Admirals de Grasse and des Touches were to divide and confuse the British Commanders, Hood, Rodney and Graves, to such an extent that finally and at the vital moment command of the sea off the North American coast passed to a fleet of 36 French battleships off Yorktown. There, on

19 October 1781, the commander of the only large British field army on American soil, Lord Cornwallis, was forced to surrender. This, the decisive event in the American War of Independence, was a magnificent achievement by the French navy. Had the Spaniards been co-operative a similar success might have occurred earlier. But in the spring of that year the Spanish Government was so intent on recovering Gibraltar that their great ships remained at Cadiz; where in fact they proved useless in either forwarding the assault on the Rock or preventing its relief.

The convoy which the British Government gathered for supplying Gibraltar and Minorca sailed from St Helens on 13 March 1781 under the protection of a fleet of 28 ships-of-the-line, commanded by Vice-Admiral George Darby, in H.M.S. *Britannia*, a 100-gun three-decker of the largest size in the Royal Navy. Off Cork they were joined by a further five ships-of-the-line, destined for the East Indies, as well as a number of victuallers and trade ships for the West Indies and America.

Darby himself was not an outstanding naval officer. His elevation to the post of commander-in-chief of the Channel fleet had been a nasty political job perpetrated by Lord Sandwich, who had originally promoted Darby to ensure the acquittal in an impending court-martial of Admiral Palliser, another of Sandwich's political supporters. But Darby, like the majority of English naval officers, was a competent seaman, well versed in the arts necessary to handle large numbers of vessels. Here he had little to do. He sailed south from Ireland, sending off at intervals the various convoys to their several destinations as he pressed on for Gibraltar. On 10 March he was off Cape Spartel. Three sail were sighted, and Darby sent ships to chase them. But the weather was foggy and in the upshot the large Spanish fleet in Cadiz made no attempt whatsoever to interfere. Firing signal guns every hour to keep together his squadron, now reduced to 29 ships-of-the-line, and the convoy of 100 store-ships, *Britannia* sailed on in regularly rising winds until all arrived on 12 April 1781 in a decreasing gale, off the Rock of Gibraltar. The convoy got safely in, but Darby and the greater part of his squadron kept cruising in the Bay and Gut of Gibraltar from their arrival until 18 April. During their first evening 13 transports, escorted by two frigates, slipped out and made their way eastwards to Minorca. Darby saw 26 enemy sail off Algeciras, but no large-scale challenge was made to him by sea then or later. After spending a couple of days at anchor off Gibraltar the *Britannia* and Darby finally collected their charges and sailed home to England on 21 April arriving off the Lizard on 18 May, with despatches from Eliott.

The second relief of Gibraltar on 12 April 1781 caused great changes in the conduct of the siege. The British had for hours before its arrival carefully noted new dispositions of the Spanish vessels off Algeciras, and an immense business of flag signals repeating from their towers. There was great activity in their batteries and new guns and mortars were installed. It was guessed that the long-awaited convoy was drawing near, and this was confirmed when at midnight on 11 April a cutter, the *Kite*, reached harbour from the approaching fleet. She carried despatches from London and messages from the Admiral; and her commander, Captain Trollop, went ashore at once and waited on the Governor.

Next morning a thick fog covered the surface of the sea around Gibraltar, but the topmasts of Darby's vessels could be seen above the rolling mists from the British signal posts along the crest of the Rock. As the day broke and the sun became more powerful the fog gradually rose, as Drinkwater described it, 'like the curtain of a vast theatre, discovering to the anxious garrison one of the most beautiful and pleasing scenes it is possible to conceive'. The convoy moved towards harbour in a compact body, under the escort of some warships, while the rest of the naval squadron lay-to under the Barbary shore, owing to a suspected danger from fire-ships. Fifteen Spanish gunboats formed line, came a little way out from Algeciras and opened fire on the nearest vessels of the convoy. But when a line-of-battle ship and two frigates sailed over towards them, the Spaniards broke up their order and fled indiscriminately back to shelter under the land. In their haste several ran aground and were abandoned by their crews, who scrambled shorewards over the rocks. The garrison was later bitterly to regret that the navy did not send in the boats to destroy these helpless craft; but the naval officers were contemptuous of these 'bum-boats', as they called them, and left them to be re-manned and safely carried off by the enemy.

So far so good. But as the leading ships of the convoy dropped anchor off the harbour, at about 11 a.m., the long-prepared Spanish batteries at last opened fire against the fortress. In all about 114 pieces of ordnance, of heavy metal, 26-pounder guns and 13-inch mortars, opened up, from Fort St Philip on the bay side to Fort St Barbara on the Mediterannean coast. The guns thundered from five large batteries and from the forts; and the mortars, some 50 in number, shot from their emplacements in the lines. They aimed at the British batteries around the Land Port Gate, at the town itself (which was largely under direct observation from various Spanish signal posts and observation towers) and at the waterfront and the shipping crowding alongside it. The Spaniards broke off for their usual period of siesta soon after 1 p.m., but reopened fire at 5 and continued pounding away for the rest of the day and throughout the night. The British batteries replied, concentrating the weight of shot and shell against the St Carlos battery, which soon slackened its fire.

On the first sight of the new relief, both soldiers and inhabitants had crowded towards the shore, shouting and cheering at the longed-for approaching end of distress and shortage. The storm of fire which fell upon the town caused panic and confusion; men, women and children fled in great discord to the open spaces at the southern end of the Rock. Fire broke out among the crowded and abandoned houses of the town. Some of the enemy's shells fell as far as the New Mole, nearly two-and-a-half miles from the cannon's mouth; their shot, which included fireballs, reached beyond the South Port. Nowhere was safe, and confusion, destruction and conflagration raged unchecked.

Not much harm was done to the convoy itself. One small vessel was sunk near the water-tanks by a direct hit, but the vessels moved to the south of the New Mole and began to disembark their supplies hurriedly there and at Rosia and Camp Bay. Five hundred men of the garrison helped to unload. This number was later increased and though enemy fire continually harassed the British shipping, the work went on unceasingly. With the exception of the 72nd Regiment, fairly safely housed in the bomb-proof casemates of the King's Bastion, and the various companies of other regiments stationed in similar strong points, the bulk of the British and Hanoverian infantry was marched south to join those already in position round Windmill Hill and on Europa Flats. There they settled into camps which during the next two years grew to look like permanent settlements.

During the afternoon pause in the enemy bombardment on the first day, most of the inhabitants dashed back into the burning town to try to rescue, many of them, not only their personal possessions but supplies of goods which they had kept concealed in order to bring forth in small quantities, when the prices suited, in time of shortage. They quickly fled again. Not only did the shower of shot resume. Their lives were put in danger from undisciplined and looting soldiers, plundering the battered and abandoned houses.

As was often the case in the British army of the eighteenth and early nineteenth centuries, when their usual harsh discipline broke down in new and unforeseen circumstances, the men quickly got completely out of hand. A retreat, a stricken field, a disaster often meant the temporary disintegration of whole regiments. At sea in shipwrecks it was the same: crews would refuse duty, break open the liquor stores and drink themselves into stupefaction. So it was at Gibraltar. Under the sudden opening of the bombardment, the soldiers, at the very moment of relief, finding after months of critical shortage that many Gibraltarians had kept hidden supplies tucked quietly away, broke into plundering, looting, debauchery and destruction among the blazing and ruined houses of the town. By the third day large numbers were adrift. Among the exploding shells and crashing round-shot, men drank indiscriminately the stocks of the abandoned wine-shops; one of the 12th died from vast quantities of raw spirits, and the life of another was saved with difficulty. Any animals found were slaughtered at once. Pigs, turkeys, ducks, geese and fowls were shot or bayoneted and immediately boiled, roasted, baked or fried at great fires in the streets. Even the government stores were invaded and robbed, while any woman who ventured into the town ran a very good risk of insult.

It was noticeable that only the British troops misbehaved. Eliott in a later despatch said 'the Hanoverians have committed no publick outrage'.

Just how serious were these riots is hard to determine. Indiscipline certainly occurred and Eliott and his fellow officers were naturally deeply indignant. The Governor specifically denied any case of rape occurring, but some of the more excitable (and less responsible) diarists of the siege use the word. Drinkwater mentions that, in their 'succession of irregularities', one drunken group of soldiery gathered in the ruins of the Roman Catholic Church in Gibraltar, 'to carouse and be merry'. One of the troops noticed in the wreckage a life-size image of the Virgin Mary, which he proposed to put in the whirligig, at this time kept permanently in position at the end of the Grand Parade for the correction of scolding women. A mock court-martial was held, 'her ladyship was found guilty of drunkenness, debauchery and other high crimes, and carried in procession to her place of punishment. There she was found by the Governor, who, despite the firing, regularly attended guard-mounting. He was deeply offended and had the image removed to the White Convent. But even there, where she should have been safe enough, Drinkwater declares, 'she was by no means exempt from further insult and disgrace'. This kind of thing sounds more like a drunken frolic than a complete breakdown in discipline.

Eliott sent the town-major and a party of well-disciplined men into the town to stave in and destroy all the casks of strong liquor they could find, and all women were ordered to move southwards away from the

10   *Lieutenant-General Robert Boyd*

*From an engraving by John Hall
after A. Poggi*

11   *Captain Sir Roger Curtis*

*From an engraving by J. Caldwall
after W. Hamilton*

12   *Admiral Sir George Rodney*

*From an oil painting after Sir Joshua
Reynolds*

13   *Admiral George Darby*

*From the oil painting by George Romney*

**14** *The naval hospital at Gibraltar*
*From a sketch by John Spilsbury*

**15** *The town under bombardment*
*From an engraving by James Fittler after Richard Paton*

dangers of bombardment and personal harm. The wives and families of officers and men went off in droves, the lucky ones to find shelter in tents which were hurriedly pitched, the others to find what refuge they might amongst the rocks. Even there they were not safe, for the Spanish gunboats ranged along the shore, shooting at the unloading convoy as darkness came on. The balls which missed the shipping fell on land. Breastworks improvised from furniture, trucks, mattresses and bolsters were of little use and many women and children spent a miserable night sheltering in crevices on the slopes. There also some were hit. Nor were their sufferings of this first night to be their last.

By the conventions of eighteenth-century warfare, the bombardment of the town of Gibraltar was a surprise and a disappointment. Civilians were not usually reckoned military objects. It was thought that, while to kill an enemy soldier was, as a rule, a right and proper thing to do during a war, indiscriminate slaughter of ordinary men, women and children was wrong. The twentieth century developed a point of view which acquiesced in the destruction of whole towns and countrysides, even whole peoples and races, so that the fighting soldier should run short of supplies, be made despondent by the loss of relations and the disappearance of familiar places and so be inclined to abandon or be unable to continue the struggle. During the time of the great siege of Gibraltar, it was thought better to slay the one soldier whom 20 people kept in the front line rather than attempt to eliminate the 20 in order to paralyse the one. Towards women and children there was often a rough courtesy. It was true that the Spaniards in the outbreak of the siege in June 1779 had been sufficiently unkind to return to the garrison children suffering from smallpox; but at least they had sent them back to their own people. In the bad times at the end of 1780 they had permitted without molestation the escape of many inhabitants. When Mrs Gledstanes, wife of the Lieutenant-Colonel of the Royal Manchester Volunteers, had sailed with her five children in October 1780, the vessel in which they left was seized by the Spanish and taken into the Spanish camp. Through glasses the anxious British had watched the little family being landed. But they were not returned to the starvation rations of Gibraltar; a flag of truce informed Eliott that they had been safely passed on to Cadiz.

To open fire at long range on houses and shops was regarded as not playing the game. Even during the Napoleonic wars, when civilian Britons in France were ruthlessly interned under bad conditions and when national feeling was high and angry, one or two bombardments by British vessels of Boulogne were scornfully described as 'trying to win a war by breaking windows'.

The authentic eighteenth-century note is struck by Drinkwater, who, when approaching his description of the Spanish bombardment, wrote:

> Our private letters had, for some time before, mentioned that the Spaniards purposed to bombard Gibraltar, if the Garrison was a second time relieved, but the truth of this intelligence was doubted, it being conceived that no beneficial consequences could arise to them from such a cruel proceeding. We however overlooked the predominant characteristic of the nation, which particularly in this instance, seems to have influenced them more than any other motive, and even to have carried them beyond that line of prudence and caution which in military affairs ought to be strictly attended to.

Even the spectacle of the enemy's guns being elevated as the British convoy approached, and the sight of gun-sponges and rammers reared against the battery walls, had not it seems convinced Drinkwater that the decencies of warfare would be so dreadfully violated.

But the decision had been made, and thenceforth there were to be few breaks in the noise, fury, fire and smoke of the assault. There was hardly a month to pass between 12 April 1781 and January 1783 without thousands of rounds of shot and shell being poured into the town and its defences. It was computed that in the first seven weeks, up to the end of May, nearly 77,000 were discharged. Only in July and August 1782, when supplies and energies were being conserved for a very special occasion, was there any slackening; a total of 780 rounds was fired by the Spaniards, all in August—a mere 25 rounds a day. But as the British contribution for these two months came to over 8,600 shot and shell, grape and carcasses (over 139 a day), the noise rolled round the Rock without much cessation.

Famine and fire-ships had failed to subdue Gibraltar. Now the Spaniards were to press the siege with remorseless bombardment. This cannonade was directed, moreover, not only from the great land works of the isthmus but by sea. The Spanish were determined to do their utmost to make life impossible for the British garrison.

The unloading of Darby's store-ships went rapidly on, under the long-range fire of the Spanish land-batteries by day and constant harassment from their gunboats at night. The bombardment on 13 April was particularly heavy, upwards of 3,000 shot and shells being fired. Eliott was not at all certain what was the chief aim of the Spanish 'present mode of acting', as he described it. No advance across the isthmus seemed to be contemplated. Perhaps a naval attack was in preparation, he thought; or French reinforcements were expected in the Spanish lines. He sent 150 men to replenish the magazines on the North Face. Stores of shells with different fuses, of hand grenades and carcasses were placed ready. Picquets were strengthened, both by day and by night, and absorbed over 400 officers and men on each period of duty.

On the whole the ships, both naval and merchant, of Darby's command escaped lightly. Damage was done to some, especially by the night fire of the once-despised Spanish gunboats. Although these attackers mounted only one 26-pounder each, they had longer barrels than those of this calibre usually carried afloat. On returning home, there was a discussion in the Commons about the damage they caused. One Member asserted it was because the powder used by the Spaniards was so superior to the British variety that they were always outranged. Admiral Darby (who was M.P. for Plymouth), in reply declared it was the length of the guns which enabled the Spanish shot to take effect; and that though their oar-propelled gunboats operated dangerously against our vessels in a calm, as soon as a breeze sprang up they were easily beaten off. There were no great naval losses, certainly. There was one nasty moment when a Spanish 13-inch shell pierced the side of an ordnance store-ship unloading at the New Mole, but, as Eliott said, it 'luckily went blind'.

Eliott asked Darby to leave some store-ships and naval vessels behind him when he finally got ready to depart. He also asked for powder from naval stores, since obviously the whole nature of the siege had changed. Darby agreed to both these proposals and further landed men to help the garrison to get their supplies ashore. Saying that 'the Garrison of Gibraltar is a very grand object', he promised that if his main fleet were to be driven off station for any reason before the bulk of the new supplies were landed, he would leave two large frigates and a couple of cutters to protect them, if necessary.

By 20 April most of the stores were on land. The wind then came from the west and the fleet set sail. Thirteen colliers which had not been emptied were drawn in as close to the New Mole as possible and scuttled there. Eliott had told all the inhabitants that if they cared they could put themselves and their families aboard the now empty transports and store-ships and leave for England. Large numbers did so, along with many officers' ladies. By this time the town was pretty thoroughly ruined, though most of the official storehouses were safe. The chief loss occurred when the shells of the besiegers set fire to the stores in the Spanish church. Boyd, acting with great energy, called out parties and under heavy fire saved nearly everything. Casks of flour were rolled into the King's Bastion and piled up to protect the casemates in the south wall, where several men had been killed or wounded during the bombardment. These temporary traverses, placed before the case-mate doors, though they undoubtedly saved lives, were soon replaced by more orthodox shields. It was found that the men regarded any flour-cask damaged by enemy action as lawful prize. They scooped out the contents and fried them into pancakes, 'a dish which they were very expert in cooking'.

# 7

## *The Bombardment*

By the time the fleet had sailed discipline had been restored. Men found plundering were executed on the spot, and their bodies left hanging throughout daylight. Eliott, reporting events home to Lord Amherst, complained bitterly of the 'scandalous irregularity of the British Regiments comprising this garrison, ever since the enemy opened his Batteries. Except rape and murders, there is no one crime but what they have been repeatedly guilty of.' Drunkenness was the most popular vice of the British nation at this moment of time. From village ale-house to the House of Commons it prevailed; in the stews and slums of London cheap gin was the popular tipple: 'Drunk for a penny, blind drunk for tuppence, dead drunk threepence.' In Parliament, when a drunken Prime Minister might be faced with a reeling leader of the opposition, port was the liquor; brandy, as Dr Johnson said, was for heroes. Schoolboys drank small beer. Soldiers drank anything they could get hold of, any time, anywhere. And when they found in the broken houses of the town of Gibraltar the carefully concealed stocks of tradesmen, they became uncontrollably savage. 'A spirit of revenge against the merchants', as Drinkwater called it, resulted in incredible waste and destruction; 'among other instances of caprice and extravagance, I recollect that of roasting a pig by a fire made of cinnamon.' During the hurried disembarkation of supplies, provisions and stores were left lying about all over the place; there they were exposed to the weather, the enemy's shot and the thieving hands of the soldiery. Such waste was peculiarly annoying to a man of Eliott's temperament, who could not understand the temptations and overwhelming desires of less abstemious men. Even after most of the indiscipline had vanished, this firm-minded officer, usually lenient, was capable of hanging a soldier at the door of a store he had been robbing. Wanton plundering of the garrison's stores was a crime which he would only with difficulty persuade himself to pardon. To highlight the responsibility and to make importance of safeguarding supplies he put a field officer in charge at each principal landing place, at the New Mole and Rosia, both by day and by night; captains were on duty at every one of the eight main storage points between the Land Port Gate and Europa, while guards were strengthened both by day and by night. These precautions were of course not because the Spanish theatened to attack, but to preserve the garrison's food and stores against marauders within the gates.

The men did not forget or forgive the inhabitants of Gibraltar. Eliott, after the fleet had departed, ordered the remaining civilians to remove all timber and combustible material out of their houses within 24 hours. They found their houses, whole or ruined, well stripped. After April 1781, there grew a bitterness between those natives who remained and the soldiers, made worse by the unceasing bombardment.

On the British side there were often long pauses in the return fire. Ammunition sometimes ran short in the high batteries on the North Face. Many of the traverses, now tested and under pressure, were found not to be shot-proof. Moreover, the extensive range of the Spanish guns came as a surprise to the British. Their shot and shell fell much farther south than had been expected. A seven-gun battery in the Spanish lines concentrated on the Rock-gun, a heavy 24-pounder, at the highest point of the cliff; it was frequently hit, and several times replaced after being dismounted or damaged. Those British defences made from earth-filled casks were found useless and had to be replaced by more regular patterns of sand walls strengthened by sandbags and very solid in construction. The British in reply to their enemy's long-range fire placed two ship's mortars in the shelter of the head of the Old Mole and aimed several shells at the Spanish main magazine. By taking great pains in aiming and reckoning charges and fuses, the artillery were able to reach their target. As the distance was 3,056 yards, this was a considerable technical achievement and caused much exultation to the great crowds of inhabitants and others who witnessed it. But little damage was done and the effect must have been mostly psychological.

Casualties mounted. The surgeon of the 56th, Dr Thomas Chisholm, was severely wounded while in a casemate on the supposedly sheltered north side of the King's Bastion; he lost a foot, his other leg was broken and he suffered head wounds also; Lieutenant Cunninghame of the 39th died from head injuries, for which he had been trepanned five times. Shells burst and buried men alive. An officers' bomb-proof shelter was damaged when Spanish gun-shots brought down upon it rocks from above its roof. In the first week Eliott reported to London that three sergeants and 20 privates had been killed, five sergeants, a drummer and 69 privates wounded. Casualties on this scale continued through the rest of April and May.

Often in the early morning, just as dawn was breaking, Spanish gunboats bombarded shipping from the sea. The merlons in the British batteries were considerably damaged, debris filled the ditches and trenches along the North Face, cannon were dismounted and by mid-May the town itself presented a pitiable sight. Spilsbury drew two little sketches in his diary, the first showing the town house, 'Crushett's', belonging to Lady Riches, as it was before the firing, the other after the third day of bombardment; chimneys are down, the roof shattered, windows broken and driven in, walls pitted with cannon-ball scars; in one place fire has destroyed everything, and daylight is visible beyond an empty window frame. Mrs Green's pleasant house, 'The Mount', was completely destroyed at the first bombardment; her diary, which had been continuous from the early days until the moment of arrival of Darby's fleet and convoy, broke abruptly off, and was not resumed until 3 June. By that time Mrs Green herself, like many of her friends, had taken refuge to the south of the Rock, in temporary huts. The days of dinner parties and regular meetings for whist were over. To make matters worse, the weather was bad, with lightning and heavy storms of rain, through which the bombardment continued.

Eliott maintained his headquarters, which were much damaged and constantly under repair. He had a bomb-proof shelter, but as the shelling continued he came to take his daily station in a large tent pitched well south of the ruined town, where he remained with his principal officers and aides-de-camp. At night he returned to town. Boyd took up a permanent position in the King's Bastion, his own house being as severely damaged as that of the Governor.

Yet in spite of this formidable attack ships from the outside world reached Gibraltar. On 27 April 1781 H.M.S. *Enterprise* returned from Port Mahon, along with the frigates *Brilliant* and *Porcupine*, the sloop *Minorca*, three privateers and 25 sail, bringing in at least a further 1,000 tons of provisions. The captain of the *Brilliant*, Roger Curtis, remained behind when his ship sailed, taking charge of the naval defences.

Curtis at this time was 35 years old, a Wiltshire man of an old naval family, and had served afloat from the age of 16. He had been on the Newfoundland and North American stations, where his commanding officers had quickly promoted him. He became a firm friend of Eliott, who constantly praised him, and played an active and noble part in the defence of Gibraltar, for which he was subsequently honoured.

It was almost as if the Spanish had given up the idea of starving the British into surrender, and were relying on hard bludgeoning and constant bombardment—except during their siestas, which they observed throughout, even on the worst days, with almost religious devotion. Vessels arrived from Algiers in May, with sheep, wine and brandy; these and other vessels sailed away for Minorca packed with the miserable men, women and children whose homes had been destroyed and whose hoarded stocks had been burnt or plundered. Casualties had been heavy among them, but were not officially recorded. Spilsbury mentions the death from a gunboat shell of three Jews, one of whom has lost all he had in town, 'near £10,000', and the killing in another place of two butchers; but their losses usually went unnoticed. Only when something unusual or dramatic or particularly horrible happened did the civilians of Gibraltar attract attention. Their misery must have been even greater than those of the British camp-followers, since they had fewer organised resources. Any bombardment by night is a chancy business, and Eliott disapproved of replying to the nocturnal attacks of the Spanish gunboats. This led to trouble, particularly after one onslaught, when heavy enemy shell-fire from close inshore killed several people in the camps near Windmill Hill. A child and a soldier were killed, and other soldiers wounded in bed. Great discontent was caused, representations were made to the Governor, and Eliott finally agreed that the artillery should return their fire when the enemy attacked again.

In spite of increased vigilance and heavy punishments, thefts by the troops continued. Two of the artificer company were hanged at the White Convent for plundering that store, and one of the 58th was executed for stealing rum. It was usual in these cases to leave the bodies hanging until sunset, and, in order to impress the lesson, Eliott ordered the town guards to be marched past the swinging corpses. This incessant plundering caused one wry incident, when a soldier, having collected several watches and much jewellery, tied all in a handkerchief and stuffed his treasure into a gun muzzle before going in the evening to his bomb-proof (where each returning soldier was searched); he lost the lot when the Spanish gunboats came that night and his richly loaded cannon was the first to be discharged.

Throughout the bombardment the garrison flag was flown on a tall flagstaff on the Grand Battery. It attracted the enemy's fire and both flag and staff were several times replaced. When necessary the flag was temporarily nailed to the stump, but it became a point of honour to show the colours for every possible hour of daybreak. On 4 June the King's Birthday was once again honoured, this time by a salute of cannon and mortars, firing in succession from the Rock-gun on the right to the batteries on the left, all shot and shell being concentrated on the St Carlos battery. For the better effect this took place during the Spanish siesta period. Little damage resulted, it seems, from this gesture. The Royal Standard was flown on the Grand Battery and the Spaniards, when they at length reopened, put three cannon-balls through it. At this period the enemy was full of activity. Line-of-battle ships, bomb ketches, fire-ships, gunboats and zebecs were constantly arriving or departing from Barcelo's fleet; small craft disembarked ammunition and stores for the Spanish camps, where large working parties were observed gathering brushwood for making into fascines. The night raids from the sea were sometimes so prolonged, the number of shells fired running into hundreds, that the British military camps were evacuated, the troops either drawn up at battle stations or dispersed. The miserable civilians fled in the darkness from their squalid shelters to take refuge in the gullies and crevices of the Rock.

After 9 June there was a slight temporary slackening in the Spanish shell-fire, for one of their main magazines was on that day blown up. A tremendous explosion took place, followed by a succession of lesser bursts, like a continual roll, as live shells and other fixed ammunition took fire. This went on for 20 minutes, but a fierce fire raged for over three hours, though the Spaniards worked like beavers to suppress it. Their drums beat the alarm and the whole Spanish army, some 13 battalions, besides cavalry, assembled before the camp. The British fired a few long-range shots at the blaze, but this particular magazine was near the hill feature known as the Queen of Spain's Chair, and a well-meant attempt to increase the damage had little effect.

This disaster brought consolation to the British for two misfortunes. One of these was a reduction in the ration of beef, only three-quarters of a pound being issued weekly from the beginning of June 1781 instead of the full pound usual before that date; the other was the belated arrival of bad news concerning the small frigate squadron, consisting of the *Flora* and *Crescent*, which had formed part of Darby's relieving fleet originally, and which had, after the relief of Minorca, returned to Gibraltar with supplies. They had left Gibraltar on 29 May to pursue two large vessels seen near Ceuta. These had proved to be Dutch frigates, and a fierce engagement took place, in which one Dutch ship surrendered to the *Flora*; but the other forced the *Crescent* to strike her flag, after inflicting heavy damage and disabling half her crew; then the *Flora* came to her aid and the victorious Dutchman made off for Cadiz, leaving her prize. Reports of this action came in from the Spanish side, naturally exaggerated. These naval activities, with various alarms and excursions connected with constantly increasing convoy and warship movements through the straits, made many in Gibraltar believe that an assault was imminent, especially when fire-ships were reported to be making ready once again. And during June extensive new encampments were seen prepared behind the Spanish lines.

Eliott reported home that incessant activity, heavy guard duties, sleep interrupted by gunboat attacks and the constantly recurring damage to his artillery was reducing the effectiveness of the garrison. However, he was never a man to suffer trouble passively, and he set to work to make gunboats of his own. He began with two, converting and cutting down a couple of brigs, each mounting four 24-pounders and with 12-pounders in the bows. The first one completed was named *Vanguard* and was moored near the New Mole. His increasing casualties caused him to appoint regimental surgeons and surgeons' mates to do duty in the hospitals; for this he gave extra pay.

So the long siege drew on to July and August, marked by bombardments by day and night of varying intensity, with quarrelling between soldiers and townsfolk, with an occasional duel, court-martials and arrests of officers and men for drunkenness (once while on picquet), by reports of slight damage or freak accidents: a musket barrel was twisted like a corkscrew by a shell, without harming the soldier who carried it; a cask of oatmeal was hurled from a house by another shell-burst, to fall on its end without damage. Three soldiers' wives were flogged by the hangman through the camp for buying stolen goods. The weather was bad, with a trying east wind and a great heat. Regiments changed quarters. The major and the adjutant of the 72nd quarrelled, and fired three pistols each at the other, without damage. The British batteries were repaired with heavy wooden caissons, bound with strong iron and filled with earth, to replace the merlons; Willis's had been particularly heavily damaged. On 20 July, 'about 10 a.m. the Dons saluted us from the lines with 28 or 9 shots and fired a feu de joye from the camp, island, shipping, gunboats etc., the whole three times over, a very pleasing sight', wrote Spilsbury. News came in that the regular Spanish troops before Gibraltar had been replaced by militia; so that the prospects of an assault grew more dim. A large fleet, upwards of 70 sail, not displaying any colours, sailed eastwards into the Mediterranean; this later proved to be a French force en route to Minorca for its blockade and siege.

Eliott knew more than anyone else in Gibraltar about this fleet, for Hillsborough had sent him news from 'one of his Majesty's Ministers at a foreign court'. According to this despatch, 12,000 men were to be embarked at Cadiz on 26 June, perhaps against Gibraltar, perhaps against Port Mahon; much ammunition was being loaded aboard, but little biscuit; possibly the 'many small baggs to be filled with earth' were designed to fill the morass which formed an important part of Eliott's defences before the Land Port Gate; and it was rumoured that the Duc de Crillon was to have the command.

To pass the time some more gunpowder experiments were put in hand. Five 32-pounders and an 18-pounder were sunk into the sand behind the Old Mole and then secured with timber baulks at different degrees of elevation and loaded with varying quantities of powder. At 42 degrees of elevation the result was satisfactory, several of the shells bursting over the Spanish camp. Musket shots fired with dried or un-dried powder were found to differ by as much as 40 or 50 yards in range.

Towards the end of July Miriam Green sailed for home. She was by then a very sick woman, the privations of the siege having completely worn her down. She came of an indomitable family, for her father had been a colonel of Engineers and her grandfather, Lieutenant-Colonel Jonas Watson, of the Royal Artillery, and the 'Chief Bombardier of England', had been killed at the siege of Cartagena in 1741, at the age of 78. Mrs Green lingered on in England for almost a year, dying on 21 June 1782 from the effects of a chill originally contracted in the dark and damp bomb-proofs of Gibraltar. It was a pity she did not live to share the honours granted to her husband after his 22 years' service on the Rock. He also had suffered in health during the siege, but was to survive her for almost 30 years.

Mrs Green was not the only civilian to sail for England on the occasion of her departure. Two Indiamen, the *Lord Townshend* and *Nottingham*, were used as transports, and Eliott sent home a number of inhabitants and invalids. This was a great relief, for the Spaniards had in mid-June passed into Gibraltar over 140 women and children they had detained, captured in vessels which had left Gibraltar at the end of April; they kept the crews as prisoners. Any means of lightening the burden of ineffectives was welcomed by Eliott, for the crowded en-campments below Windmill Hill and on the flats by Europa were poten-tial breeding grounds for disease and misbehaviour. Both July and August seemed excessively hot to the inhabitants and soldiers; to many it seemed the hottest and most oppressive they could remember, but this may have been because they were encamped, living under canvas or in small wooden huts. Luckily, with the diversion of enemy effort to Minorca, there was a marked slackening of Spanish fire from the land batteries. Only when the British attempted anything unusual were they stimulated to take action. Thus when the captain of artillery at Willis's endeavoured to clear his field of fire by setting alight the rank canes and weeds in front of his pieces, he found them too full of sap and moisture to do anything more than cause smouldering great clouds of smoke; the Spaniards at once opened a brisk cannonade. But this excitement quickly died down.

So regularly did the Spanish fire a steady three shells a day that the British likened them to the Trinity, nicknaming them in the jocular and blasphemous way so common to English troops, 'the Father, the Son and Holy Ghost', and pretending to see in this an attempt to convert them to the true faith.

Gunboats still harassed the garrison on many a night, but few shots came over in the daytime, and only a shell or two in the hours of dark. Both sides spent their energies in repairing their works, all much knocked about in over three months of heavy bombardment. The British were also busily employed in making streets in their infantry camps and generally doing what they could to make their new dwelling places neat and tidy. Spilsbury's little sketches show a military passion for straight lines, orderly palisades, regularly spaced embrasures and battlements, sentry boxes, formal paths and hutments like tiny dolls' houses arranged on the rough and untidy lower slopes of the Rock. One drawing, entitled 'An Officer's Hut—Mine', shows a low plank-walled cabin, a door in one end, two rectangular windows tucked under the eaves, with a tiny chimney cheerfully smoking and a small flat-roofed extension at the back. Another sketch, of an artillery officer's home, is of a stone-walled, tiled-roof single-storey building, probably a cattle byre in normal use, but with two chimneys, and a small railed-off enclosure around it; it abuts on a rough crag, 'in which was a large cave which sheltered them from the gunboats'. Such places, and similar makeshifts, provided accommodation very different from the kind of quarters in which British officers on foreign service usually lived. For the men, the change was not nearly so marked. Barrack life and the tented field, whenever British soldiers served, was always crowded, always lacking in comfort, never private. Gibraltar in particular, then and for long after, was notoriously uncomfortable and cramped. Whether in the casemates of the King's Bastion or the Grand Battery or in the huts and tents near Rosia or on guard at Willis's or the isolated posts at places like Catalan Bay beneath the towering precipices of the eastern face, these regular troops were very little worse off in war than they would have been in peace.

News came in from the outside world on 7 August, accompanied by a neat and successful naval action. The wind was westerly, but very light, and the morning was hazy when at 7 o'clock a strange brig hove in sight from the Spanish look-out towers. Their signals were seen above the mist from the British posts on the summit of the Rock, and the alert was sounded. As the fog dispersed a vessel was seen, becalmed but rowing with the current towards the garrison. Captain Curtis ordered the British gunboats, now two in number, the *Vanguard* and the *Repulse*, out to sea, while three naval barges were sent to help the strangers. The barges were commanded by the captain of H.M.S. *Porcupine*, Sir Charles Knowles, a baronet of a naval family already full of honours and action, though not yet quite 28 years old. On their side, the Spanish sent 14 gunboats from Algeciras to the attack. The brig, which proved to be H.M.S. *Helena* carrying 14 four-pounder guns, opened fire; the Spaniards came close, circling round and firing round-shot and grape. At this point they were all some league-and-a-half from Europa. One of the barges pushed on through the cannonade in spite of the circling enemy gunboats, came alongside the *Helena*, took aboard the despatches she was carrying for Eliott and came back again unscathed. Then, as the morning breeze sprang up, the incomer broke away from her attackers and came in easily. Although they had come close and hot musketry fire had been exchanged, the Spanish gunboats had not dared to board. The *Helena*'s rigging and sails were much cut about, but she had lost only one man killed (her boatswain) and two seamen wounded. She was 16 days out from Portsmouth.

All this provided a thrilling spectacle to the garrison; especially as at one point, when the Spaniards were crowded around the British ship, becalmed miles from help, and with other Spanish warships approaching, they had given her up for lost. The British attributed *Helena*'s escape partly to the fact that the enemy's cannon, intended to fire on Gibraltar from a distance, could not be sufficiently depressed to bear upon her hull.

The news first brought by the *Helena* (duplicated in H.M.S. *Kite*, which made Gibraltar on 19 August) and also carried in other vessels which later arrived with fruit, tea, onions and salt was not encouraging. The year 1781 was to prove in retrospect the decisive year of the War of American Independence. Then, after six years of bitter and fruitless effort by land and sea, the British Government was to realise that to bring the 13 colonies back to the Crown was an impossible task. It was the year of Yorktown, the year when under its complicated load of responsibilities the Royal Navy was to fail at the decisive moment.

On the American stations, the decisive area of the conflict, rumours concerning French convoys and French fleets and squadrons resulted in Rear-Admiral Thomas Graves at New York, Rear-Admiral Sir Samuel Hood with 15 ships-of-the-line en route to Cuba and the Chesapeake, and Vice-Admiral Sir Peter Parker, commanding at Jamaica, manœuvring without co-operation or co-ordination during July and August. In the same period the Frenchman, de Grasse, showed his one stroke of genius in a lifetime of mediocrity. He concentrated 28 line-of-battle ships off the Chesapeake by the end of August, at the moment when General Cornwallis was at bay in Yorktown, with some 7,000 troops and no hope of rescue save by sea.

Nearer at hand to Gibraltar, Minorca was in desperate trouble. James Murray, the general commanding there, was a sound officer, one of Wolfe's brigadiers of 1759 and a former Governor of Canada, and had been at Port Mahon since 1774. But to defend a whole island with a force of two weak British regiments and a couple of Hanoverian battalions was a very different business from holding a concentrated and naturally defensible position like the Rock of Gibraltar. When 8,000 Spanish troops and 100 heavy guns (the whole commanded, as Eliott had been forewarned, by the French Duke of Crillon), landed on 20 August 1781, there could be only one end. This came, inevitably; but was to be delayed, because of a prodigious resistance by Murray and his soldiers, until February 1782. Then, to the cheers and compassionate tears of their French and Spanish conquerors, 600 worn-out men crawled out from Fort St Philip at Mahon to lay down their arms. To Eliott, well acquainted with Murray, it can have been no surprise that he would resist bravely; but he must have been prepared for the loss of Minorca, when once the Bourbon allies had clearly shown they were determined to take it. About the possibility that Gibraltar, equally plainly a Bourbon object of onslaught, might also be taken, Eliott never seems to have felt any tremor of doubt. He asked his government for supplies, for food, for powder, for guns and mortars to replace those worn out by incessant use, for large and heavily armed warships to keep the Spanish gunboats at a distance. Never at any time in the long series of despatches he sent home did he ever express the slightest doubt that he could hold Gibraltar against the utmost strength of the enemy. His tone is always one of moderation and common sense. No heroics and high-flown phrases were used. Eliott had a job to do and with the means at his disposal he did it. The fact that history records his ultimate success should not blind historians to the great perils he ran, or to the intelligence and energy he showed in meeting many dangers. Moreover, Eliott was not content merely to counter the moves made by his attackers. From the first bombardment he opened in September 1779, to the building of his own gunboats and the encouragement of many highly ingenious and novel methods of fortification, of food conservation and of artillery practice, the Governor of Gibraltar made his besiegers realise that they too had problems to solve which were solely due to their opponent within Gibraltar.

Towards the end of August 1781 the enemy once more tightened their blockade. When the wind was west, two zebecs and four gunboats anchored off Cabrita Point, cruising at night across the entrance to the bay and in the straits. In easterly winds, a frigate, a zebec and four gunboats cruised between Centa and Europa, others in the Gut, and one zebec lay-to off Europa Point. At Algeciras a battleship lay, with the rest of the numerous gun- and mortar-boats ready for night bombardment duty. So vigilant were they, that Spilsbury, noting the signals 'the Dons' fired to keep stray vessels away, laconically commented that 'a stranger would suppose we had the plague here'.

In spite of these precautions, vessels slipped into Gibraltar, for the extra little provisions they brought proved very profitable. Sometimes an old ox, survivor of the siege to date, was slaughtered and sold for as much as eight reals a pound. Now and again there were unexpected supplies of cow meat, when enemy shells killed grazing cattle; 'when a shell falls,' said Spilsbury, 'they go and smell it.' Fresh meat, newly arrived, cost a great deal: mutton and goat at 10 reals, veal (very scarce, naturally) 12 reals; one day in August four hens fetched 15 dollars. Grapes brought 2 reals a pound, onions 3 dollars and 6 reals per measure of 25 lb. In the midst of this growing shortage, and with memories of former privations, it was critically noted 'that there was but one chest of tea and a little coffee in the Garrison, and that the chest and 300 lb. of the latter was taken to headquarters'; though not for the delectation of Eliott himself, one supposes.

On the afternoon of 12 September 1781 at 5 o'clock the Spanish army turned out in style and fired a triple feu-de-joie. Many English gloomily thought this might be to celebrate the capture of Minorca. This was not yet the case, although de Crillon had taken all the island, including Port Mahon, except Fort St Philip itself, at his first landing on 20 August. He had offered Murray any price he cared to name to surrender, and would not have credited that a further five months of constant endeavour lay before him.

September wore on, with a gradually increasing fire from the Spanish side, continued night attacks from the sea and harassing fire levelled against the Spaniards and their working parties; and its quota of losses and dramatic incidents. For the third time in the siege one of the British cannon, waiting ready loaded for action, was accidentally exploded by an enemy shell; the first time this happened it had been the British 'morning gun' which fired. Many guns were so worn out by constant use that their range was much shortened. Several shells burst on leaving the muzzle, their fuses, seven years in store, being worm-eaten. The Rock Mortar itself was split, by a shell bursting prematurely in its barrel, mortally wounding the gunner who discharged it. One evening an enemy shell struck a house opposite the King's Bastion in which the two majors of the 39th were sitting with the Town Major, a promising and popular young officer called Burke. The shell brought down the wall, broke Burke's thigh, and penetrated the floor before exploding, blowing Burke to the ceiling and burying him in the ruins. He was carried to the hospital, where his leg was amputated, but died soon afterwards. The two majors, Mercier and Vignoles, managed to get out before the explosion, but they, with a sergeant and his daughter who were in the cellar of the house, were both wounded. Men deserted, or were captured in the attempt. One of them, from the 56th, was hanged; another, of the 39th, hanged himself. There were complaints about medical arrangements: too few stretchers ('cradles' was the term used then) were prepared for carrying the wounded; dressings were not kept at advance posts for prompt use; some surgeons were reported as afraid to venture from their bomb-proofs during a bombardment, so that men bled to death while waiting. One hospital doctor, in spite of great shortage of space, kept a whole ward to himself for personal accommodation; there were other interlopers in what should have been the safest place in the fortress (though occasionally a stray shell hit the hospital and killed or further wounded the patients). The hospital surgeons were 'little better than butchers', while regimental doctors were not trusted with medicines. A short course of training was given to sergeants and corporals in the regiments by their doctors, to teach them how to stop blood by the use of tourniquets. The *Helena* and *Kite* sailed for England carrying invalids and an officer who had lost his leg.

This monotonous siege life continued during October, with hunger, suffering and endurance. Men were constantly being killed and wounded, continually under threat, living in squalor and gunsmoke, amid noise and explosions. Occupied in working parties, noting the small changes in the enemy's works or the death-fall over a precipice of a drunken private of the 58th, the robbery of an officer by a Hanoverian or a bloodless and pointless duel between one officer of the 12th and another of the 72nd: these are the visible signs of a long ordeal. Casualties by the end of September amounted to well over 400, 86 of them killed. Each day a thousand men of the garrison laboured at the works, often on the exposed North Face. Amongst their tasks was the breaking up of the scuttled colliers, which had been dragged close ashore and largely emptied; much of their timber was used to buttress the defences of the batteries; a good deal of their cargo was still unrecovered on the bed of the sea when the siege ended.

On the enemy side, the torpor of the summer wore off. New works appeared on the isthmus. A signal tower, built near the Queen of Spain's Chair, was used to signal to their batteries when British working parties were going up the hill, with a subsequent increase in the rate of fire. Slowly the numbers of rounds increased, until once more over a thousand a day were coming over from the Spanish guns.

It was distressing to discover, on 4 October, at this moment of mounting pressure, a mutiny aboard the naval cutter *Speedwell*. Nearly half the crew were concerned. Their plan was to murder the officers of the watch, cut the cable and run away with the vessel to Algeciras, where they reckoned they could sell their prize for £6,000. This sum they proposed to split between themselves and then all were to return to England. They were waiting for a favourable wind in the evening when their plot was confessed by one of the party; a boy who had deserted from a Spanish vessel. Four of the ringleaders were seized and put in irons aboard another ship. The commander of the *Speedwell* was a certain Lieutenant John Gibson, R.N. Drinkwater states it to have been 'somewhat singular, that Mr Gibson had been so unfortunate as to have the cutter he then commanded run away with by the crew into a French port, while he and his officers were ashore'. Almost certainly a brutal discipline exercised without mercy caused this disgraceful business. The plot was so naïve that only desperation could have forced British seamen to act so senselessly. The practice of pressing men into naval service caused great unrest amongst those unlucky enough to find themselves snatched from merchant ships into the Royal Navy. Even the crews of vessels laden for Gibraltar with essential stores had to be protected by special passes. Pressed men often sought desperately to escape; Drinkwater noted that four men who deserted to the Spanish in August, 1781 from the *Repulse* gunboat had been pressed a short while before from a privateer in the bay. Harsh discipline and a sense of grievance might lead to dangerous violence and mutiny.

The classic case of the results of such treatment was to be that of the *Hermione*, a 32-gun frigate whose crew, goaded beyond endurance, murdered the officers and carried her off into the Spanish port of La Guaira in September 1797; under the same captain, one Hugh Pigot, the men had fought in actions against the enemy well and bravely. But the results of any such mutiny were almost inevitably fatal to the mutineers. The *Hermione* mutineers were exterminated when caught. The chief astonishment felt about the mutiny in the *Bounty* in 1789 was not so much that it occurred as that no satisfactory explanation emerged about the disappearance of the chief ringleader, the acting Lieutenant, Fletcher Christian, until long after his death. Mutineers who escaped were ruthlessly tracked down, and many were executed, often years after the date of their offence. In the same way, the utmost effort was always put forth to recover ships lost through mutiny. The *Bounty* was hunted all over the Pacific for years before the discovery in 1813 that she had been destroyed many years earlier at Pitcairn. *Hermione* was recovered in October 1799 in a most daring operation, being cut out from under Spanish guns at Puerto Cabello by boats of H.M.S. *Surprise*. John Gibson's first official encounter with mutiny, when his crew took his cutter *Jackal* to France, was wiped out by the recapture of the vessel in 1781. The aim was to drown even the memory of a mutiny in blood and vengeance. Army discipline during the eighteenth century was harsh and brutal; naval discipline was merciless.

By October 1781 the garrison in general had come to the conclusion that the enemy was about to attempt a storm against the fortress. The Spaniards stepped up their rate of fire until 'a person would think it impossible for a bird to escape, amidst such showers of shot'; although in fact casualties were surprisingly light; 'the Dons' worked very hard, and 'crowded their work with traverses'; a new battery of six embrasures was finished, over against the Old Mole and Water Port Gate, in spite of heavy fire from Montague's Bastion and the lofty emplacements on the North Face; it was set on fire by howitzer shells, but was made ready for action, nevertheless. The Spaniards deeply strengthened this battery by piling great heaps of gabions and sand in front of it; and, when the British increased their fire, even the gun embrasures were masked by sandbags, the whole forming an enormous heap against which even heavy ordnance was ineffective. When the British at length abandoned their attempt to destroy this work, nearly 1,600 heavy shot and over 500 shells had been discharged against it. Among them were a few shot of a new nature: these were cannon-balls which had been made red-hot in furnaces before being loaded into the gun-muzzle. The difficulty of loading an incandescent body into a power-filled gun had been overcome by pushing a thick wet wad, thoroughly drenched in water, down the bore, to lie between the powder and shot. The operation was tricky, but the experiment was continued. And in due course the 'red-hot shot' of Gibraltar were to become famous.

The gun- and mortar-boats came regularly over to harass the camps, and engaged several vessels attempting to reach the British. Some they captured, to the dismay of those who crowded the seaward works to watch these distant naval engagements; despite the risks they ran, soldiers of the garrison looked on such spectacles as welcome relief from the monotony of life under siege. The moment anything unusual was to be seen, the troops flocked to the line-walls to watch. When, as happened at the end of the month, the blockade was broken, there was always a great upward surge in spirit. Then a small ordnance cutter, the *Unicorn*, accompanied by four small vessels from Portugal, came safely in, bringing sheep, poultry, and fruit. Eliott bought up all the onions and lemons for the use of the hospitals to combat the scurvy, now once again on the increase; and some of the visiting crews, being suspected as probable spies, were kept under lock and key. When these vessels were unloaded at the New Mole, crowds attended, eager to bid for almost anything which would relieve their monotonous diet of salt beef, biscuit and cheese (which at this period was issued in lieu of butter). Onions sold for 2s. 5d. a pound, common green tea at £2 5s. 6d. a pound, loaf sugar at nearly 17s. a pound; a hen cost over 12s. and any orange or lemon which escaped Eliott's clutches was eagerly bought for as much as 7½d. a piece.

Although casualties among the British troops were never particularly heavy at any one time, they never ceased. Officers and men were killed or injured, two or three in a single night, then none for a week, then perhaps a single death. The Spaniards continued steadily to labour at their defences and batteries, which by mid-November were approaching the northern edge of the inundation, and were not much more than half a mile from the main works of Gibraltar facing the isthmus. Their precise intentions were uncertain. It seemed to some British observers that their chief aim was to reach positions from which they could command the whole extent of Gibraltar's waterfront from the Old to the New Mole and even beyond, right down to the Naval Hospital. Even on the South Parade, where the guards assembled on parade before marching off to relieve their several posts, the Spaniards managed to drop their long-range shots. Shells burst as far south as the tents of military encampments, and near the magazines and barracks by the

Princess of Wales's lines. Some were reckoned to have travelled as much as 4,000 yards before landing. Moreover, the Spaniards copied the British trick of measuring their fuses so accurately that they could burst their shells in the air, harassing working parties and forcing men to take shelter. Some relief was obtained from the fact that many such projectiles failed to explode; this was thought to be due to the Spanish workmen stealing the gunpowder and substituting sand. But the threat was serious. Running the blockade was always a difficult business, depending on wind strengths and directions, and on the strong currents which swept around Europa Point. The Spanish gunboats, not so dependent on sails as were all vessels from England which attempted to reach Gibraltar, could move freely in the morning mists or during the flat calms which left the bay as smooth as a mirror. Only on a comparatively narrow extent of the westward-facing waterfront could vessels moor to unload. If this stretch should fall within range of constant Spanish gunfire from the isthmus batteries, the town might find itself once more contending with famine; and, with hunger and shortage, disease might bring disaster. This was to be the pattern of events at Minorca.

*A zebec*

# 8

## *Sortie*

Eliott this time took the initiative in a most unexpected and lively manner. If it was regarded as suicidal for the Spaniards to attack on foot across the isthmus it might well have been thought equally foolish for the British to sally forth. This, however, was what the Governor planned to do. He may have chosen the actual date because of information gained from a corporal of the Walloon Guards who deserted, with a companion, during 21 November. This man declared that there were 21,000 men in the Spanish camp, waiting only for the arrival of a combined fleet to attempt to storm Gibraltar. At this time there were fewer than 6,000 officers and men in the fortress; most of them were weary from continual duty, tired from the almost ceaseless bombardment, short of food and it would seem without much hope of rescue from outside. At the actual moment of decision, nearly 600 of them were lying sick or wounded in hospital. Twice relieved in the nick of time, threatened if not actually afflicted by the diseases of scarcity, with very small naval resources of their own, faced by actively hostile Spanish and French military and naval forces, and now for many months deprived of even the semblance of neutrality by the Moorish rulers of nearby North Africa, the British must have appeared pretty well exhausted. Certainly Eliott took great risks in preparing the sortie which took place on the night of 26–27 November. Had the attempt failed, had the 2,200 fit men who sallied forth in the darkness been betrayed or unlucky, Gibraltar might well have fallen shortly afterwards.

The weather had been wild and stormy for a few days before Eliott moved. Rain fell heavily and the winds were so strong that tents were blown down and the boom which protected the harbour was frequently broken, to be immediately repaired amidst rough seas. In such circumstances movements were always restricted, men on both sides keeping in shelter. When the normal evening gun was fired on 26 November and the gates were officially closed (a routine which Eliott maintained formally throughout the siege), new orders appeared. All troops were ordered to repair at once to their own quarters in casemate, barrack or camp and the wine-houses and grog-shops were immediately shut.

The assaulting force comprised the 12th Regiment of Foot and Hardenberg's Hanoverians in their entirety; the picked men of all other infantry corps, their grenadier and light infantry companies, made up to full strength from the ordinary battalion companies, were ordered to assemble at midnight on the Red Sands below the ruins of the town; 100 artillerymen with four officers and ten N.C.O.s, a party of 22 engineers and skilled men, 40 artificers and 160 workmen were also paraded, with some seamen. Each soldier carried 36 rounds of ammunition (powder and ball); each musket had a good flint fitted, and another was carried in the soldier's pocket; only two drummers went out with each regiment, and no swords were carried. The countersign used was 'Steady'. In support the 39th and 58th regiments were paraded at the same hour on the South Parade, under the command of General Picton.

Brigadier Ross commanded the detachment destined for the onslaught. His men were in three columns, Hardenberg's Regiment forming the bulk on the right, the 12th on the left. The ultimate destination of each column was clearly indicated. The right, under Lieutenant-Colonel Hugo of Hardenberg's Regiment, was to move first, marching through the barrier at Forbes's, moving across the far side of the inundation and the abandoned gardens towards the middle of the Spanish advanced works. The centre party, under Lieutenant-Colonel Dachenhausen of Reden's Hanoverians, was to follow hard on their heels, going through the Bayside Barrier and making for the Spanish mortar batteries constructed under the old guard-houses and a ruined windmill in the middle of the isthmus; while the left, containing the 12th Foot and commanded by its Lieutenant-Colonel, Thomas Trigge, brought up the rear and made for the gun-batteries near the western shore. The 12th and Hardenberg's were to take station as sustaining corps between the enemy's main line and the advanced batteries which were the main object of attack, and to defend those charged with destruction duties from interference. Other groups of grenadiers and light infantry companies were to guard the flanks; and a reserve, under Major Hamilton Maxwell of the 73rd Highland Regiment, of four other companies of picked men, was destined to hold a line on the northern edge of the gardens beyond the inundation.

Artificers and workmen were provided with tools and materials for burning and destroying the enemy works in their advanced lines, and at

2 a.m. on 27 November the whole moved quietly off, after the waning moon had set.

The men of the sortie were in high spirits at the prospect of action and, in spite of their long inaction, they carried out their duties admirably. Their forward movement, despite all precautions, was quickly discovered. The Spanish sentries stationed before their works on the fringes of the old gardens were early on the alert; they fired their muskets and ran through the darkness towards their own lines. Hugo at once pushed briskly on, found no opposition and began the destruction of the parallel and batteries. Part of Hardenberg's mistook the place where they were supposed to halt and form and discovered themselves in front of the battery called St Carlos; they were fired on by the enemy, but pressed on and took possession of the fortification and were found there when Dachenhausen arrived with the centre column. Dachenhausen's advance party, the flank companies of the 39th, mistook them for the enemy and some shots were exchanged until the use of the password prevented more. Trigge's column was equally successful and in a very short time all opposition was overcome and the British were in undisputed command of all the enemy gun- and mortar-batteries, their stores, trenches, barricades and traverses across the middle of the isthmus. The troops designated for the purpose took post between these captured works and the main Spanish lines to prevent any possible assault, while the workmen, artillery and engineers laboured to destroy as much as was possible. There was very little resistance by the Spaniards encountered in the works; though one officer and a few others put up a strong fight, they were quickly overcome. Keys to the magazines were found on a captured artillery officer. Another officer, Lieutenant Baron Helmstadt of the Walloon Guards, was also captured, with 16 others; the Baron was badly wounded, but was carried into Gibraltar along with the other prisoners.

The work of destroying the enemy's works took an hour. Ten 13-inch mortars and 18 26-pounder guns were spiked and ruined, the batteries and stores were set alight by means of the fire faggots carried by the workmen, and trains of powder laid to the magazines. During this time the Spanish reaction bore all the signs of panic and surprise. Columns of fire and fiery clouds rolled away from their burning fortifications, lighting up all around them; as Drinkwater said, the troops and neighbouring objects were 'beautifully illuminated . . . forming all together a coup-d'œil not possible to be described'. In spite of this clear view, the Spaniards directed their artillery against the town and upper batteries of Gibraltar, which, when the sortie was firmly

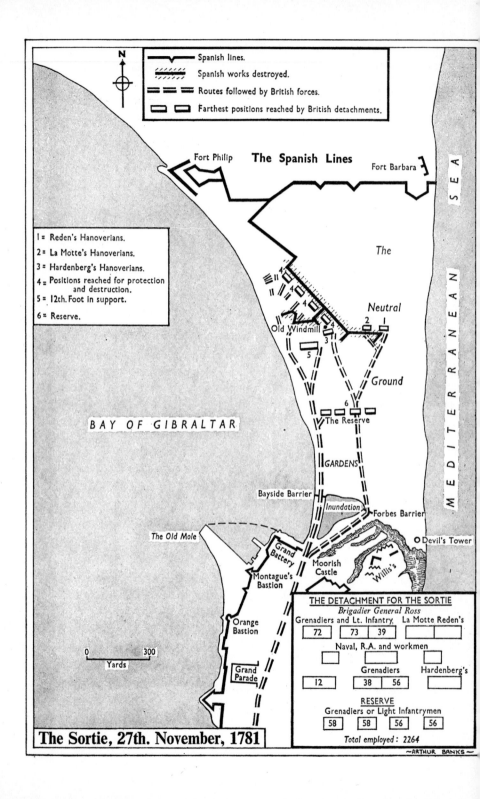

**Key (top legend):**
- Spanish lines.
- Spanish works destroyed.
- Routes followed by British forces.
- Farthest positions reached by British detachments.

**Side legend:**
1 = Reden's Hanoverians.
2 = La Motte's Hanoverians.
3 = Hardenberg's Hanoverians.
4 = Positions reached for protection and destruction.
5 = 12th. Foot in support.
6 = Reserve.

Fort Philip

**The Spanish Lines**

Fort Barbara

S E A

The

Neutral

Old Windmill

Ground

The Reserve

M E D I T E R R A N E A N

B A Y   O F   G I B R A L T A R

GARDENS

Bayside Barrier

Inundation

Forbes Barrier

The Old Mole

○ Devil's Tower

Grand Battery

Moorish Castle

Willis's

Montague's Bastion

Orange Bastion

0     300
Yards

Grand Parade

**THE DETACHMENT FOR THE SORTIE**
*Brigadier General Ross*

| Grenadiers and Lt. Infantry | | | La Motte Reden's | |
|---|---|---|---|---|
| 72 | 73 | 39 | | |

| Naval, R.A. and workmen | | |
|---|---|---|
| | | |

| | Grenadiers | | Hardenberg's |
|---|---|---|---|
| 12 | 38 | 56 | |

**RESERVE**
Grenadiers or Light Infantrymen

| 58 | 58 | 56 | 56 |
|---|---|---|---|

*Total employed : 2264*

**The Sortie, 27th. November, 1781**

~ARTHUR BANKS~

established, had opened a fierce fire on the Spanish major forts in their principal lines of defence. Even during the withdrawal the British troops were not harassed, though they must have made a very obvious target; all the more so because, when it came to the turn of Hardenberg's Hanoverians to retire from their position on the British extreme right, they found the barriers at Forbes's locked, 'by some oversight', and had to march across the face of their own defences and return through the palisades at Bayside. There they followed on the heels of the 12th Foot. With that zeal for noting every coincidence and casual occurrence so noticeable among soldiers, it struck Drinkwater as 'not a little singular that these two regiments, who at the memorable battle of Minden had fought by each other's side, and, according to the natural course of events, could never expect to meet again, should be employed a second time on the same occasion, and be the only entire regiments out'. These two corps were the largest formed bodies of troops employed by Eliott; Hardenberg's Hanoverians mustered 348 officers and men, the 12th numbered 486; they had played a valuable role in the first attack; and, had the Spanish reacted swiftly and sent out strong parties against those in the sortie, their disciplined strength would probably have enabled the smaller groups of British to whom they gave shelter a chance to form on the reserve and get quietly and quickly away into the garrison. As it was, they were the last to return, when everything Eliott had required was successfully accomplished.

The main work of destruction naturally fell to the artillerymen, engineers and artificers. Each column had a detachment with it, supplied with hammers, axes, crowbars, fire-faggots and other burning materials, with soldiers or seamen under their direction to do the rough work. But these unskilled labourers, though full of zeal, were too ignorant to do the job properly. Eliott, in spite of the obvious risks he ran, accompanied the sortie in person; and when he saw the difficulties, he sent back to the garrison for the remainder of Green's company. They hurried to the spot, were rapidly distributed along the line and completed the destruction with great efficiency. It was discovered that the Spanish engineers and artillerymen had built their batteries with considerable skill; behind a dense wall of sand guns and mortars had been embedded in well-protected bays, each guarded from blast from side and rear by baffle walls; many of the long guns were used dismounted from their normal carriages and half buried in the earth at such a high angle as to obtain the maximum possible range. So unprepared had the Spaniards been for any attack against these works by infantry, however, that they had not troubled to build banquettes, the usual raised and protected walks for sentries which could be manned by musketeers in case of assault. Thus, even had greater numbers of guards been in their advanced works during the sortie, they would have been as helpless as were the few who were trapped there.

All the lines of approach and communication, traverses, bomb-proofs, artillery, beds and carriages and platforms and other works were left ruined; and, as the British troops withdrew, explosions behind them indicated the blowing-up of the abandoned enemy magazines. The largest blast took place just as the last party of the British attachment had got within the garrison; then the principal magazine blew up with a tremendous explosion, 'throwing up vast pieces of timber, which, falling into the flames, added to the general conflagration'.

This remarkably successful affair cost the garrison four killed and 25 wounded; only one officer figured in the casualty lists, a lieutenant of the 12th being wounded; and one man was reported missing, 'supposed to be left wounded in the batteries'. Hardenberg's had two of the killed and 12 of the wounded. Considering that the Spanish had some 78 officers and men actually in the works attacked, that the entire action took place nearly three-quarters of a mile from the British defences and within a few hundred yards of well-established enemy batteries mounting 135 pieces of heavy artillery, the butcher's bill was extraordinarily light. Moreover, the British lost no musket or even any working-tool. The principal loss of material appears to have been a kilt; one of the 73rd detachment apparently returned without his, to have a new one promised him by the Governor, who was naturally delighted with the success of his venture. One souvenir brought back was the written report of the Spanish commanding officer, due to be sent in the morning to his general. Written a little too early to be entirely accurate, it stated 'nothing extraordinary had happened'.

Confusion among the enemy continued for several days. On the night following the sortie they opened a heavy fire of cannon and musketry on their own abandoned works, still sullenly smouldering, apparently in the belief that the British were out again. They made no immediate attempt either to put out the flames or to reoccupy their positions, although their patrols of cavalry were much more active and more numerous than they had been previously. And Drinkwater recorded the execution in the enemy's camp of several men, 'who probably might be some of the unfortunate actors in the late disgrace'. When the works finally ceased to burn, only heaps of sand remained, among which, from the summit of the Rock, a few ruined and dismounted mortars and guns could be discerned. Even as late as 12 December, over a fortnight after the assault, smothered fires were still breaking out, and flickering over the ruined works.

Some at least of the credit for this business must be given to that controversial character, Charles Ross. After leaving the garrison for a short time, he had managed to get back on 13 November, in the *Phoenix* cutter, which contrived to evade an enemy patrolling squadron of a zebec and three gunboats and got in without firing a shot. It was generally supposed he had come back to take command of the 72nd. He immediately made himself noticed, first turning out a major, a captain and a subaltern from a house on Scud Hill, then moving to another on Windmill Hill and dispossessing a captain and five subalterns. But it was to Ross that Eliott entrusted the direct command of this vital effort. Within the next few days letters arrived from England announcing Ross's promotion to major-general; he sailed on 21 December, during a brisk levanter, for Portugal and England.

Chief credit for success must go to Eliott. After over two years of close confinement his troops were still sufficiently well trained to undertake that most difficult of all operations, a large-scale night assault on an entrenched enemy. Everything shows signs of careful intelligent planning: the strong parties to protect the workmen, the equipment used, the placing of the reserve, the simple yet comprehensive orders, the short notice and quick action throughout the whole affair. Secrecy about any possible intention of a night attack was absolutely essential. Desertion from the British lines was still occurring: three men had deserted during October; and on the morning of 22 November a soldier of the 58th Regiment who had been missing for several days was seen to run from his shelter and take refuge in the Spanish fort of Santa Barbara. The merest hint of any danger from the garrison might have meant that the sortie would have run into strong opposition and very possible disaster. As it is, it is difficult to understand why the Spaniards did not at any rate fire on the British troops marching and working quite plainly on the isthmus in the glare of the burning fortifications. A few squadrons of cavalry might also have been usefully employed in the darkness. But nothing was done.

The Governor was of course delighted with 'this glorious occasion', as he called it in orders, and Ross also commented not only on the great honour conferred on him by being given command of the attachment but on the 'firm, good behaviour' shown by all the officers and men concerned.

In a despatch written on 1 December 1781 Eliott gave his reasons for making the sortie as not only due to the extent of the enemy's works, and the many new batteries recently erected; as these were of great height above the ground and only 1,200–1,500 yards away from Gibraltar's own defences, he thought that they could have been used to conceal many men in preparation for an assault. He also revealed that he knew the Spanish system of moving men and relieving guards; only some 700 in all were on duty in their lines, and their methods were too slow in action to allow any quick reinforcement. Even so, he had anticipated more annoyance from Spanish gunfire than was actually received during the retirement, when not one man had been killed or wounded. As one reason for this, he quoted Captain Curtis, R.N. (in whom he always showed the utmost confidence, speaking in terms of high praise) as saying that the gun sills in the Spanish batteries, built to allow firing against the Rock on a height and at a distance, were too high to allow the barrels to be sufficiently depressed. As his principal gains from the sortie, Eliott listed the inevitable delay in the replacement and reopening of the enemy batteries, the loss of some 14 months' work and the gain of time by the garrison; he also reported that despondency reigned in Madrid, because of this setback. This despatch was marked 'Most Secret' and was endorsed in London as received there 5 January 1782. With other public and private letters it had left Gibraltar on the night of 12 December 1781 in the *Unicorn*; the *Phoenix* cutter sailed the following evening, similarly burdened, in a gale.

There is no doubt that all of Eliott's labours were very considerably lightened by the energetic and meticulously accurate plans and sketches of all the Spanish defences which were regularly prepared and brought up to date by Green and his engineers. These were as clear and detailed as if made on the spot and at leisure in times of deepest peace; beautifully drawn and tinted, sent home regularly, they kept both Government and garrison fully acquainted with the enemy's ground dispositions and works.

Delight at his success did not blind Eliott to the still harsh realities of life. He reported that scurvy was increasing; and asked for money, powder, shells (especially 12-inch), recruits and medicine. He made detailed lists of what was needed: camphor, cream-of-tartar, gum ammoniac, Glauber's salt, emetics; capital instruments and trepanning (four sets), 24 scalpels in cases, six dozen lancets not in cases, a dozen bone nippers ('we find them very useful'), lint tow, old sheets, thread, four dozen stump caps and four dozen stump pillows.

Early in December, several exchanges under flags of truce occurred between Spanish and British. Letters were brought into the garrison from Englishmen made prisoner in cutters which had been captured while trying to run the blockade. News of the Spaniards taken in the batteries was sent to General Alvarez, the Spanish commander. One of the prisoners, Baron von Helmstadt, had been wounded in the knee. The Governor visited the wounded man frequently, and it is said that it was because of his reasoning with him that Helmstadt, after demurring, finally agreed to have an operation. The Baron was a young and handsome man, engaged to a beautiful Andalusian girl; his plight attracted much pity from all in the garrison. His leg was amputated. The Spaniards and his fiancée sent messages of thanks for the care taken by the British; also gifts of poultry, fruit, clothing and money for the use of both Helmstadt and the other officer, a lieutenant of artillery named Don Vicente Freire. But Helmstadt's health broke down completely; not it would seem from the results of his amputation but from 'some inward malady, probably a fever', according to Drinkwater. Daily messages about his condition were exchanged, but on 28 December the Baron died, to the deep regret of his captors. The war was suspended while his body, dressed in full uniform, and lying in a handsome decorated coffin, was escorted to the New Mole by Eliott and other principal officers marching in procession, accompanied by Don Vicente; a company of grenadiers of the 12th Foot also attended, with reversed arms; a military band played a dirge; although Eliott himself was not particularly sympathetic to the religion of his enemies, he kept the proprieties, allowing boys carrying candles, a crucifix, and holy water, and the vicar of the Spanish church, repeating part of their funeral service, to accompany the coffin. Three volleys were discharged as the body was put into a boat and carried off out into the bay, where a Spanish vessel came to receive it. The British craft was accompanied by a naval barge commanded by Sir Charles Knowles, Curtis's principal lieutenant, and bearing also Eliott's Adjutant-General as his representative. Eliott took particular care to observe all the niceties of such an occasion. The fowls, fruit and money which remained of the Baron's gifts were returned to his friends. This was at a time when potatoes were selling at 1s. 8d. a pound and while he had over 640 sick in his own hospitals; but it was much better to make a gesture of indifference than to attempt winning a dishonourable and in practice negligible gain.

The weather during December was exceptionally wild; though Christmas day itself was delightful. Strong winds threw down the tottering shell-blasted walls in the battered town, while rain spoilt many of the garrison's makeshift stone and clay houses and tents in their encampments. Fuel grew so short that even in the officers' hospital wards no fires were lit. Sickness increased to the point where officers' servants (usually exempt from working on the fortifications) were called on for duty. Even so, Eliott found it necessary to reduce by 100 the number so employed.

Bad weather did not prevent the enemy from at least beginning to work on their ruined batteries. Heavy fire was opened on them, which was returned. One evening a single Spanish shell, exploding near an entrance to a large cave in the Queen's Lines, wounded 11 men of the guard, including the sergeant and drummer. To shield themselves from observation the British put up screens of canvas before the batteries on which they were working; and the remaining now-empty colliers, beached and useless, were cut up by the engineers and used to strengthen the defences; squares and oblongs cut from their sides, complete with ribs and strengthening timbers, were carried whole into position, and found to be of greater permanence, properly supported, than any similar type defences used before. Eliott himself, in a cipher despatch, reckoned that the garrison had lost during the year 1781 no less than 127 dead, 46 permanently disabled and 324 wounded; from the beginning of the siege, the dead numbered 260. And the year closed, as one anonymous diarist remarked, 'without producing the least appearance of peace'. In truth, there seemed little prospect of either victory or even reasonable terms at that stage for either Great Britain or her lonely outpost at Gibraltar.

The year 1782 opened locally on rather a better note, calculated to maintain the high spirits which the sortie had raised. A small armed ship arrived from Port Mahon and Leghorn on 4 January having 22 Spanish soldiers aboard, captured by General Murray. Like the enemy over against Gibraltar, those under Crillon in Minorca knew they had a war on their hands. During September Murray had sallied out from his refuge in Fort St Phillip (where his guns kept the harbour at Port Mahon partly open to friendly vessels) against Crillon's headquarters; he had destroyed one battery and taken 100 captives. But at the time when this detachment reached Gibraltar, the dreaded scurvy had taken such a hold over Murray's garrison that men were dropping dead at their posts, and there was no hope for the survivors. And this same scourge had a firm grip over many on the Rock. To escape from their worries the Gibraltar garrison took to drinking harder than ever; but this was no remedy at all and deaths increased. To check this trend, Eliott ordered officers to pay duty on their liquor, much to their annoyance.

By the end of January the Spaniards had almost completely renewed their advanced batteries, remodelled on a new plan, unmasking howit-

**16**  The sortie, during the night of 26–27 November 1781. On the right of the picture (from l. to r.) are: Ensign A. Mackenzie, Maj.-Gen. G. A. Eliott, Maj. C. Wallotton, Lt. G. F. Koehler, Lt.-Col. J. Hardy, Brig.-Gen. C. Ross, Capt. A. Whitham, Capt. R. Curtis, Lt.-Col. T. Trigge and Lt.-Col. von Hugo

*From the oil painting by John Trumbull*

17  *The store-ship 'Mercury', commanded by Lieutenant Heighington, fighting her way between*
*a Spanish frigate and a zebec*

*From the oil painting by E. Jukes after Nicholas Pocock*

18  *The preparation of the floating batteries*

*From an engraving by Bergmiller*

zers and building high walls of fascines. This time they constructed the banquettes omitted in their earlier defences on this site. Sketches of these new works show them well equipped with sentry posts approached by steep slopes in the front, by ladders and steps within the walls. Any future sortie would meet with much more useful and well-organised opposition than had been possible in the previous November.

The British tried hard to set these new works alight by shooting carcasses at them; but the Spanish guards and workmen soon extinguished any fire. Many of these carcasses were blind shells originally fired into the fortress; perforated with three large holes, the cavity filled with an inflammable composition and shot back at the enemy works, these shells sometimes burnt for as long as a quarter of an hour, even when smothered in sand, which was the mode used by the Spanish to render them harmless. At one time the Spaniards tried to copy the British plan of working behind canvas screens; but the posts on the summit of the North Face were far too lofty for this subterfuge to be effective, and the screens were soon abandoned. On another occasion they sent a number of men against the British barriers by night, and opened a hot musketry fire; but this attempt was not followed up. It was noted that the new works were equipped with barriers, in which were hung gates, closed at night. Such obstacles would have made the sortie in November much more difficult, had they existed then.

While awaiting the new artillery assault which was obviously at hand, the British Engineers prepared depots of an increased size near their batteries in different parts of the defences; fascines, sandbags, and other materials were assiduously piled up. Some ordnance stores and other supplies arrived towards the end of January in two cutters; *Viper*, an exceptionally large vessel for this rig, mounted 28 nine-pounder guns, *Lively* the more usual 14; they had been chased by Spanish gunboats, but in a freshening wind had quickly slipped them. Their green tea fetched a guinea a pound, corned beef 18*s*. 8*d*.; cheese and butter cost 4*s*. 10½*d*. a pound; a sheep over £14.

February was marked by trials of another experimental weapon. This time it was a 'depress gun-carriage', the invention of Lieutenant George F. Koehler of the Royal Artillery. Drinkwater described it:

> The gun was fixed in a bed of timber, the underside of which was a plane parallel to the axis of the piece; from this bed, immediately under the centre of gravity, projected a spindle eight inches in diameter. This spindle passed through a groove formed for its reception in a plank, the upper side of which was also a plane: upon the under piece the bed and gun recoiled, being attached to it by a key passing through the spindle.

The bed and gun by these means were at liberty to move round upon the axis of the spindle, and when fired, slided upon the under plank in the line directed by the groove. The under piece was then connected, by a strong hinge in front, to two cheeks of a common garrison-carriage, cut down to be little higher than the trucks. The gun could be laid to any degree of depression under twenty degrees, by a common quoin resting upon the cheeks of the carriage; but when greater depression was necessary, two upright timbers, with indented steps, were fixed to the cheeks; by which, with the assistance of a moveable plank, to slide in upon the steps, and a quoin, the back part of the plank, upon which the gun slided, was elevated at pleasure by iron pins in the uprights; and the gun depressed to any angle above twenty, under seventy degrees.

Besides the great amount of depression possible (which was of particular importance on such a gun-platform as the Rock) this invention had two other advantages; the recoil was absorbed by the plank on which it slid, and the gun could be easily returned to its former place; and, at the place of farthest recoil after discharge, the gun could be swivelled round to lie across the carriage, so that the sponging and reloading operations could be conducted under cover of the merlons at the side of the gun embrasure. Of the first 30 rounds fired, in the presence of Eliott and other officers during the afternoon of 15 February 1782, 28 landed in one traverse of the St Carlos battery, to the delight of all the British who witnessed this interesting event. Spilsbury, always handy with his pencil and keenly interested in all that went on round him, put a couple of very clear sketches of Koehler's invention into his diary. He also drew a 'depress mortar carriage', made on the same lines, about which little is heard.

Besides bombardments and continual work on batteries by both sides during February, the month was further marked by a good deal of naval activity. Ships passed through the straits in both directions. There were several brisk little engagements, during which ten or so vessels slipped through the blockade. One of them, the *Mercury*, had left in January, ostensibly for England; in this belief, several inhabitants had taken passage in her. But her captain had received secret orders, which he faithfully kept. He put in to Lisbon and took in a cargo of wine and fruit before sailing again; he had recommended his passengers to take ship for England in the ordinary Lisbon packet, but they liked their accommodation too well to make the change. The captain, still keeping his own counsel, set sail directly back to Gibraltar. And it was that all-too-familiar bay that his guests found themselves looking at on the afternoon of the 23 February, along with a squadron of Spanish zebecs and a frigate, with which the *Mercury* exchanged cannon-fire before escaping. Her lemons were particularly valuable; and it was to prevent any suspicion that she might return with this particular cargo that Eliott and the *Mercury*'s captain, a naval officer called Heighington, had put up this elaborate pretence. Not only Gibraltar but Lisbon had its spies. For this successful manœuvre Heighington was deservedly promoted, largely on Eliott's strong recommendation.

Spying went on continually on both sides. Eliott frequently sent home news which could have reached him only through such secret sources; and occasionally a spy was actually seized in Gibraltar itself. Such one was Antonio Juanico, a mariner, who had reached the Rock late in 1781 aboard a vessel from Faro. He was suspected, arrested and interrogated. Of his guilt there could be soon no doubt, and Eliott sent home the results of his enquiry. Juanico's purpose had been to gather information for the Spanish Commander-in-Chief at San Roque. Eliott's sentence was of death; the spy was to be hanged by the common executioner on 4 February 1782, but the execution was postponed three times; in the end Eliott pardoned him and sent him to one of the naval vessels which called at the fortress during March 1782, on condition of his constantly serving on board during the course of the war, and with a stern command that he should never again set foot on Gibraltar.

On the afternoon of the same day (23 February 1782) on which Heighington brought his unwilling passengers back to the noise and confusion of Gibraltar instead of to 'the exhilarating coast of Britain', the Spanish fired a great feu-de-joie repeated several times. Once again all the Spanish and French shipping in the Bay at Algeciras was dressed over-all. Eliott and the garrison had a shrewd idea what it might portend, but not until 1 March, by a flag of truce, did they officially learn that Minorca had fallen on 5 February.

Gibraltar was obviously going to receive the benefit of undivided attention from its foes. Fire-ships were reported preparing at Algeciras. The Spanish laboured like beavers to extend their trenches and traverses. Powder and stores were landed on their beaches. New magazines were built, fresh guns and mortars installed. According to one deserter, the Spaniards had been working their cannon so continuously that in many batteries guns and mortars had been replaced three times already. Now all were once again renewed and made ready. Not even the heaviest defensive bombardments could prevent the Spaniards from reaching the northern edges of the long-abandoned gardens, on the place where Maxwell's reserve had been stationed on the night of the sortie. Several times heaps of fascines were set on fire and flames rose from the batteries as the range shortened. The Rock-gun was worn out once again, so that a shell burst the instant the match was applied and wounded an artillery officer. All the same, as the steady flow of plans regularly sent home clearly showed, the threat from the north was becoming more severe. A new cavalry encampment was observed in the distance, a new cart road constructed leading down to the main Spanish lines. As a part counter to this threat, the masonry bridge on the ditch at the Land Port Gate was pulled down, so that a formidable and uninterrupted obstacle ran across the British defences from underneath the impregnable North Face to the very edge of the sea. To fill the ditch if assault should come portable *chevaux de frise* were prepared and kept in readiness.

Eliott maintained his stream of requests for help. Now and again he apologised for the number made, pointing out that many were duplicates. The number code was used: '527 3174 242 1476 1912' was interpreted as 'Much more powder will be wanted' by the cipher clerk in Lord Hillsborough's office. Early in April, Eliott stated that he had bread to 12 June 1783, beef to 30 May and pork to 7 December of the same year, but pease only to 20 December 1782 and butter to 10 October 1782. Other stores he listed in varying quantities: oil, vinegar, kidney-beans, rice, raisins, currants, candles, soap, macaroni, grouts, sugar, wheat and lamp oil; all in all, fit for only a very plain and limited life. Nor was this dull food improved in the cooking. In those days the only method in general use was that of boiling up everything in a sort of glorified stew. Among other requests Eliott asked for another 100 iron cooking pots wanted for his troops, 'of ten to thirteen gallons each'.

In the meantime, Eliott had received some important stores and had been reinforced by a new regiment. News of this long-awaited relief had come on 25 February, when the *St Ann* ordnance ship arrived; she not only carried the timbers and frames, ready-made but unassembled, of two gunboats, as well as other stores, but information that the timbers of another ten gunboats were to arrive in the *Vernon* store-ship. It took patience to await the *Vernon*, which did not reach Gibraltar until before midnight of 23 March; but she came in good company, for with her were two frigates, *Apollo* and *Cerberus*, as well as four transports, bearing the 97th Regiment of Foot, besides 70 drafts for the garrison. The drafts came from one of the least reputable sources of recruits for the British army. They had been collected from deserters from various regiments confined in the Savoy Prison: 10 men for the 12th, 20 for the 39th, 19 for the 58th and 21 for the 72nd. At least on the Rock of Gibraltar they could be made to work; and they would have not only their own comrades but the besiegers to guard them. The 97th were, like the 72nd, a corps raised during the course of the war, their actual date of formation being 23 July 1779; their colonel was named Samuel Stanton. The men had been enlisted, not for life as was the rule in ordinary times, but for three years' service. They had no particular connection with any special town or district; it was only during the year 1782 that 'territorial' titles were generally granted, and for a century afterwards such designation was to be in most cases very loose and usually inappropriate. And when the war was over this particular regiment was disbanded and disappeared. On their arrival at Gibraltar they were very sickly. Although the siege had in fact less than a year to go before the fighting stopped they were to lose 113 officers and men through death by disease, more than twice as many as of the 'old' regiments who had been there from the beginning. They were also to lose 12 men and a drummer killed or died of wounds in this short spell, so that the cost to this one short-lived and long-forgotten regiment of the great siege of Gibraltar should not be overlooked in any accounting. Their commander, who had been promoted to brigadier by Eliott soon after his arrival, was not to survive for very long, for he died of sunstroke early in June 1782. Eliott said in a despatch home that Stanton's death was due to a fever brought on by exhaustion, for he had been most diligent in his constant attendance on the many sick men of his regiment both in barracks and hospital. Most of the 97th were to pass through long spells of fever before they recovered and became acclimatised to the Rock. And Spilsbury, writing down the fact that when at a moment of strain and heavy bombardment in April Eliott required the 97th to send out a group of picquets, remarked 'but they could not furnish it. So much for young regiments.' To the hard-bitten and long-suffering veterans of the Rock, after nearly three years of confinement and distress, practical ability was a primary consideration. Not until 17 June 1782 were the 97th able to put a picquet of men into the field.

As a matter of fact, Eliott was doing well to receive any men at all. Besides the regiments lost at Saratoga, those sent to India and the West Indies and the men shut up and, as it proved, irretrievably stationed at Minorca, well over 7,000 had capitulated in October 1781 at Yorktown, where Cornwallis had surrendered to a combined American and French force. The bulk of these were British troops, in regiments so far reduced by fighting and sickness that even battalions of the guards were down to less than 500 men apiece and others were only a couple of hundred strong.

Moreover, not only was Eliott fortunate at such a moment to be reinforced: he was lucky that what was actually sent to him finally reached Gibraltar Rock. Both French and Spanish naval forces were on the alert. American, Dutch and French privateers were becoming increasingly audacious, raiding the British coast from Aberdeen to Flamborough Head; squadrons and large single ships were all over the world snapping up British vessels ranging from 50-gun ships to frigates and sloops. The *Vernon*, on her way to Gibraltar escorted by H.M.S. *Success*, a 32-gun frigate, had fallen in off Cape Spartel with a large Spanish ship, the *Santa Catalina*, on the look-out for them. According to the Spanish accounts, the British had made their approach under the Dutch flag, had passed across the enemy's bows and at the critical moment had hoisted their true colours and raked the Spaniard several times, shattering her hull and dismasting her before she surrendered. Then the other part of the Gibraltar convoy, with *Apollo* and *Cerberus*, had come into sight, *Success* had sailed off homewards with her prisoners and the wrecked prize had been set alight and sunk. Among the papers taken out of this captured ship were found a list of 30 Spanish men-of-war at sea searching for this one single convoy, with detailed descriptions of the various vessels and their cargoes; even the names of officers aboard as passengers appeared. The *Santa Catalina*, a much larger and finer ship individually and with a larger crew than any of the English vessels, seems to have been foolishly surprised and badly fought, as well as being under-weaponed; these were common faults in Spanish vessels of the time. But the whole incident shows very clearly how extended were British resources by the winter of 1781–2, how precarious was British control of the sea, and by what a narrow margin Gibraltar was held. It also indicates how much the possession of Gibraltar was becoming a matter for national pride. After all its adventures, its reliefs, its narrow escapes from fire, starvation, disease and bombardment, the Rock was becoming a symbol for Great Britain as well as for Spain.

Besides men, ordnance stores, and gunboats, there arrived at Gibraltar many other invaluable supplies: eight cwt. of 'portable soup' for the hospitals, medicines, clothing and boxes of necessaries and gifts sent to officers by their friends and relations at home. Also enclosed with despatches were many official letters. The Governor was allowed to give leave of absence to officers who were ill to return to Great Britain, 'if you have no objection'. He received copies of the new Mutiny Act, along with warrants which permitted him to hold courts-martial. The old warrants had run out or were on the point of doing so, as Eliott had informed Government on several occasions; and so legalistic was the attitude of the times, and so inimical to any possible abuse of military and royal power were so many opponents of the Crown, that Eliott, quite properly, had been very anxious to conform to the letter of the law.

The Governor also received a further instalment of the lengthy correspondence connected with his staff appointments. The first announcement of these in June 1779 had been accepted dubiously; in April 1781 the promotions of Ross, Picton and Green to the rank of brigadier, each with a major of brigade, had led to further protests from home and requests for caution. Each of these extra staff meant increased expenditure; hence the doubt expressed; but Eliott, in spite of being repeatedly told of the need for economy, kept every post and man he had nominated, constantly pressing his need for such help and begging that an early favourable decision on their additional pay might be made.

The gunboats were quickly assembled, and the first was in the water by 17 April. Everyone confidently expected an assault. Losses were steadily mounting; the 12th alone lost 30 men during February, and early in the next month had an officer killed by a shell-burst as he was marching off duty; by the same shell his servant lost an arm 'and the drum was broke to pieces on the drummer's back'. One spectacular disaster occurred on 25 March 1782, when a shot entering Princess Amelia's battery on Willis's 'took off the legs of two men belonging to the 72nd and 73rd regiments, one leg of a soldier of the 73rd and wounded another man in both legs; thus *four* men had *seven* legs taken off and wounded by one shot'. It was while making this comment that Drinkwater mentioned that two boys of the artificer company were possessed of such exceptional eyesight that they were regularly stationed on the works to warn workmen of approaching shots, being so uncommonly quick of sight that they could spot the flight of missiles almost from the moment they left the gun muzzle. On this occasion the lad at Willis's had it seems just turned his head after reproving the men for not attending to him when he saw this shot, and his warning was too late to take effect. One of these lads, called Thomas Richmond (not 'Richardson', as Drinkwater wrote) was nicknamed 'Shell'; the other, John Brand, 'Shot'. Such events, along with noticing the constant replenishments of the enemy's supplies and additions to their works, kept the garrison alert in the midst of their monotony. The arrival of a Spanish 'regiment in blue' was news; so was the fact that the anniversary of the opening of the bombardment on 12 April passed with only a long slow fire from the enemy's lines; one wag suggested that perhaps they were spending the day with fasting and prayer, firing minute-guns to express their sorrow that so much powder and shot had been wasted for so little result. It was news when a man of the 39th, who had stolen a watch, ran off from the Land Port defences one evening under a hail of musketry and grape which brought him down just as he reached the enemy's works. It was even more interesting news when Eliott had grates prepared for heating red-hot shot in the batteries along the North Face. But they were not actually used; this was a disappointment for most of the garrison at the time, for they could have done with a tonic. Eliott, however, decided to keep this particular defensive weapon in reserve, for he had just heard of a new threat to Gibraltar.

# 9

## *Assault by Battering-Ships*

The Governor reported home on 1 April that a dozen ships in Algeciras were being prepared as battering-vessels. This news he had from a seaman, who described them as 'lining with cork and cables'; the Duke of Crillon was to take command of a new attack on the Rock. The news proved to be almost exactly accurate and was soon widely known in the garrison. By 11 April the main outlines of the enemy's plan were common knowledge. Crillon was to be supported by a French engineer called Michaud d'Arcon, a man of great ability; 20,000 French and Spanish troops were to join those already in the lines; besides the battering-ships, ten sail-of-the-line under Admiral Don Bonaventura Moreno were to reinforce the squadron in the Bay. So it was rumoured, and the gossip was not badly informed.

There was certainly great activity by the enemy. Many vessels, both of peace and war, sailed through the straits. By 16 April there were three frigates, four large zebecs, a cutter, and a bomb ketch at Algeciras, besides other large vessels apparently being cut down and remodelled; a large zebec, a cutter, a lugger and a bomb ketch lay off Orange Grove, the principal beach of disembarkation for Spanish supplies going to their lines on the isthmus; off Cabrita were another large zebec, a smaller ship of the same rig, and a sloop-of-war; while also in the area were 15 gunboats and eight mortar-boats, besides many smaller craft. The largest single fleet seen for some time appeared on 26 May, when 114 sail arrived in the bay, and in the course of the next few days disembarked some 9,000 men, who were quickly encamped behind the Spanish lines. There was in fact immense activity at all points on sea and ashore wherever the besieged British looked. One diarist said, when he heard that 'the regular siege against this place will commence': 'In the name of all that is horrible in war—what is meant by a siege, if bombarding, cannonading and blockading on all sides, in the manner here related, is not one?' Drinkwater remarked, about 4 May: 'from seven in the evening to the same hour the succeeding afternoon, both the garrison and the Enemy were silent. This was the first twenty-four hours in which there had been no firing for the space of THIRTEEN MONTHS.'

In spite of all this naval force, a few vessels contrived to run the blockade in both directions during April and May. One incomer brought sheep, another 30,000 oranges (which sold at nearly 5d. each). A little convoy under *Cerberus* and *Apollo* sailed on the night of 8 May, braving not only the zebecs but three Spanish frigates in the Gut; an engagement occurred, and three of the four transports (*Thompson, Loyal Britain* and *Valiant*) were triumphantly brought back across the bay next morning, captured by the Spanish. But the remaining transport, with the frigates and ordnance ships, got safely away. By mid-June, however, 19 British vessels had been taken and 287 seamen were in a Spanish prison at Ronda, with 27 officers. Most had been captured while inward bound for Gibraltar; their lives were hard, since all provisions at Ronda were very dear and the British had only their pay to live on; Eliott supported a plea made by the captive merchant navy officers that they might be given passports and allowed to go to Portugal.

In the meantime the Spaniards worked steadily away at the vessels they were converting off Algeciras. Several old vessels, men-of-war or 'galleons' (as Drinkwater termed them), were cut down; yards and topmasts were struck, upperworks removed and the sides and decks strengthened with extra timbers. By June, although members of the garrison were still speculating as to the exact purpose of these operations, Eliott himself had no doubt. He sent home, in code, a most detailed and, as events proved, an accurate account of these ships. After they were cut down, a roof was formed over their top decks and made bomb-proof; guns were to be used on one broadside only; sandbags, neapolitan oak and cables were woven together to reinforce the sides; only the main and foremasts were left standing; iron chains were aboard for mooring purposes. He even advised that the attack which these floating batteries were destined to make would probably be against the Old Mole and the northern part of Gibraltar's defences; a French officer was in charge. This was all correct although three months were to pass before there was the final proof. Eliott also reported, thankfully, that although the Spaniards had collected considerable numbers of workmen for these operations, they had very largely suspended operations on land against him, concentrating all their efforts on the preparation of their new naval assault. The general appearance of these battering-ships was like 'an oblong floating hay-rick'. To combat them, Eliott asked once again for a squadron of King's ships. No doubt acting on Curtis's advice, he believed that an active naval force which could operate in strength at sea was the best way to counter this new threat. But he was to be disappointed. Although the new gunboats were to prove successful, and although 1,900 barrels of powder arrived in three store-ships during this period, government did not spare him any large vessels. In this they were almost certainly right, for dispersal in penny packets of either naval or military strength against so powerful and numerous enemies at such a time would have invited destruction; particularly at Gibraltar, where facilities for mooring and repair were limited, and very close to which large hostile naval squadrons could operate with ease.

June was marked by a spectacular accident. On the morning of the 11th, between 10 and 11 o'clock, an unlucky 13-inch shell from the Spanish lines fell through the splinter-proof at the door of an expense magazine on Princess Anne's battery at Willis's. It burst, and ignited the powder, which blew up with so violent an explosion that it seemed to shake the whole Rock. It was reckoned that 100 barrels of powder went up in a single instant. Debris was thrown far away into the sea and three merlons were hurled down on to the lines and gun positions immediately beneath the source of the disaster. So violent was the shock that the doors of the other magazines in the battery were forced open; but luckily none took fire. A drummer and 13 men were killed at once, and three sergeants, three drummers and nine rank-and-file were wounded; this party had been employed at the time working on the flank of the battery. At once the Spanish redoubled their fire. Their men turned out with loud cheers and their drums beat to arms. Some English observers thought the enemy moved forward as though thinking of an immediate assault. But in spite of the heaviness of the blow, all the rest of the British defences were intact. There was no panic or widespread disorder and everyone stood firm. The danger passed, though fire broke out the following day in the ruined magazine three times. But the Spanish did not notice it, and only the normal general bombardment continued. To have lost 29 men to a single blow was hard, especially in the extended state of the garrison. Once again the officers' servants had to go on fatigue work, to lighten the labour of the regiments. Even so, the damaged battery was soon back in service. The rubbish was quickly cleaned away and several shots were fired from the position even on the evening of the fatal day, both to encourage the British and to impress the enemy with the fact that nothing particularly vital had been damaged.

Through the hot summer days and nights the Spaniards worked steadily away at their battering-ships, closely watched and carefully recorded by the garrison and its diarists. Various terms were used for them: 'floating batteries' and 'junk ships' were popular. 'Junk' was a term much used at this time for old rope and cable, material which because of its fire-resisting qualities and absorbent nature was put thickly on the new strong wooden roofs and sides strengthening the original hulls, gradually altering their appearance completely. The enemy camps behind their lines steadily expanded. On one occasion 5,000 Frenchmen arrived in a single day. So interested were the new-comers that a large party of French and Spanish general officers with their following aides-de-camp and personal friends came into the lines to gaze at the formidable North Face. One general with other officers came down and stood before their most advanced works having various features pointed out to him; whereupon, says Drinkwater, 'our artillery thought proper to give them a shot, which the General in the advanced works probably took as a hint to retire; for he immediately pulled off his hat and returned into the battery.'

On the British side labour was incessant. Nine hundred men were employed on each shift, so that between guards and working parties and parades (for Eliott had formed a new parade ground well south of the town's ruins) the soldiers were kept ceaselessly employed. The usual disposition of strength was to have two whole regiments on the North Face, two others massed and ready to move southwards toward Europa Point to counter any possible attack there, and to keep the other two (three when the 97th became fit for duty) and the Hanoverian Brigade lining the sea-walls and manning the posts at Windmill Hill, along the crest and at Catalan Bay. All of them, crammed into the little space available for camping, in the casemates facing over towards Algeciras or in the batteries of the North Face, always conscious of the enormous Rock in whose shade they lived, led the dullest of lives. Work, drill and danger were their daily portion, enlivened only by liquor. Desertion continued. Spilsbury, describing an escape by 'one of the Savoy lads' who had been placed in the 58th, says he got clear away to the Spaniards, though fired at by the British; this was this particular man's fifteenth desertion. One man even got away from the hospital. Several were recaptured; one, a sergeant of the 72nd, was duly hanged after court-martial; he had been discovered, hiding in an attempt to find a suitable moment for his final break, after four days' search; the wretched man, trying to descend the steep precipices, had found himself on a rock face unable either to climb back or to go on, and had been obliged to call out for help. He had left a letter stating his intention of deserting, so had no hope of mercy. Other soldiers were flogged. Four seamen also deserted; they had pretended to go out to visit some lobster-pots, but made their escape to the enemy. Drinkwater mentioned that two of these sailors had been earlier involved in the conspiracy to run away with the cutter *Speedwell*, as previously recorded. There was indeed great boredom.

One Highlander of the 73rd, who believed he had 'the sight', prophesied after a dream of the future that Gibraltar would be taken three weeks after it was attacked. Eliott's method of dealing with such melancholy prophets (of whom the time and the circumstances produced several) was to lock them up in close confinement until the period of their prophecy was expired; when they were well flogged and restored to their comrades. Partly no doubt to keep the men occupied, partly because some kind of attempted assault on foot was not out of the question, the regiments in turn were taken down to the coast and given musketry practice with powder and ball. Six rounds a man were fired, at targets placed along the line-wall or at casks thrown adrift on the current. Not all the men obeyed orders strictly. One shot hit a store-ship, another lodged in an officer's coat. Such expressions of anonymous disapproval have been known to occur in other places at other times. In the normal way, drummers were not armed with muskets; they were usually trained as stretcher bearers. Nor were sergeants so equipped, carrying a halberd (very useful for drill and control) and sword. But Eliott now ordered that both drummers and sergeants were to carry firelocks and accoutrements in case of alarm. Musicians, another generally privileged class of soldier, were similarly armed; and their names were also added to the rosters of those who had to turn out with shovels for labour on the fortifications.

Another symptom of the strange mixture of boredom and tension found in life within a besieged fortress was a new outbreak of duelling and minor insubordination among the officers. There were several 'affairs of honour', over trifles too routine or uninteresting to be recorded, in which shots were exchanged with little or no effect.

For the garrison even liquor ran short, or perhaps was deliberately reduced in the quantity available. Grog-shops were cut down to a supply of four gallons a day, so drinking for the men became a matter of 'first come, first served'. Officers were allowed to buy only a quarter of a pint of rum a day, which was so troublesome that getting spirits became hardly worth the bother. Nor did food provide much joy. Flour was so full of weevils 'that a plum pudding has the appearance of a currant one'. A dead cow sold at nearly 6s. a pound. Sugar cost almost as much a pound in cheaper times and brought over that price on occasion. Small supplies of such stores were occasionally auctioned, hence the variation in cost.

The weather was oppressive, with much heat and little wind. Dysentery and influenza took their toll. On one day, of the 13 captains and subalterns of Reden's Hanoverians, only one was fit enough to report for duty; and nearly 700 men were in the hospitals.

It was during this long period of waiting, visibly confronted with the steadily rising risk of imminent and novel assault, that there began what is to people of today one of the most notable features of the Gibraltar defences: the subterranean galleries in the heart of the Rock itself. It is said that on a day in May 1782 while Eliott, his Chief Engineer and staff were inspecting the batteries on the North Face, he found one idle while the artificers were repairing it. The Governor is supposed to have said aloud, while meditating over the ruins, 'I will give 1,000 dollars to anyone who can suggest how I am to get a flanking fire upon the enemy's works.' Whereupon Sergeant-Major Ince, who was with his commanding officer, Colonel Green, stepped forward and suggested the idea of forming galleries in the solid rock. Certainly Ince was put in charge of making such a gallery, six feet high and six feet wide, begun on 22 May. Eliott wrote home and asked particularly for miners to be sent out: any who had served in sieges were to be preferred. At first the idea was for a fully protected covered way, leading to the Royal Battery. A dozen miners, with labourers, were put on to the task, later reinforced. This first project was succeeded by others. One gallery, which ran along behind the face of the rock above Faringdon's battery, had an opening blown in the outside wall on 15 July 1782. 'The mine was loaded with an unusual quantity of powder,' said Drinkwater, 'and the explosion was so amazingly loud that almost the whole of the enemy's camp turned out at the report. But what must their surprise be, when they observe whence the smoke issued!' The aperture was enlarged, the tunnel widened to take the recoil, and a 24-pounder was mounted, bearing on almost all the enemy's works on the isthmus. By September a total of five such heavy weapons was installed. Later a complete new battery, similarly constructed, was hollowed out nearby and armed; this was named 'St George's Hall', because of its extensive capacity.

Whether Sergeant-Major Henry Ince ever received the 1,000 dollars he was supposedly promised is not known. According to one story, he contracted for his subterranean work, at the rate of one guinea per running foot; another has it that the total cost ran at one real ($5\frac{1}{4}d.$) per foot cube. Ince certainly left an indelible mark on the history of Gibraltar, on which he had first served as a private in the 2nd Foot. A Cornishman by birth, he was one of the first members of Green's company, being appointed a sergeant on the date of formation. He had been promoted sergeant-major in September 1781 and served not only throughout the siege but for long afterwards. A special rate of pay was granted to him, of 4s. a day, besides his 2s. 10d. a day as foreman; his charge included the constant development of the underground caverns, batteries, galleries and magazines built in the heart of the Rock. Very short in stature, but wiry and hardy and of great industry, his contribution to Gibraltar's successful defence was considerable.

Eliott placed great reliance on Green and his company. By July, 1782, its strength was down to 92 of all ranks; 22 had been lost in the siege, including six dead. The Governor wrote home, asking for reinforcements and an increased establishment. These were granted, and a recruiting campaign was launched in England by the Duke of Richmond, then Master-General of the Ordnance and ultimately responsible for the company. Although the recruiting of highly skilled tradesmen for military duties is always a particularly difficult operation of that uncertain business, the fame of Gibraltar's defence and the honour gained by this new corps were so attractive that masons, carpenters, sawyers and smiths came forward in considerable numbers. These reinforcements reached Green in October 1782, putting the company's strength in N.C.O.s and artificers up to 234. During the siege the total casualties of this invaluable company were 72 of which 23 were dead through sickness. None of the artificers deserted to the enemy, but two men (not included in the total already given) suffered death by hanging (on 29 May 1781) for plundering the King's stores.

There also appeared during this time of waiting one of the curious little foreign corps which have so frequently played an interesting, if not particularly decisive, part in British military history. Often during the course of wars fought for trade and trade posts up and down the length of the world's shipping routes, the British government has picked up as allies people who were not so much the friends of Great Britain as the devoted enemies of Great Britain's foes. Such at this period were the people of Corsica.

Pasquale Paoli belonged to a Corsican family which for generations had struggled for the island's independence from Genoese domination. He very largely succeeded in dominating his native land by 1755; but in

1768 Genoa formally ceded Corsica to France. Paoli resisted strongly, but was evicted during the following year. He settled in London, where he not only received a pension from the British government but became a warm friend of Dr Samuel Johnson and Boswell. Naturally enough many of Paoli's Corsicans fought bitterly against the French during the War of American Independence, and many were regularly employed by British commanders in the Mediterranean.

Towards the end of May 1782 a vessel arrived at Gibraltar with some supplies from Leghorn. It also carried a dozen Corsicans and an officer who had voluntarily embarked to offer their services to Eliott against the French. These men were at first distributed among the British regiments, where within the fortnight two of them had quarrelled so violently that one died from a knife wound; the killer was subsequently acquitted by a court-martial. This was not a particularly promising opening to the story of Anglo-Corsican co-operation, but better things were to follow.

The British consul at Leghorn, John Udney, had early in March forewarned Eliott that a Corsican party was being organised there. He warmly recommended its leader, a man called Leonetti, Paoli's nephew, as a lively ally who had raised his little force at his own expense; Leonetti's cause was also sponsored by Horace Mann, British representative in Florence. Leonetti himself turned up with his followers on 25 July, when two vessels arrived. These were the *St Philip's Castle*, an armed ship chartered by the British Government, and the cutter *Hector*, from Algiers. There were five Corsican officers, 12 N.C.O.s and 58 privates, 'with some small remains of refreshment', according to Eliott's despatch. Leonetti had had some military training in the Grand Duke of Tuscany's service, and many had also been engaged in Minorca, escaping before Murray's final encirclement and surrender. 'I am not without hopes that this little corps may be made useful', said Eliott, and he formally embodied them on 4 August 1782. Leonetti received the title Captain-Commandant, supported by a Captain-Lieutenant, a first and a second lieutenant and an adjutant; by the time they were organised they also included four sergeants, four corporals, two drummers, 68 privates and a chaplain. They were armed with musket and bayonet; each man carried a horse pistol on the left-hand side and two cartridge boxes. Eliott quartered them on Windmill Hill, which post he committed to their charge. During the siege they suffered few casualties; an officer was wounded (he recovered) and two men died of sickness; naturally enough, there were no deserters.

*St Philip's Castle*, besides this welcome reinforcement, brought some immensely good news. This was of Rodney's overwhelming defeat of the main French fleet in the West Indies off Dominica, near the group of islands called Les Saintes, on 12 April 1782. There de Grasse, the French Admiral, had been captured and his fleet dispersed. Thirty-three British line-of-battle ships had encountered and fought a French fleet 29 strong, destined originally for the capture of Jamaica. During the battle five French vessels were taken or sunk; the captured flagship, *Ville de Paris,* 110 guns, was regarded as the finest ship afloat; she had been well fought and had hideous losses but was finally carried off in triumph. The victory might have been even more decisive, as subsequent enquiries revealed. But it was incontestably a great achievement, and helped to reconcile the British Government and people to accepting the bitter and unmistakable fact that the American colonies had gone for good.

In North America Cornwallis's surrender had proved fatal to the British cause. There were still plenty of battle-hardened British troops there, ready to fight and in good spirits. They held New York and Charleston. But the heart was out of the fight, not so much in America as at home in London. There had always been much opposition to the idea of subduing the colonists by force. Chatham's last speech in the Lords, during which he collapsed and died, had been in favour of conciliation. The Duke of Richmond, Lord Rockingham and Burke had long been in favour of recognising the United States as a new country. George III and Lord North had tried to continue the war, but by February 1782 the desire for a new government was so strong that a motion that a speedy surrender should be made in America was supported by 193 members of the House of Commons, and North's majority shrank to a single vote. During the next month he was replaced by a ministry led by Rockingham, and including Fox, Shelburne and Burke, all men who had condemned the war. It was to Shelburne, as Secretary of State, that Eliott henceforth addressed his despatches, until he took over the leadership in July, after Buckingham's death. The war against America was for all practical purposes abandoned.

To give up Gibraltar without a fight was quite another matter. George III, although the changes in Parliament and cabinet had much reduced his personal influence, was still the King. He himself was deeply impressed with Eliott's actions, which were indeed unique at the time in that nowhere could he be blamed for failure. George gave orders that all the despatches from Gibraltar were to be laid immediately before him as they arrived.

Certainly on and around the Rock there was no suggestion that danger was over and the war nearing its end. On the contrary. As the French and Spanish realised that America was almost certainly free, their attention became increasingly concentrated on the capture of Gibraltar. One great object had been attained. To seize Gibraltar seemed not only desirable but highly probable. This isolated fortress, under pressure for over three hard years, insignificantly reinforced, short of food, ravaged by sickness, without hope of relief in the midst of battle, must surely succumb to the double might of Spain and France and a double threat from land and sea?

Eliott and the garrison showed no fear. They celebrated the news of Rodney's victory with a magnificent feu-de-joie; just as they had during the 4th of the previous month, precisely at 1 p.m., discharged the regulation salute, now of 44 guns, in honour of the King's birthday. News kept coming in about the enemy's preparations: the ten ships were being strengthened to six or seven feet thick on the larboard side, with green timber bolted with iron, packed with cork, junk and raw hides; the roofs were bomb-proof; guns were of heavy metal; the bombardment was to be supported by large boats, full of troops, and fitted with hinged platforms which could be lowered to facilitate landing, so that an assault from the sea could be made if opportunity offered. Off Algeciras gun-shots were heard, where the enemy tested their cannon. There was great noise at night on the isthmus, as the French and Spanish troops toiled at their defences and preparations, employing many hundreds of mules and thousands of workmen. The heat and oppression of the weather was made worse by clouds of smoke and waves of hot air rolling down from the parched brown hills on the Spanish mainland, which were being burnt off in the usual manner. A kind of influenza, which was blamed on the moist warmness of the air, afflicted both armies.

On their side the British were equally active. New covered ways were made behind the ramparts facing the sea, using the wrecked houses as material for the traverses. Deep ditches were dug for shelter. New trenches were cut at Willis's, and the subterranean gallery at Faringdon's battery extended until a shelter 140 feet long was cut out of the solid rock. Light balls were fired at night, just to make sure that the Spanish did not advance their forward works any more; and a sentry post of four privates and a trusty sergeant was sent out every night, to put a man as near to the enemy lines as possible to listen and to report; this was withdrawn every morning before daybreak and had orders not to fire except in extremity. The cannon at Willis's and on the heights were kept loaded with grape, so that as heavy a toll as possible could be extracted, should the enemy meditate a storm on foot across the few hundred yards which separated them from the foot of the British defences. These precautions did not prevent the enemy from springing a surprise on the night of 15 August, when they constructed a new shelter-trench 500 yards long, with a communication trench nearly three times that length, which linked their advanced works on Bayside to the eastern shore of the isthmus. This took the British aback next morning, for they had suspected nothing on such a scale was being performed. Some 10,000 men were employed; over one-and-a-half million sandbags and thousands of casks full of sand had been used, with immense numbers of fascines; the whole took place without any interruption from the garrison and within half a mile of their posts. In the shelter of these works the enemy began to build three new batteries for mortars.

All this activity gave point to information brought by a deserter from the Spanish lines. This man, originally a member of the garrison at Minorca, had enlisted with the French after the surrender, but now reached Gibraltar by swimming round the Mediterranean end of their lines. He stated that 25 August was the day appointed for the opening of the bombardment, which the enemy confidently believed would be on such a scale that the British batteries would be 'beaten to powder'. He also reported that there was not much love lost between Spanish and French and that although there were 40,000 men in the camp, the soldiers, many of them now levies and not well disciplined, were deserting daily in large numbers, carrying off their arms. This man, with another like him, was put into one of the English regiments.

On 19 August, at midday, a boat arrived in Gibraltar bay with a flag of truce; it had a crimson awning and the rowers were in uniform. A British boat put out to meet it, in calm and foggy weather, and brought back letters for Eliott along with a present of ice, fruit, game and vegetables; there was also a packet of letters for several of the inhabitants. All these came from the Comte d'Artois, brother of the King, who had just arrived from Madrid. Crillon sent them with 'the strongest expressions of esteem' to Eliott, saying he wished to become his friend, after proving himself worthy of the honour by facing him as an enemy. Eliott replied in suitable terms, with 'a thousand thanks' for the handsome present in accepting which he had broken a resolution made at the beginning of the war, to put all gifts up to public auction. Eliott also begged Crillon not to send anything more, since 'the English are naturally fond of gardening and cultivation', and there was really no need. These courtesies did not stop Eliott, when describing the events in a despatch home, from writing that the exchange was 'intended, I presume, to inform me of the arrival of the Princes [for the Duke of Bourbon had arrived with d'Artois], in order that they might not particularly be singled out by our gunners or marksmen'. Nor did they prevent the British from firing a shot over the truce boat, when it was noticed she was approaching too close to the town front; nor the Spanish that same night from raising a semicircular parapet with sandbags for a new battery in their advanced works.

That matters were working towards a climax at sea was shown by some trials in the open waters (but still very close to Algeciras) of some of the Spanish floating batteries. They were observed to put out under sail; ensigns were flown and what were apparently salutes were exchanged. It was also noted with some interest by the British that, when these large and awkward craft attempted to return to their sheltered anchorage near the isle of Algeciras, one of them needed to be towed by ten gunboats.

The floating batteries were constructed to the design and under the close superintendence of a Frenchman, Michaud d'Arcon, a highly celebrated engineer. The long-awaited attack was at this moment being keenly anticipated in Paris, where at one theatre a drama enacted nightly, before wildly applauding audiences, the capture of Gibraltar after bombardment from d'Arcon's vessels. Various novel means of seizing the Rock had at times been contemplated by inventive Frenchmen. Among them were reported: the use of poison; a mounted charge from the sea by soldiers on horses made of cork; the building of an immense cofferdam round the fortress which could then be flooded by pipes; and even the construction of an artificial mound higher than Gibraltar itself. But all these wild and whirling notions had disappeared before the reality of these great vessels, more strongly reinforced and strengthened than any previously built, and fitted out with the utmost ingenuity.

On the whole both sides spent most of August in strengthening their own works, one side for assault, the other for defence. There was a brisk exchange on the North Front during the afternoon of the 21st; but new palisades and covered ways, strengthened roofs to bomb-proofs, furnaces built in the shelter of traverses to heat shot red-hot, and a shift of the few wretched remaining inhabitants as far south as Eliott would permit, were the chief British activities. From the British naval craft men were landed and formed into a marine brigade, under command of Captain Curtis, whom Eliott appointed a brigadier-general. The ships themselves were drawn in close to shore and a

19  *The Spanish fleet, led by the ten battering-ships, in the Bay of Gibraltar*

20  *The battering-ships open fire, 13 September 1782*

*Both from eye-witness drawings by G. F. Koehler*

21　The North Front of Gibraltar, as seen from the Spanish lines during the land and sea attack, 13 September 1782

From an engraving by T. Malton after G. F. Koehler

strengthened boom defence was prepared. Only the gunboats and ships' boats were kept ready to put to sea.

On the Spanish side an occasional whole day would pass without their firing a single shot; but 64 new embrasures were opened in their new works, with magazines in the rear; a deserter from the Walloons said that no fewer than 90 pieces of cannon had been brought forward, to supply a constant flow of weapons to replace those which might be damaged or overheated. The floating batteries, using sweeps, gradually drew out and anchored in line on the far side of the bay; the British watched as loads of powder and shot were put about them. They also saw some hundreds of men, escorted by cavalry, march down to the beach and go aboard, early in September, after a large body, moving 'in a very irregular manner', had gone ashore and into camp. These latter were supposed to be the artificers, the first group presumably members of the crews, forcibly put aboard the battering-ships. These were days when convicted men and hardened criminals in Spain and France often served their sentences aboard penal galleys. Even in England, the land of the free, press-gangs were actively encouraged to fill the crews of warships, and condemned spies (like the man already noted), military deserters and jailbirds were sometimes given the option of embarking as seamen.

On the British side a large redisposition of forces took place in early September. Field officers took charge of guards in the lines; the sailors, about 900 strong, were put in charge of Europa Point; the 39th were encamped in South Port Ditch; the 73rd were posted in shelters of the ruined town, with the 12th behind the New Mole and the 72nd in the King's and Montague's batteries. The Corsicans remained at Windmill Hill; but the 97th, placed at Rosia, were disappointed ('much shag-reened' to use Spilsbury's words) at not being put on duty. Other corps were placed ready in reserve. Details of guards mounted on the 7 September 1782 show 32 officers and 957 'other ranks' of the infantry alerted for the town, lines and southern defences, out of a total strength of some 7,530 men. In addition, some 700 men were on picquet duty; and the engineers and artillery were also carefully organised, controlling over 1,700 workmen. With the orderlies, servants and soldiers used in administration and on hospital duties, half of the total garrison at least was employed at any given moment. At this time 400 men were lying sick or wounded in hospital. Every man not definitely attached to a specific unit with clearly defined duties was given his alarm post, either with a musket or to carry shot, in case of emergency. It was obvious that such tremendous exertions could not be sustained for long.

It was also very clear, from the busy activities of the Spanish and French, that the crisis was rapidly approaching.

The enemy batteries in their advanced lines on the isthmus, though now once more full of men, constantly labouring, were far from ready. Some of the embrasures were blocked with sandbags, and though guns and mortars were evident, their trenches and firing platforms, magazines and shelters, were not nearly so complete as those in the British lines. Afloat, however, they had more nearly perfected their arrangements. Lights at sea were seen at night; gunboats were noticed withdrawing from near the Old Mole head early one morning through the dawn mist, though they had not opened fire or betrayed their presence. It was thought that they had been taking soundings in readiness for the great assault from the sea. A certain amount of movement was also noticed on the isthmus at night, and farther inland, where strange fires and lights burning in a line were seen. These also were regarded as preparation for marking the place of anchorage for the vessels waiting to come in for the attack.

The ten battering-ships, all roofed, all equipped below decks, were by now putting the final touches to their rigging, which was very much simpler than that used by sea-going vessels. Three tall masts, with topmasts, a long bowsprit, gaff and boom at the stern for a spanker or driver and a couple of crossed yards on each mast, with a minimum of cordage, was all most of them carried. A conspicuous feature was an extremely long jack-staff mounted on the stern, on which to fly an enormous standard.

Once again the garrison reacted against enemy threats of their own volition. There was nothing of the rabbit hypnotised into helplessness by the stoat about Eliott and his men. Boyd was responsible, so Eliott wrote home, for the initiative this time. Accepting his suggestions, at 7 a.m. on 8 September the British batteries opened a heavy fire against the enemy's advanced lines and batteries. Red-hot shot were used in large numbers for the first time. They proved highly successful. By 10 o'clock one Spanish battery of six guns and another with two guns were ablaze. The enemy returned the fire, but not until over two hours had passed. They worked with astonishing bravery to extinguish the flames and keep damage under control. But by 5 o'clock in the afternoon not only were the first two batteries destroyed; the parallels were beaten down and another 13-gun battery had been heavily battered and was burning. The British continued to fire until darkness, but the Spanish and French ceased during the afternoon. The British lost several men during this cannonade; later they learned that 140 had been killed among the French alone.

Next day the bombardment continued heavily on both sides, the Spaniards bringing into service a 64-gun battery which was not nearly complete, and employing in all over 100 cannon and 66 mortars. They opened fire simultaneously, the signal being two rockets fired from their forts at 5.30 a.m. The discharge was tremendous, a rude awakening for any of the garrison still asleep. The onslaught was particularly against the North Front, the Grand Parade, the Land Port and the two adjacent bastions of Montague and Orange. At times, 10–20 shells could be seen in the air at once, trailing their slow arcs of smoke as they fell to earth. The shot, on the other hand, discharged at point-blank, arrived almost as soon as the flash of discharge was spotted. Guards were quickly put under cover, but again there were several casualties. So accustomed were the British to the slow formality of Spanish operations that their unorthodox behaviour in opening fire from batteries not completely ready took them quite by surprise.

The allied fleets also took a hand. Seven Spanish and two French line-of-battle ships, accompanied by other craft, sailed in line ahead on the morning of 9 September to the camp at the Orange Grove and then stood along the coast within gun shot, firing as they went, down to Europa. There they put about and sailed northwards, still discharging their broadsides, before returning to their anchorage. In the evening they sailed over once again and fired a few more shots. The garrison very naturally returned the fire, grateful for some action. Little damage was done by either side. In spite of this naval onslaught, a small craft from Algiers managed to get into Gibraltar, bringing four bullocks, 30 sheep, some wine and general stores. As night fell 16 enemy gunboats came over to within gun shot of the King's Bastion. This time it was not to take soundings, but to form line and bombard; they retired after about half an hour's brisk exchange of grape-shot.

The same pattern was repeated on 10 September, the wind still standing steady from the east, while the land bombardment continued. The desire to miss nothing at such an interesting moment brought the off-duty men of the garrison in crowds to peer over the line-walls. Eight were killed and 17 wounded in these attacks, during which it was reckoned about 6,000 shot and shells were hurled against the defences. The British looked on these attacks from the sea with a kind of lofty contempt, cheering heartily when a shot went home on an enemy craft, and particularly when it was seen that the bowsprit of one of the attackers was damaged. On one occasion, Spilsbury remarked: 'It was ridiculous enough to see one of the ships put about while firing, and the men at some of the guns, not being informed of it, kept firing the same guns, being then the contrary way.' Nevertheless the continual struggle kept the British busy all night, clearing the debris which fell into the ditches and replenishing the magazines in forward positions. The rate of fire from the Spanish lines increased daily, until it reached 6,500 shot and 2,080 shells every 24 hours. During darkness the Spaniards also came daringly close to the lines near Bayside below the batteries; they set the palisades on fire and shot several volleys of small arms towards the Rock. After a round or two of grape had dispersed these men, a heavy cannonade was resumed, many short-fused shells being aimed at the parties of British workmen labouring in the trenches. Besides the damaged palisades (which burnt for several days and were left full of gaps wide enough to admit eight men abreast), the *chevaux de frise* in the ditch before the Land Port Gate were much destroyed, the covered ways obstructed and breaches opened in the wall. As the gunboats also resumed their nightly bombardments, the pressure on the garrison intensified.

The two frigates, *Brilliant* and *Porcupine*, with other vessels, were scuttled close inshore. Fire was always the greatest danger of sea warfare, and the risks of confusion and concealing smoke due to British ships aflame beneath the Rock's defences were too great to run. It was reported that one of the enemy's attacks had been broken off very suddenly because a red-hot shot was discovered to have hit a Spanish vessel. Their experience of this new menace in the lines on the isthmus had frightened the enemy; and the British were correspondingly anxious to exploit their success. New furnaces were built, shot prepared and men trained. Along the North Face, near the western entry and along the sea front from Bayside to the New Mole all was made ready, so that a constant fire could be maintained of these deadly missiles.

By the morning of the 12th, after new squadrons of Spanish and French vessels had arrived, an immense fleet of 44 ships-of-the-line (three of them three-deckers, then the largest warships in the world), several frigates and zebecs, as well as the usual gun- and mortar-boats, now totalling 90 in all, had moored in the bay; at least six admirals' flags were counted. Besides these regular men-of-war, there were many armed vessels, the boats already noted prepared as landing-craft, and 300 troop-carrying transports. It was thought to be the most numerous assembly of warships ever seen in the Bay of Gibraltar. The core of the whole forthcoming attack, however, lay in the ten floating batteries, now completed and waiting in heavy menace for action.

These vessels varied in size and armament. The *Pastora*, carrying the squadron's commanding officer, Rear-Admiral Bonaventura Moreno, mounted 21 guns; the smallest, *Los Dolores*, only six. In all the ten of them carried 142 guns; another 70 cannon were in reserve. Their crews mustered 5,260 officers and men. Each battering-ship was clad on its fighting side (for these craft were specifically designed for the sole operation of beating down the defences of Gibraltar in one single action, continued to success) with three successive layers of squared timber, three feet in thickness. Within this wall ran a body of wet sand, and within that again was a line of cork soaked in water and calculated to prevent the effects of splinters. Over 200,000 cubic feet of timber had been used in these strengthening operations. The whole of this fortified sea-wall was bound together by strong wooden bolts. A hanging roof of strong ropework netting, covered with wet hides, was constructed at a slope, to protect the crews from shells or dropping shot. Underneath this roof, which shelved at such an angle that shot could not lodge there, was a reservoir of water, from which many pipes led off, like the veins of the human body, through the sides of the ship, giving a constant supply and keeping the wood, sand and cork thoroughly saturated. Their designer, Michaud d'Arcon, had planned in this way to prevent any risk of combustion from the British red-hot shot.

The largest vessel was originally of 1,400 tons burthen, the smallest of 600 tons. The crews varied from 760 to 250 men; 36 men were allotted to work each gun, in relays. The guns were nearly all of brass and were all new. These ships' powers of manœuvre were limited, for only one large sail was hoisted. But it was confidently expected that, when once in position, moored by iron chains, their uninterrupted fire pouring out without cessation at close range, the British defences would crumble, unable to retaliate.

At about 7 o'clock in the morning of 13 September 1782 this immense project was put into motion. Escorted by great numbers of vessels, the ten battering-ships drew out from their position near the island of Algeciras, crossed the bay and by 9.45 a.m. were in position. Admiral Moreno and the *Pastora* anchored opposite the middle point of the King's Bastion, the others in admirable order astern and ahead, and about 1,000 yards from the shore. The moment all were in place and were letting go their anchors a tremendous cannonade opened on them from every British gun which would bear. The floating batteries at once replied from all their ordnance, joining the 186 guns and mortars firing at the British works from Spanish forts and batteries on the isthmus. It was reckoned that over 400 cannon were at work.

So far all had gone well with the attackers. The ten ships had taken their stations pretty well where planned, in line ahead, the nearest (*Pastora*) only 900 yards from the target, the most distant at about 1,100 –1,200 yards. They had, it is true, achieved no surprise. British seamen had anticipated that the enemy would try to take station by night, as they themselves would have done in the same circumstances. But the activities of the morning, along with the fact that great crowds of spectators were seen to have gathered along the shore (at a safe distance) and on the many hilltops north of the Spanish lines, gave warning enough, so that all batteries were manned and the grates and furnaces lit and prepared for action. Each kiln, it was reckoned, could heat 100 cannon-balls in an hour; but it was to be over two hours from the first shots before these red-hot missiles were ready; and a further two hours passed before any large numbers were used.

The spectacle was terrific. Immense clouds of smoke wreathed the face of the Rock and spread out across the sea. Through this murk the guns flashed and shells and carcasses soared through the gloom trailing fire. The day was fine, with a steady but light north-westerly wind, which gradually rolled away the gunsmoke south of the Rock, and enabled both sides to maintain aimed fire. The 80,000 watchers on the heights, many of whom had come from villages far inland to see this well-advertised performance, saw a sight unique in their lives. On the slopes of the hills near their numerous camps, the Spanish and French troops stood, brightly uniformed, in ranks and squadrons, ready to move forward. Crillon had under his orders 16 squadrons of cavalry, and seven companies of carabiniers and mounted grenadiers, totalling 2,440; and his 35 battalions and hundreds of companies of picked men, grenadiers and fusiliers, numbered over 24,620, according to one French account. Crillon, with his five supporting lieutenant-generals and other senior officers by the score, awaited the final success which surely would reward the immense effort. Nothing quite on this scale, in such a picturesque and dramatic arena, staged with such magnificence in a comparatively small space, had ever been seen before.

For hours the two sides exchanged shots at full pressure. At first the battering-ships tended to fire low, wasting their shot in the waters between themselves and the town shore. But they soon corrected this, and every cannon-ball crashed home. Long stretches of the line-wall were destroyed, and the neat merlons and embrasures of the Grand Battery, Montague's and the King's Bastions much battered and muti-lated. The enemy battering-ships seemed to focus their attention on the King's Bastion, which was grievously mauled, though not to such an extent that its fire ever ceased. On the North Face Willis's suffered. The remains of the houses in the town were much knocked about. Casualties mounted. Four artillery officers fell: Captain Reeves lost an arm and died, Captain Groves was burnt when an ammunition chest blew up, two lieutenants were wounded. Bodies lay in the streets and batteries. Even so, considering the weight of the bombardment, the total was comparatively low; in a few hours of desperate and decisive battle, 17 of the garrison were killed and 86 wounded.

For some hours the battering-ships lived up to their reputation of invincibility. The heaviest 13-inch shells rolled harmlessly down the sloping roofs or burst without effect above them. The 32-pounder shot, striking the reinforced walls, seemed unable to damage them. On occasion smoke rose from one or other of the bombardment vessels; but immediately men ran out from cover and put out the threatened conflagration with water-hoses. By midday the kilns and furnaces had succeeded in heating their cannon-balls red-hot, and these 'roast potatoes' or 'roasted pills' were immediately used. At first it seemed that even these were going to prove useless. The weary and battered men toiling at the British guns, faces and hands blackened by powder, eyes bleary with sulphur fumes, toiling in the heat of the sun and scorched by handling with tongs these dangerous and glowing balls from forges and furnaces kept steadily at their task. All were thirsty.

Some of the enemy's mortar-boats and bomb ketches tried to second the efforts of the floating batteries; but the wind changed to the south-west and blew a smart breeze, causing a heavy swell which prevented this attempt to joint the onslaught. Don Moreno's flagship began to smoke at about two o'clock in the afternoon. This appearance of flames aboard *Pastora* was encouraging to the British. Men were seen on the roof, however, and once again the Spaniards triumphed. Fire was steadily continued, although the rate of fire from the battering-ships began to fall away, and by 7 o'clock only a few of their cannon were still in action.

Aboard the Spanish vessels conditions were by now much worse than in the British batteries ashore. The crews suffered greatly from the heat of the day. Crammed in between low decks devoid of ventilation, motionless on the heaving water, unable to see what was happening outside, conscious of the steady thumping of cannon-balls into their enclosing structures, weary and thirsty from their own violent exertions, the men could hear of no visible success. One vessel, moreover, fell out of action through panic. This was the *Talla Piedra*, one of the largest battering-ships and carrying 21 guns. She was commanded by the

Prince of Nassau, and also had on board d'Arcon himself, present as a
volunteer to watch the success of his own inventions. After over four
hours of continuous action and some two hours' exposure to red-hot
shot, one of several of these incandescent balls which hit the hull struck
at a place very difficult to reach. To pull away and throw overboard the
smouldering woodwork was a prime necessity. The guns were abandoned for the time being and all hands turned to quenching the blaze.
But the cessation of firing meant that the *Talla Piedra*'s own concealing
shroud of gunsmoke cleared away, so that she lay clearly exposed to a
concentrated fire of all the British guns which would bear. The blaze
spread, and the crew, in panic fear of an explosion, flooded the magazines and rendered the whole strength of her battery useless. The confusion aboard her and in *Pastora* grew, and other vessels also in the
Spanish line were soon in equal difficulties. D'Arcon showed great
courage. He remained aboard *Talla Piedra* until after midnight, when he
set off in a small boat to seek help from the admiral in *Pastora*. By him
he was sent ashore to see de Crillon; but by the time he reached the land
headquarters de Crillon was not to be found, and d'Arcon learned that
an order had been already given to set all the craft on fire.

By 8 o'clock in the evening and at night-fall only one or two ships at
the northern end of their line were still in action; there they had not
attracted so great a weight of fire as those opposite the King's Bastion
and the main town lines. By nine o'clock all the Spanish guns afloat
were silent, although the land batteries continued their cannonade.

By midnight it was plain to see from the shore that *Pastora* was
beginning to burn, and an hour later she was in flames. Rockets and
distress signals were sent up from other vessels, also ablaze. Ship's boats
came in to rescue the crews. Violent screamings from the battering-
ships could be clearly heard on shore; but the British, roused to new
efforts by visible signs of victory, continued to fire heavily, mingling
grape-shot with their red-hot shot so as to intensify casualties. About
midnight a piece of wreckage was blown ashore, with a dozen men
clinging to it; they were the survivors of a crew of 60 of a Spanish
launch sunk while going to the aid of the stricken vessels.

By 2 a.m. on 14 September 1782 it was clear that the grand assault
from the sea had utterly failed. Curtis put out with a dozen British gunboats from the New Mole and formed line on the flank of the burning
battering-ships. The gunboats advanced, firing grape-shot; whereupon
the Spaniards abandoned their attempts at rescue and fled, those who
could move, to the westward. Only the ten wrecked floating batteries
remained, blazing from stern to stern; for, when the Spaniards and

22 Lt.-Gen. Eliott and his officers watch the defeat of the battering-ships. In the foreground (from l. to r.) can be identified: Lt.-Gen. R. Boyd (fifth from left, with arm extended), Maj. C. Walloton, Lt.-Gen. G. A. Eliott (writing), Brig. W. Picton (in white wig), Brig. W. Green (with roll), Maj. G. Lewis (sitting), Lt.-Col. G. Mackenzie (wearing kilt)

*From the painting by G. Carter*

**23** *The defeat of the floating batteries during the night of 13–14 September, 1782*
*From an aquatint by C. Tomkins after F. Jukes and J. Cleveley*

**24** *Sir Roger Curtis rescuing Spaniards from the burning battering-ships*
*From an engraving by J. F. Sherwin*

French had fully realised the completeness of the disaster, Don Moreno had not only left his own vessel, but had given orders that all of them should be set alight and forsaken. Curtis's arrival and the devastating volleys from his gunboats interrupted this operation, so that many hundreds of the crews were still aboard.

Curtis at once set about the dangerous task of rescuing these poor wretches, whose shouts and groans and screams roused horror in the hearts of all who heard them. 'At the utmost hazard of his own life', to use Eliott's words, Curtis and his men went alongside and dragged the Spaniards from the flames. Eliott wrote: 'For some time I felt the utmost anguish seeing his pinnace close to one of the largest ships at the moment she blew up.' The danger was very real; Curtis's coxswain was killed and others wounded at this moment, and large holes caused by falling timbers were stopped by seamen's jackets stuffed into them, keeping the pinnace afloat long enough to enable other British craft to arrive. One of the British gunboats was also sunk; but over 350 Spanish seamen and gunners were rescued and brought ashore. So violent was one concussion that doors and windows at the Naval Hospital, well over a mile away, were forced open. With the flaming wrecks and the bright flashes of cannon lighting the undersides of drifting clouds of gunsmoke, the nightmare scene was brilliantly and dramatically illuminated, both for the garrison crowding their own ruined walls, and for the massed spectators along the Spanish shore, now silent before this terrifying sight. Even Curtis was moved. In his despatch home he wrote:

> The scene at this time before me was dreadful to a high degree. Numbers of men crying from amidst the flames, some upon pieces of wood in the water, others appearing in the ships where the fire had as yet made but little progress, all expressing by speech and gesture the deepest distress and all imploring assistance, formed a spectacle of horror not easily to be described.

By 4 a.m. three of the battering-ships had blown up and sunk. All this time and throughout the night the Spanish land batteries on the isthmus had continued to fire heavily, for in the noise and confusion and owing to the poor communications of the day they had no certain knowledge of what was really happening. In all, from the first shots when the floating batteries arrived to daybreak on the 14th it was calculated that nearly 40,000 rounds had been expended. It was one of the most tremendous bombardments in history.

When morning came the Bay of Gibraltar presented a terrifying scene. The water was covered with wreckage, among which lay the burning hulks of the remaining battering-ships. To some pieces of broken timber a few survivors clung; other men were adrift on rafts. Bodies also floated there. At 10 a.m. two more ships blew up and one after another others exploded, until only three remained. Of these, two burnt down to water-level before sinking, and there was for some time hopes of saving the third and bringing her in as a prize; but she was too far gone, and sank at her moorings, still fast to the iron chains so hopefully lowered on the previous day. The final order for her destruction was given by the British naval officers sent to inspect and if possible to salvage her. The Spanish land batteries turned their attention to the British, active among the floating debris, and finally the bay lay deserted. Brought ashore was the huge colour flown by the Spanish admiral; it was taken to the South Parade by the seamen who found it and presented to Eliott, where he stood with his principal officers congratulating one another on their complete and overwhelming triumph. A large crowd shouted and cheered at the sight. Eliott gave money to the sailors and the great flag, reversed, was tied to a gun and left displayed as a visible token of victory. Two Spanish launches were also seized by the British and fetched under the cover of the garrison's guns. Wounded prisoners were sent to the hospitals, and the others (amongst whom were three priests) were put in a camp on Windmill Hill where for some days they were kept incommunicado. The Corsicans provided the guards for these prisoners-of-war.

The 14 September was marked in the afternoon by a great march of Spanish and French troops, with colours flying, down from their distant camps to a position behind their main line of forts across the northern end of the isthmus. At the same time many enemy warships loosed their topsails, and craft packed with soldiers were seen in readiness. It looked as though a general assault was about to be made, and the British stood to their guns and their alarm posts and the kilns were kept lighted. Few men had been lucky enough to sleep very much during the previous 24 hours; they were all dog-tired; and many artillerymen were so parched with thirst that they even drank the filthy water in the buckets used to cool and moisten their sponges. Men of the 39th and 72nd regiments, who had been in reserve during the previous day, were pressed into service to help keep the batteries manned, and the guns firing. The Naval Brigade, who had also provided gun-crews, drew the envy of the soldiers, from the issues of grog served to them at their labours.

The threatened attack came to nothing. It seems one was definitely contemplated; but Crillon forbade it to be made, saying he thought the only result would be the destruction of the soldiers and sailors engaged in such an undertaking.

A westerly wind threw up on Gibraltar beaches the debris of battle, including many horribly mutilated bodies; it surprised the garrison that so many of these corpses, like many of those taken prisoner, should appear elderly, long past the age of vigorous warfare. Other relics came ashore: large wax altar-candles; barrels of salt provisions; ammunition boxes, each containing ten rounds of powder in linen cartridges; and mahogany and cedar planks, adrift from the sunken wrecks. Eliott later had a handsome set of tables made for his official residence from these timbers; Drinkwater commented that when the cannon holes had been filled with sound wood, cut in various figures, they formed 'a beautiful contrast with the burnt part'.

The destruction of the battering-ships did not mark the end of the bombardment, which continued in regular style for the rest of September and for much longer. The Spaniards usually began to fire about 5 or 6 o'clock in the morning, when the night picquets were going in, and kept it up briskly till about midday, when they knocked off for a couple of hours for their customary nap. The resumption was usually leisurely, their cannon ceasing about 7 p.m., when mortars kept up a desultory fire of shells throughout the night. Their usual daily consumption ranged from 1,000 to 1,600 rounds, a number which, with their very great expenditure during the grand assault period, notably diminished the massive piles in reserve stored in their artillery park. British casualties for September included 84 dead and 305 wounded. This total does not include a man hanged on the 25th; 'the noted Dennis Murray, 39th; his brother, a very good man, was killed the 11th, at night, and hoped not to live to see him hanged', recorded Spilsbury.

One of the prisoners died; a marine captain, Don Joseph Ambulodi, he was buried in the Roman Catholic cemetery in Gibraltar with military honours. Captain Curtis, R.N., attended and the grenadiers of the 39th fired a volley over his grave. The other captured officers, French and Spanish, eight in all, with the three priests and 11 captured French private soldiers, were sent back on 17 September; and 260 Spanish prisoners-of-war were returned by agreement on 6 October. At that time there were still ten captives in hospital. Fifty-nine declined the offer of repatriation and enlisted with Eliott; ten went into the 39th, ten to the 58th and the rest to the Corsican volunteers.

The news of this total disaster was received by the Bourbon courts in Madrid and Paris with incredulity and despair. The Spanish king, in his palace of Ildefonso, listened to the news in horrified silence.

Behind the French and Spanish lines furious controversy raged about responsibility for the disastrous failure of the Grand Assault. Many enquiries were held and several books published. Crillon attracted most of the blame. He was supposed to have mislaid d'Arcon's chart of soundings, so that the battering-ships were not anchored on their proper stations. Certainly their line appears to have been too far extended to the south. The supply of gunpowder to the isthmus batteries failed at a critical moment in the afternoon. Co-ordination had been lacking. It may be that Crillon was never really convinced that the battering-ships would be able to do the job on their own. He believed a united assault by the whole fleet, supported by the floating batteries, would be needed. D'Arcon was confident that his invention would be sufficient. In spite of the many months of preparation, the final movements had in fact been performed in a hasty manner. Experiments with d'Arcon's pumping arrangements had not been satisfactorily completed when Crillon had given the definite order to attack to Admiral Moreno, on threat of his removal if he delayed or refused. Yet a great combined fleet had just arrived off Algeciras, which on the vital day proved quite useless; the final decision to abandon and destroy the remnants of the battering fleet shows that no plans had been made to tow them away. A postponement for another 24 hours might have enabled French and Spaniards on land and sea, to concert their efforts so that the battering-ships would not have gone into action virtually unsupported. Whatever the mistakes d'Arcon may have made in design, no blame can be attached to Moreno and his crews. They all fought hard and suffered heavily. Crillon must, as chief commander, take much of the blame—always supposing that the capture of Gibraltar was in any way possible under the circumstances of the time and place. Perhaps, however, like the British attempt to conquer the Americans, the aim was impracticable, whatever men might do.

In Paris the Chevalier de Parry published a bitter lampoon on Crillon, part of which ran:

> Mes amis, vous le voyez bien
> Vos bombes ne bombardent rien;
> Vos bélandres et vos corvettes
> Et vos travaux et vos mineurs
> N'épouvantent que les lecteurs
> De vos redoutables gazettes;
> Votre blocus ne bloque point,
> Et grace à votre heureuse adresse,
> Ceux que vous affamez sans cesse
> Ne periront que d'embonpoint.

This last statement at least was grossly unfair: food on the Rock was still very short and restricted; scurvy was ever-present; and a few pounds of loaf sugar sold at auction towards the end of September fetched over 18*s*. a pound.

# 10

# Final Relief and Truce

Despite his resounding success, Eliott did not relax. Nor did he fail to inform those at home of the still pressing need to guard and sustain Gibraltar. He pointed out that the daily expenditure of powder was very great (716 barrels of powder were used on 13 September, as well as 8,300 rounds); that bedding and stores were wanted; and that although he had adequate supplies of bread, beef and pork, soap, candles and train oil, his butter stocks would last only until the following December, his pease and oatmeal only until February 1783, and that only small amounts were in store of rice, raisins, sugar and macaroni. He also made formal application for prize money to be distributed among the garrison as a reward for the destruction of the Spanish battering-ships. Early application in such matters was indeed advisable; it was not until November 1782 that Eliott heard that the pay warrant for the half-year ending Christmas 1779 for his staff appointments made that year was even then just being prepared.

The enemy fleet which arrived off Gibraltar just before the battering-ships began their attack came from the English Channel. There in June and July 1782 they had been stationed, under Admiral Cordoba, to intercept British convoys and to challenge any British squadron who might come their way. They seized 18 vessels of a convoy outward-bound for Newfoundland, but had failed to make contact with 25 British sail under Howe returning to England. Cordoba's 40 warships were too strong for Howe to tackle, so the English fleet, secure in its seamanship and confident in its ability to outsail any pursuit, sailed home by night between the Scillies and Land's End and reached safety. At this moment the British position at sea even round its own coasts was not safe. Convoys from Jamaica and to the Baltic were at sea, and what with the French and Spanish in the Channel and a powerful Dutch fleet in the North Sea it was impossible to be strong everywhere. On the other hand, a huge convoy, destined in part for America and in part for India, was gathering in the Channel. The decision was made to combine the escort duties for some of these merchant vessels with a third relief for Gibraltar, as had been done with Rodney two years earlier. Towards the end of July orders were given to load vessels with supplies, ready to sail under Howe's orders when once the Channel should be clear.

Cordoba left the mouth of the Channel at the end of July; but it was not until the end of August that the British ships for the Gibraltar convoy were ready. It was during the assembly of this convoy that the celebrated incident occurred of the loss of the *Royal George,* a 100-gun ship and one of the most powerful in the world; she was heeled over for underwater repairs off Spithead when she suddenly filled, overset and sank at her anchors, with the loss of some 900 in all; not only were many women and children drowned but also Rear-Admiral Kempenfelt, whose improved signal code was to be made still more effective by Lord Howe. Changes of plan and foul winds continued to delay Howe, and it was not until 11 September that the merchant vessels, transports and guardian fleet actually sailed from Spithead. Howe had with him 34 ships-of-the-line and a dozen smaller naval craft, with some 140 other craft, unarmed vessels, of which 31 were destined for Gibraltar. Besides many stores and supplies two regiments were embarked as reinforcements, the 25th and 59th Foot.

Howe's task was difficult. The French and Spanish fleets were greatly superior in number, although the 35 Spanish men-of-war were in bad condition, having been continuously at sea for months; their crews were sick and weary, the ships' bottoms encrusted with barnacles and foul with weed. Howe's ships, on the other hand, were freshly equipped, their bottoms sheathed with copper (now a common feature in British warships) and everyone aboard anxious to take help to Gibraltar, whose long and vigorous defence was assuming legendary proportions. Howe himself was a first-rate seaman, with a long record of victory. He had been in action and wounded at the age of 20, had fought at Quiberon and operated successfully against the French off the American coast in the early years of the American war. During the Yorktown operations he had been in voluntary retirement, as he disagreed profoundly with North's ministerial policy. Now he was in arms again, a man who possessed the full faith and devotion of his officers and men. His flagship was H.M.S. *Victory,* already one of the most famous and fortunate of British men-of-war.

Even so, Howe was lucky. His sailing date, two days before the grand attack on Gibraltar, was too late to bring aid to Eliott, who in the event proved not to need it. Bad weather delayed the fleet still further. A violent storm before Howe reached Cape Finisterre scattered the vessels, but the full tally of 183 sail was gathered and counted before the various 'trades' parted from Howe's fleets. Not until 8 October did Howe appear off Cape St Vincent, whence he sent a frigate ahead to gather information. Two days later she returned, bringing definite news that Gibraltar was still well held, and that Crillon's assault had been made and had failed completely.

On the same day a fresh storm arose, but Howe was able to keep his warships and the vessels for Gibraltar together. Things were very different with the allied fleet at Algeciras. As night fell the gale increased until it was blowing a hurricane, with driving clouds of rain. Some French and Spanish warships had been preparing for sea and were caught half-ready; others were driven from their moorings. Many had been at single anchor, prepared to ship and put to sea to engage Howe's approaching fleet. The wind blew hard from the south-west: and the garrison, which had earlier noted much activity and many signals in the enemy fleet, heard in the darkness many guns obviously fired as distress signals.

As day broke, the British were delighted to see the enemy squadrons in complete confusion. One French ship-of-the-line and a frigate were fast ashore at the Orange Grove, along with many smaller craft, another had badly damaged masts and rigging, others had been driven out of sight. Best of all, a large Spanish two-decker was seen only a few hundred yards away, not far from the King's Bastion. She had lost her foremast and bowsprit and could do little to save herself. Fire was immediately opened upon her as she drove helplessly ashore, finally running aground near the line-wall off the Ragged Staff. She hoisted an English flag over her Spanish ensign as a sign of surrender. Curtis went aboard and took possession of the ship. She was the *San Miguel*, a 72-gun vessel with 650 men aboard, commanded by Don Juan Moreno. Officers and crew were at once disembarked and marched away to camp, at Windmill Hill; they had lost two dead and three wounded in this brief encounter. Another vessel, also in range at daybreak, was more fortunate. She was hit by some red-hot shot, but threw her powder overboard and so lightened made her escape.

Later that day, 11 October 1782, Howe's fleet was sighted by the garrison. Howe expected a battle, and sailed ready for one. Of his three divisions the third and centre squadrons sailed in line of battle ahead, the second in reserve. *Victory* had pride of place, leading the third

**25**   *Admiral Howe's relief of Gibraltar, October 1782*
*From the oil painting by Richard Paton*

26   *The victorious Governor of Gibraltar: Lieutenant-General Eliott, with the floating batt*
*burning in the background*

*From an engraving published by Robert Sayer*

squadron. The convoy had been given clear and stringent orders to make straight for Gibraltar. At 5 p.m. the relieving fleet was in sight from the ramparts; they were not unexpected, for incessant flying of signal flags from the Spanish watch-towers along the coast had forewarned the garrison. But the enemy made no attempt to challenge, and the British vessels had only the weather to contend with. By nightfall one British frigate, *Latona*, and four of the convoy were safely anchored near the town. Nightfall, hazy weather, fluky winds and (according to one account) inattention to Howe's strict orders by the merchant skippers took the rest of the fleet beyond Europa Point and into the mouth of the Mediterranean. There on the following days Howe once more collected the transports and lay-to ready for battle.

Little by little most of the convoy came into Gibraltar. They were immediately unloaded. The two regiments of foot embarked on some of Howe's warships (where in action they could have been used as marines), landed about noon on 18 October, under the line-wall near the New Mole, and were in camp by 10 o'clock that night, the 25th behind the Barracks, the 59th on Windmill Hill. Eliott complained bitterly about their condition. They were almost destitute, because a brig, *Minerva*, which had been loaded with their clothing, camp equipage, baggage and provisions, as well as the regimental wives and children, were missing. Later it was discovered to have been captured off Malaga, after being dismasted in the storm.

During the week which these events consumed the Spanish and French had been very active. They kept up a heavy bombardment, firing a good deal towards the *San Miguel* in an attempt to destroy her. On occasion the Spaniards sent in their gunboats at night, trying to set her on fire. She had proved a fine vessel, newly built at Havana, with beams of cedar and decks of mahogany. She had been in the combined fleet in the English Channel and had taken part in the naval bombardment which had preceded the assault by the battering-ships. Now she lay helpless on a sandbank beneath the Rock. Not until 100 soldiers had been detached to help the navy was she refloated on 17 October and towed to a beach behind the New Mole. There Sir Charles Knowles was given the command, she was refitted, rechristened the *St Michael* and taken into the Royal Navy.

As men, powder and shot were disembarked, Eliott replied freely and vigorously to the enemy fire. But most attention was concentrated on naval matters. Howe kept at sea, prepared to fight, while the combined fleets did their best to refit and reassemble their warships. By 13 October they were ready and put to sea. They took two hours to clear the bay, a French rear-admiral, the last of the rear division, leaving at three in the afternoon. They included six three-deckers and 38 two-deckers; frigates and 29 zebecs and other armed vessels accompanied them. Howe awaited them in line ahead and order of battle, sheltering those transports which had not yet succeeded in reaching Gibraltar.

At sunset the two fleets were close to one another, but no exchange of shots occurred. On the next two days various harmless evolutions were carried out by the French and Spanish fleets, but they did not make any serious attempt to annoy Howe. When the wind came east, Howe edged in towards Gibraltar, shepherding the remaining store-ships, and keeping Eliott informed by frigates passing between them. By the 18th all the convoy (except for the brig lost off Malaga) was safe; and Howe was even able to let the Governor have an extra 1,500 barrels of gun-powder.

The British fleet, its main work done, stood through the straits towards the Atlantic. Howe kept on past the narrowest part of the gap; where, because of tricky currents and the close neighbourhood on either hand of hostile territory, he did not wish to give battle. The allied fleet pursued him. But on 20 October 1782, having gained a bearing off Cape Spartel, Howe formed line of battle at one-and-a-half cables' distance, backed his topsails and awaited his enemy. These, the frigate *Panther* signalled, were 43 sail-of-the-line, and approached in a moderate breeze, under single-reefed topsails, and topgallantsails, foresails and staysails. The French and Spanish, who had the wind and could give or refuse battle as they pleased, approached in a very half-hearted way. The vans of the two fleets engaged and fought for some hours, during which no ship on either side was crippled or taken, though some 600 casualties in all were sustained. Then the combined fleet broke off the engagement, and Howe sailed on for England. With him went Curtis, who had embarked in *Panther* to take Eliott's reports to the naval commander-in-chief. He took passage in H.M.S. *Victory*, of which Howe shortly afterwards made him captain. The Governor, in letters home, once more stressed Curtis's activity and influence, and asked for his speedy return. Howe's fleet regained Spithead on 14 November, having successfully carried out the third and last relief of Gibraltar.

Howe's disappearance was hailed as a great victory by the Spaniards. Admiral Don Louis de Cordoba described the engagement as ending with a complete rout of the British fleet, with Howe under all press of sail fleeing from his brave pursuers. Nor can Cordoba be blamed for his boast, for in solemn fact the Spanish navy had few enough laurels to show for their long and weary war. And it should be noticed that the spectacle of a British fleet, inferior in numbers, apparently being chased through the straits by their enemies, had a depressing effect on the garrison. It was 'no very pleasing prospect for a British garrison to behold', said Drinkwater, and Spilsbury described 'the Dons' as being 'after them in full chase'. The noise of the succeeding cannonade reached the Rock over the water from the distance, although the action took place many miles away and no ships were in sight.

Eliott once again had plenty of food and stores at his disposal. Bread, flour, beef, pork, pease, oatmeal: all were freely available. He even had butter in hand for another six months. And he celebrated the replenishment of warlike stores by a continuous bombardment of the Spanish works. Throughout November and December and into January 1783 the Rock batteries were wreathed in smoke shot through with flame. Grape showered down on the enemy works, even though the French and Spanish regiments were marching steadily away. Over 45,000 shot and shell (nearly a quarter of the garrison's total expenditure during the entire siege), besides scores of carcasses and light balls, were hurled against the enemy's diminishing resources, which did not return a quarter of the amount. Whatever else Gibraltar and Eliott were going to do, they were not in any way relaxing their grip or lessening their noisy defiances. Crillon, as reported to London by the Governor, was supposed to have told his troops that they would take a rest during the winter, but would resume the siege in the spring. According to private intelligence, Crillon had promised a resumption and had assured the Court at Madrid he would take Gibraltar. Among the plans Crillon had in mind were a search for a mine begun during the siege of 1727, the throwing up of a trench in a single night very close to the North Face, the building of new batteries and the construction of 50 new mortar-boats lined with copper and iron. In the meantime, whole camps were struck, all the French regiments and volunteers were gone and the Spanish numbers were reducing. Cannon and mortars were moved from their artillery parks down to the shore, ready for embarkation. Soon only 15,000 men stood against Gibraltar, and a single enemy ship-of-the-line lay off Algeciras. Their fire sank to a mere 150 rounds a day, spasmodic and ill-directed. There were times when the Spanish gun-boats stood in, throwing rockets at night and firing a few shots at the St Michael or the unloading store-ships, but their efforts were fitful and generally useless; a 'dishonourable and cruel mode of prosecuting the war', said Drinkwater.

Eliott's plentiful stores were for official use. Private people had to make their own arrangements, and luxuries were still very costly. Sugar at auction brought over 12*s*. a pound and a pair of ducks almost 18*s*. Much indignation was roused over these high prices and a committee of officers met to fix amounts calculated to allow reasonable profits; according to their tariff, sugar should have been no higher than 2*s*. 6*d*. a pound, a pair of ducks 9*s*. 9*d*. This attempt failed after about a fortnight. The traders refused to land or sell their stocks, saying they preferred to carry them off to Lisbon. Then those 'who preferred self-gratification to the public interest' began to buy again at the old high prices and exorbitant profits once again were pocketed by the speculators. Anything from 150 to 300 per cent was made, and blockade runners still arrived. One or two were intercepted by the Spanish, but cargoes of sugar, tea, rice and pilchards came in. Fresh meat and fruit were still scarce, however. During November a couple of sheep sold at 10 guineas each, raising mutton to over 5*s*. a pound; apples fetched over 2*s*. 6*d*. a pound. Tea rose to almost £2 a pound.

During this period the garrison was kept busily employed. The two newly arrived regiments were quickly at work. Ince's Gallery was enlarged to 100 yards in length and a new battery of the same kind cut in the Rock, to hold two guns. The bastions heavily damaged during the grand assault were rebuilt in solid masonry, a prodigious effort by the engineers under Green's direction. Men died in the hospital (where 900 sick were in the wards) or were killed in the lines and batteries. By a piece of extraordinary bad luck, one man was killed at Rosia by a shell fired from the isthmus over 5,000 yards away. On one occasion a shot from a gunboat set fire to the *St Michael*; when smoke poured from her gun-ports, the Spaniards turned out and cheered. But the flames were soon extinguished, after 80 barrels of powder had been thrown overboard, and the re-rigging of this fine vessel continued. During January 1783 several gunboat attacks took place, fiercely met by the cannon of the King's Bastion and by counter-attacks from the British gunboats, now all raised and back in action. At least one Spaniard was sunk and British losses also occurred. Thieves were flogged. A soldier of the 73rd, who had robbed his master, was hanged. There were even cases of desertion. Other crimes, such as casual stabbings and robberies, were tried by courts-martial. Similar misdeeds, due no doubt to close confinement and boredom, occurred. Some young officers invaded a dance organised by the sergeants of the 73rd Foot and caused a riot. Another example was found of naval mutiny, when the seven sailors of a guard-boat rowing round the *St Michael* rose against their officers, a lieutenant and a midshipman; the lieutenant had drawn his hanger and cut at the rebellious crew's spokesman, but had been knocked unconscious by the coxswain with the tiller of the rudder. The mutineers reached the Spanish lines and handed the boat over. Both officers were later returned to Gibraltar.

Flags of truce were exchanged. The Spanish officers and crew of the *San Miguel* were returned. Regularly drawn-up conventions governed such matters; the agreed rates ranged from 60 men for an Admiral of the Fleet (or Field-Marshal) to three for a midshipman and two for a petty officer. In exchange, the baggage and women (about 150 in all) taken in the *Minerva* came to join their men in Gibraltar. To Spilsbury's disgust, 17 of these women were 'disordered'; the Rock had been free of the disease for several months. A party of officers once broke into the hospital ward where lay these women ill of the pox and 'attacked' them, to use Spilsbury's words. The baggage and clothing were especially welcome, for in the cool winter weather, with squalls of rain and strong east winds, the men of the 25th had been set to work to make canvas jackets for work. Some of the transports sailed for England, carrying away 150 Jews. A dog went mad and an order went out for all dogs found loose to be killed. Also sent home was one of the Corsicans, Captain-Lieutenant Masseria. Ostensibly he was on official business for the Governor; but in a private and confidential letter Eliott said that the man had once been dismissed from being 'immediately about General Paoli', that General Murray had suspected his good faith and that close observation had found him acting suspiciously. Eliott did not want him returned to Gibraltar, but he was to be kept on out of harm's way.

The besiegers attempted to carry out Crillon's threat to use the old 1727 mine. Some hundreds of men were employed on the project, which seemed so nonsensical to the British that they refused to take alarm, though these activities, said Drinkwater, 'began to engage our curiosity'. Some of the Corsicans were given the special task of firing on these enemy parties. As the face of the Rock above the cave rose to heights between 800 and 1,000 feet Eliott himself was little disturbed. Much more dangerous and annoying was the weather, which now and again blew so hard that tents were torn loose from their pickets and guy-ropes. One hard gust drove the *St Michael* from her anchors and into the bay; luckily an eddy brought her about, and Knowles was able to run her ashore within the New Mole.

Despite all this warlike activity, the fighting was very nearly over. As early as 17 December 1782 a Spanish aide-de-camp had told a British flag of truce party that the preliminaries of a general peace were expected to be signed during that month.

The guns which thundered around Gibraltar were almost the last to be heard in this long war. As far as America was concerned, Yorktown had to all intents and purposes ended the struggle. Lord North and his government still officially held out for further campaigns; but men and money and the will to victory were all lacking, both at Westminster and in North America. The failures of Germaine and Sandwich in their over-all direction of the war were too gross to be hidden. Clinton, the Commander-in-Chief, was given permission to return home, and the fighting died away. In the West Indies there were various engagements during the early months of 1782, involving both military and naval forces. By the end of the year several sugar islands had changed hands, mostly to the advantage of the French, who at one point even contemplated an attack upon Jamaica, the largest and richest of the British possessions there; but the war in the Caribbean was dying away. Only in far-away India was there very much activity. There the armies and navies were still busy. Hyder Ali kept up his vigorous struggle until his death in December 1782, a few months before Sir Eyre Coote, his British antagonist, died at Madras. At sea Admirals Suffren and Hughes were playing their intricate dance of nautical manœuvre. So remote from the centre were these theatres of war that both the last battle on land (Cuddalore, 13 June 1783) and the final naval encounter between the evenly matched French and British squadrons (also near Cuddalore, south of Madras, on the coast of the Carnatic, 20 June 1783) were fought long after the peace terms had been agreed. But this was due to delay resulting from distance, not from any impetus derived from London or Paris.

Lord North and his ministers, after long political intrigues, were driven from office in March 1782. They were succeeded by a ministry under Lord Rockingham, pledged to end the American War. Rockingham himself died in July, and was followed by Lord Shelburne as Prime Minister; but there was no change of policy, for it had been Shelburne who had been negotiating with the Americans. America was abandoned. Troops and ships were redeployed to defend the West Indies and the English Channel. But the chief aim was to secure a universal peace, not only with the revolted and successful colonials, but with France and Spain. In the succeeding negotiations, the possession of Gibraltar played a highly important part.

As far as America itself went, there was not much difficulty. Shelburne was perfectly ready to recognise the independence of the United

States, and hoped to gain their friendship and co-operation by generous treatment. His government realised the depth and strength of feeling involved, and that reconquest was impossible. Quite apart from the accidents of war which had ended with the disasters at Saratoga and Yorktown, it seemed that only total extermination of the colonists might have led to a British victory. And this end was only possible as an achievable aim in the days of Genghis Khan—or the twentieth century. So the problems of North America were quickly settled and terms agreed upon.

With France agreement was more difficult. The re-establishment of British naval strength after the battle of the Saints stopped the more extravagant claims of the French for West Indian islands, highly desirable sources of trade wealth, even if they were pestilential grave-yards for soldiers. In the event only Tobago was lost by Britain to France. Other French trophies of conquest (Grenada, Dominica, St Kitts, Nevis, Montserrat and the Grenadines) were restored to the English, who in their turn gave back the conquered French island of St Lucia. The French, however, were bound by agreement with Spain. The Convention signed at Aranjuez in April 1779 between the Bourbon powers pledged them to fight together until Spain had recovered Gibraltar. It was this agreement which had brought about the decisive entry of Spain into the war and opened the long siege. And in 1782 the obsession of Spain with this aim and the demands of honour on France to support her delayed the conclusion of peace. As far as the court at Madrid was concerned, so long as there was the slightest hope that Gibraltar might be taken by force of arms, there could be no talk of terms. But when once the possibility of gaining Gibraltar by negotiation appeared, even the Spanish became interested.

Shelburne, a dark and secretive man, was well suited to dealing with such matters. For one thing, he knew quite clearly what he wanted: peace on the best possible terms. With America the preliminary agreement was signed on 30 November 1782. Gibraltar then became the all-important factor in the negotiations with both France and Spain. The French, represented by their Foreign Minister, the Comte de Vergennes, were almost as anxious for a general peace as the British, for the long war had strained their financial resources past breaking point. The Spanish, however, wishfully believed that a grand assault on Gibraltar might yet bring them the one resounding victory which would, in the eyes of the Spanish court, make the whole war worth while. Not until their disasters on 13 September 1782, and Howe's relief of the Rock

during the following month, did hard facts convince them that, whatever the future might hold, Gibraltar was not going to fall to their
arms.

So it was that once again the British Government seriously contemplated handing over Gibraltar to the Spanish, in return for friendship with Madrid (never to be honestly contemplated at any time so
long as Great Britain kept Gibraltar), possession once more of Minorca
and trade and territorial concessions in the West Indies. Even George
III agreed to these possibilities being discussed.

Eliott, one must suppose, knew nothing of all this. He had been
repeatedly told how pleased his King was with the defence of Gibraltar
and with its Governor. As late as 27 October 1782 he had been informed by Thomas Townshend (Lord Hillsborough's successor in
charge of colonial affairs in Shelburne's cabinet): 'The eyes of all
Europe are upon you; it has fallen to the lot of few persons to have
attracted so much attention or to have exhibited such a spectacle.' This
was indeed the truth. Eliott's successful defence of Gibraltar was the
one undeniable and outstanding British achievement of the American
war. Public admiration was immense. Shelburne himself undoubtedly
considered the proposed cession of the Rock to Spain as the strongest
card he could play. A provisional agreement, yielding Gibraltar to
Madrid, was made and early in December 1782 was discussed by the
British Government. There was immediately a great quarrel in the
Cabinet, where the Duke of Richmond (Master General of the Ordnance) wrote to the King protesting against the loss of 'the brightest
jewel of the Crown'. He had many supporters, both in the administration and in the country at large. The idea of quietly handing over this
well-defended fortress to enemies who had met only overwhelming
disaster in every attempt they had made upon it would have wrecked
any government.

Shelburne therefore suggested to Vergennes that, if the Spanish
would forget Gibraltar, the British on their side would forgo not only
Minorca but the West Indian islands mentioned in the negotiations;
and would moreover leave Florida to Spain. To the relief of both
Vergennes and the British cabinet, the Spanish ambassador in Paris,
Aranda, who had been conducting these transactions, agreed at once.
Thus by January 1783, after several months during which all the
governments concerned had been well aware that a definitive peace
was merely a matter of time, the end was plainly in sight. The Spaniards,
British and Hanoverian soldiers and seamen who died in the bombardments and encounters of December and January were doing their duty.

But it was, as proved by the signing of the peace preliminaries in Paris on 20 January 1783, an unnecessary duty.

Despite the constant clatter and banging of the bombardment and the many alerts of attack, there was a feeling of triumph in the garrison. On the last day of December a party of seamen fished up a cannon from the wreck of one of the battering-ships. To celebrate the new year this gun was drawn in procession by a naval team from Ragged Staff to the Mole Battery. The cannon, a very plain iron 26-pounder, nine-and-a-half feet long, draped with a captured Spanish ensign, was escorted by the band of the 12th Foot, playing 'God Save the King'. Other guns were soon brought ashore, most of them of brass. Such weapons were valuable; their sale-price was added to the prize money already granted by Parliament for the destruction of the ten floating batteries and the *San Miguel*. Since the first grant was for £30,000, and a later one for £16,000, every man in the garrison had reason to rejoice. Eliott as Governor received a sixteenth (£1,875 in the first distribution); captains had over £43, private soldiers £1 9s. 1d. Other distributions were made later, bringing a private soldier's total reward to £2 12s. 4d., and Eliott's to over £3,375. Gallantry during the eighteenth century was given a definite cash value.

Another symptom of the approaching end of the siege was the resumption of inspections and reviews. But as late as 29 January a fierce engagement developed, when 28 Spanish gun- and mortar-boats took station off Europa and Rosia and opened heavy fire on the *Brilliant*, anchored off Buena Vista, and the *St Michael*, now commanded by Sir Charles Knowles and moored by the New Mole, and completing her refit by getting up her topgallant masts and finishing her rigging. The Spaniards had the best of this final engagement, sending over 230 shot from their vessels, which damaged and repelled the British gunboats; while their batteries on the isthmus opened a heavy fire, discharging 800 shot and shell. The 59th lost six killed and lamed from the total British casualties of 14 (three dead and 11 wounded). Eliott's last casualty list, for the months of January and February 1783, showed one sergeant and 17 men killed, three sergeants and 41 men wounded during this final spasm of the siege; a Corsican lieutenant was also wounded.

Firing completely stopped and hostilities finished on the evening of 2 February 1783. On the fine, warm afternoon of that day the usual truce boats had met to exchange letters, when the Spaniards jumped up with cheers and shouts of joy, exclaiming 'We are all friends!' Eliott stopped the fraternisation which threatened to break out between the sentries on the isthmus; but sent orders which stopped shots being fired at Spanish vessels which approached close to the Rock. Crillon told the Governor that the blockade was lifted as from 5 February. At noon on that day, as Gibraltar was once again being proclaimed an open port, the last shot was discharged, an elevated gun being 'wantonly fired' (to use Drinkwater's expression) over the Spanish works. With relief the garrison then learnt that Gibraltar was definitely to remain in the possession of Great Britain.

It was all over and the siege was ended.

> This return of tranquillity, this prospect of plenty and relief from the daily vexations of so tedious a siege [wrote Drinkwater] could not fail to diffuse a general joy throughout the garrison. Indeed such feelings are seldom experienced; they baffle all attempts to describe them; far beyond the pleasure resulting from private instances of success or good fortune, ours was a social happiness, and the benevolent sentiments acted upon the heart with additional energy on the prospect of meeting those as friends with whom we had been so long engaged in a succession of hostilities.

The unsportsmanlike and thoughtless behaviour of the Spanish had occasionally deeply wounded Drinkwater's moral feelings, but he was a generous enemy. Ancell of the 58th (which had suffered over 100 serious casualties, including 24 dead) remarked: 'Would you believe that last night every post appeared solitary, by the silence which everywhere prevailed, and the hours of slumber seemed uneasy, for want of that martial noise with which our days and nights have been so long accustomed to.' Spilsbury, a more laconic observer, simply noted the casualties incurred from the opening of the enemy's bombardment on 12 April 1781, and the total numbers of shot and shells supposed to be fired in the same time.

An abstract of the total loss of the military garrison gave 536 dead of sickness (exclusive of those who died of the scurvy in 1779 and 1780), 333 killed or died of wounds, 138 disabled by wounds and discharged, 181 discharged from incurable complaints, and 43 deserted; a minimum butcher's bill of 1,231, besides 872 officers and men wounded but recovered. Proportionately to the numbers in each corps, the Royal Artillery and the Soldier Artificer Company suffered most severely. Naval losses, apart from those employed ashore in the Marine Brigade (12) are not included in these totals; nor are those of the civilian population, either inhabitants or soldiers' dependants. These losses, all in all, must be regarded as severe.

The actual numbers in the garrison had always been short of the 8,000 soldiers which Eliott had always stipulated as the desirable minimum.

To the total of 5,382 in June 1779 there had been added the 1,052 men of the 73rd landed in January 1780; then the 97th, 700 strong, disembarked at Gibraltar in March 1782; while in October 1782, after Howe's relief, when there were nine regiments of foot on the Rock, the total force numbered some 7,116. This figure includes the company of military artificers, whose establishment of 234 was maintained by recruitment both at home (141 had landed in October 1782) and in Gibraltar itself, although no fewer than 72 casualties occurred. These men, tradesmen all, had higher rates of pay than private soldiers, although they wore the army's scarlet coat, both in full dress and working rig; their uniform, when the company was fully accepted in 1786, kept many civilian type accessories, such as a plain round felt hat, and a long duck coat for labour; they were also privileged to wear civilian clothes and to move about outside their quarters without a written pass, when General O'Hara commanded them after the siege. From their personal records, these military artificers were on the whole much better educated, more humanely treated and a good deal more fitted to take their place in civilian life after service than the rank-and-file of most other British corps. Only the Royal Artillery men could match them, either in training or proportion of casualties; it seems that their 485 of all ranks sustained a total loss of 196.

The garrison had expended nearly 8,000 barrels of powder, and 53 pieces of ordnance had been damaged beyond repair or destroyed; they had discharged an estimated 200,600 rounds, to which should be added 4,728 shot from the British gunboats. From the enemy's batteries 244,104 rounds, all of a heavy nature, had been fired, their gunboats adding a further 14,283 shot and shell, in a siege which was calculated to have lasted for three years, seven months and 12 days.

How did it come about that, amidst all the disasters of the War of American Independence, Gibraltar was successfully defended? One reason is undoubtedly that the place was extraordinarily well held; another that in spite of all appearances the Rock was highly defensible; and it is a fact that the enemy made many mistakes, the principal one being that several different methods, each promising well, were tried in isolation instead of being combined.

Eliott's character must come into the answer. He was no romantic figure, nor did he attempt to build up or exploit his own personality. There are few apocryphal stories about the man. On one occasion he is supposed to have first reprimanded a sentry for not holding his musket properly, then taken over his post and sent the man to seek relief when he found he had been wounded in the hand. He had a certain laconic humour: when, late in 1783, he was asked about the placing of Royal Artillery men on the right of parades, he said that all guards were drawn up 'as I found it on my arrival. Grenadiers march in front; perhaps it was thought proper for a Guard of Honour; or perhaps it looked pretty.' Although he always observed the niceties of courteous behaviour, he had no personal flamboyance or panache. His own austere way of life meant that no one could suspect for a moment that self-interest or indulgence could motivate him. The siege was a clear case of 'fair shares for all', and this in itself was a powerful morale-builder.

Moreover, on several occasions, Eliott took such resolute action that he imposed his will upon the enemy. It was Eliott who opened the cannonade in September 1779. His sortie in November 1781 upset the Spanish plans for bombardment. Even the final hurried staging of the battering-ships' assault was partly due to his intensified cannonade and the free use of red-hot shot. For the rest, it was a matter of keeping his own men fit and well, ready to endure monotony, hard work and danger. No martinet or stickler for unnecessary polish or display, he regularly held formal parades and went through commonplace military routines, such as guard-mounting and flag-flying, with enough formality to ensure discipline. The actual defences of Gibraltar in the event proved adequate to all strains put upon them; they were kept throughout in good repair as well as being enlarged and extended. Novel, useful experiments, such as prepared fuses, new fire-balls, red-hot shot and depress gun-carriages, and such activities as the preparation and launching of gunboats, caused the garrison always to have some new interest. By training infantrymen as gunners or engineers, by beginning serious musketry practice and aimed firing (comparatively unknown in those days of mass-produced volleys) and by giving cash rewards for specially fine individual performances, Eliott provided incentives and variety.

Eliott was fortunate in his subordinates, such men as Boyd, Green, his artillery commanders (Colonel John Godwin, who went home on promotion in 1780; Lieutenant-Colonel Abraham Tovey, who died during the siege; and his successor, Major George Lewis), and Captain Curtis, were either outstandingly good or at worst completely adequate. Eliott himself worked hard, set a fine personal example and shared all the dangers and fatigues of his men. He was no 'Hangman Hawley' or relentless flogger, but he insisted on sound, firm discipline. Men and officers of the garrison came to have complete faith in the Governor, knowing he was doing his intelligent best for every one of them; and he was well supported at all levels.

Eliott was also lucky in that his three reliefs came at critical moments. Rodney's arrival proved the Rock was not forgotten; when Darby appeared, he brought supplies and food most urgently necessary; Howe's fleet was a living proof, not least to the French and Spaniards, that not only could Gibraltar be held by Eliott and his men alone against the worst that the enemy could do, but that British naval strength and the British Government's determination to aid the garrison were powerful enough to thrust aside their foes. All warfare is a matter of morale, good or bad. To beleaguered men these arrivals from England at psychological moments were immensely inspiring. In the same way, the allies were depressed.

In such matters as the onslaught of disease Eliott's good fortune held. The scurvy which defeated Murray in Minorca was overcome by lemon juice luckily obtained. Other frightful and highly infectious scourges of the day, such as dysentery, the 'bloody flux', relapsing or yellow fever and typhus ('spotted fever'), never obtained a strong grip. A high morale helps to explain this fact, for despair and lack of hope open the way for these diseases associated with filth, crowded quarters, and bad food; and no one can deny that men living in Gibraltar during the Great Siege were as exposed to these dangers as any man ever was.

Given even adequate leadership, however, it is possible that under the conditions of the time Gibraltar was impregnable, so long as there were enough men and supplies. Successful attack on foot across the isthmus was generally regarded as impossible; it was certainly never tried. The guns and shells of the day proved impotent to destroy the British batteries, however hard the Spaniards bombarded them. French and Spanish warships failed to stop up all entries and escapes by sea; their blockade was never absolutely effective. Yet there were many foggy and misty days on the isthmus and round the shores of Gibraltar, suitable for sudden onslaught by land and sea; but no serious attempt was made.

Then again, the many measures adopted by the enemy were never made in co-ordination. Blockade; fire-ships; bombardment by land; naval assault on a massive scale; incessant raids by marauding gunboats: all were tried. Some nearly succeeded in causing at any rate some breaches in the defences or confusion among the defenders. But after each very partial success (the fire-ships of 1780, the destruction of the town in 1781; the annoyance and distress caused by nocturnal fire from gunboats; the occasional large explosion or concentrated destruction in the British batteries) or complete failure, there came a long pause, a chance to the garrison to regain its composure, repair the damage, plan measures to avoid similar risks. Eliott never seems to have been in doubt about what expedients his enemies were about to try. Nothing came to him as a surprise. Spanish preparations for blockade, bombardment, naval assault or attack by fire were made at length and quite openly. When finally launched, each new endeavour was completely met by the garrison, which had had plenty of time for making ready and whose spirits were raised by each successive success. The British, though often physically weary, and thoroughly fatigued in mind and body as month followed month and year succeeded year, were never jolted into panic, stunned by surprise or bewildered under a multitude of blows. The allied approach was like the ritual of a bullfight, each phase separate and distinct; but at the end the matador's stroke was futile and the bull remained triumphant. Some at any rate of their failures must be ascribed to Spanish and French inferiority of techniques, when compared to British expertise. This was particularly true afloat. Twenty years after the end of the Great Siege, an English naval officer and historian wrote:

> A force of 30 sail of the line in the ports of the Peninsula, with six months' provisions and 5,000 troops, would appear formidable in a French or English newspaper, but nowhere else. I have seen Spanish line-of-battle ships 24 hours unmooring; as many minutes are sufficient for a well-manned British ship to perform the same operation. When, on any grand ceremony, they found it necessary to cross their top-gallant yards in harbour, they began the day before; we cross ours in *one* minute from the deck.

The same man, Captain E. P. Brenton, R.N., an arrogant but truthful commentator on naval affairs, declared briefly: 'as enemies, the Spaniards have rarely deserved our notice'. Both ashore and at sea, the Spanish proved themselves brave and hardy; but also slow and ineffective in action. They never seemed able to concentrate all their energies at any one time or place. They were slow in planning, lethargic in execution, easily bewildered by the unexpected, apparently always convinced that time was on their side and for them to spend, baffled by the steadiness shown by the garrison and apparently unable to believe that men in the situation of the British would or could keep up the struggle.

Seen against the background of the war as a whole, the successful defence of Gibraltar is of considerable importance. The great efforts made, at moments of immense risk, to save the Rock almost certainly had little influence on the outcome of the American War. This, when not clearly won in the first couple of years of open fighting, was as good as lost. Saratoga and Yorktown on the face of it were small incidents; it was in their setting that surrenders of a few thousand men in two unimportant places became decisive. The loss of Gibraltar at any time after 1780 would have become a symbol and a proof of disaster and shame. The keeping of it was glorious. It made 'the steadiness of Gibraltar' one of the most meaningful phrases in the English language.

# 11

---

## *The Peace and its Aftermath*

It was all over. But a great deal remained to be done at Gibraltar. In the first place, there were ceremonial occasions and rejoicings. Secondly, there was the general restoration of order and of peace-time procedure. Thirdly, the observation of terms of peace; and, inevitably, the disbandment or regrouping of the garrison.

Ceremony took precedence, as was inevitable in the eighteenth century, when the due performance of expected courtesies occupied a startlingly high proportion of men's thought and time. The very day on which the port of Gibraltar was declared open and the last accidental shot fired was marked by a review of the Highland Regiment in full dress. Then the Corsicans were put on parade; and when the 97th, still sickly and always laggard and little regarded by their comrades, proved unready to be reviewed, they were put off duty to prepare themselves, and scoffingly termed 'the second battalion of the Corsicans'. Almost daily flags of truce and parleys passed between Crillon and Eliott, who did not receive official confirmation from London that the war was over until the frigate *Thetis* arrived on 10 March, bearing not only despatches but Captain Curtis; he had been knighted for his services in the siege, particularly for his conduct during the repulse of the battering-ships. This was followed by a personal meeting between the two commanders. Eliott and Crillon met on the beach, about half-way between the palisades at Bayside and the Spanish works, now rapidly being disarmed. Dismounting, they embraced and remained in conversation for some time. Crillon later sent Eliott a present of a grey Andalusian horse. The Governor, accompanied by General Green, who must have been keenly interested in all he saw, was then taken on a conducted tour of the Spanish trenches and batteries, as well as of the Spanish cave and mine near the Devil's Tower; they dined together at San Roque. On 31 March the Duke returned the visit, arriving with a large suite; he was greeted by a salute of 17 guns from the Grand Battery and cheered through the streets by the British soldiers. The officers of the garrison were introduced to the Duke. He toured the British batteries on the North Face, being greatly astonished at Ince's subterranean galleries; and after dinner at the Convent with Eliott and his generals and brigadiers Crillon rode on to Europa through the various camps, where each regiment turned out without arms and saluted him with three cheers, which gave the visitor great pleasure. In the dusk he returned back home. It was unfortunate that the flash of the 17-gun salute on departure so startled his horse that the Duke was thrown; but no harm was done. Crillon, besides paying many compliments to the Governor and garrison, was impressed by the youthful and well-turned-out appearance of the British troops. A few days later the Duke left his army for Madrid; his successor, the Marquis de Saya, was a very aged officer who had served against Gibraltar in the siege of 1727.

Both Houses of Parliament formally passed votes of thanks to Eliott for his defence of Gibraltar. He was also rewarded with a pension of £1,500 a year and the King conferred upon him the Order of the Bath. Sir Roger Curtis had brought instructions that the Deputy Governor, Lieutenant-General Boyd, should act as his Majesty's representative and invest Eliott with the insignia of the order. Whereupon the engineers constructed a colonnade on the ramparts of the King's Bastion and a grand celebration was prepared.

The formal news of his honours reached Eliott early in March, whereupon he replied to Townshend in words surprising in a man of such level head. After declaring his gratitude and the fact that as a soldier he had only done his duty, he said: 'My sovereign's approbation —that, Sir, Oh, that, Sir, is all the world to me'.

On St George's day, 23 April 1783, this ceremony was held. At 8 o'clock in the morning detachments from each corps, with all officers not on duty, assembled in three lines on the Red Sands. Eliott read them the official letters of thanks and added his own. A general salute was given, the artillery fired a 21-gun salute and the troops a grand feu-de-joie, and after three cheers the parade moved off. A grand procession followed through the ruined streets of the town, with bands and music. The colonnade, a handsome and colourful structure decorated with flags and crowned with regimental colours, had been made from masts and yards salvaged from the sunken battering-ships. The ceremony was short and impressive, and when Boyd had placed the red ribband of this ancient order over the Governor's shoulder, the combined bands of the garrison struck up with 'God Save the King', the grenadiers fired a volley and a grand discharge of 160 cannon on the seaward lines took place. Non-commissioned officers and men continued the celebrations with a pound each of fresh beef (a very special treat) and a quart of wine. Eliott, his senior officers, their personal staffs and all the field officers sat down to a splendid feast at the Convent. At dusk, different coloured lamps were lit in the colonnade and all turned out to watch a firework display from the bastions. Spilsbury, as a captain, bitterly commented that only the junior officers were neglected in these festivities. He recorded that the day was cloudy and disagreeable, with an easterly wind, and that storms of rain in the evening blew out the lamps and spoilt the fireworks. There was a certain amount of drunkenness and uproar. Spilsbury concluded his account by saying: 'never was a worse salute performed by the artillery . . . a worse feu de joye fired by troops, worse weather, worse musick, worse fire-works, or worse entertainment.' But at any rate, like the siege, the celebrations were finished.

Besides these festivities (during which the Governor said that Boyd behaved 'with the most obliging attention'), Eliott had many other matters to decide. There were problems about the disposal of the existing garrison. Now that peace was established, it was inevitable that many regiments were to be disbanded. The 72nd, 73rd, 97th and some of the Hanoverians were sent home. For the time being the 25th and 59th were to be in garrison. The Royal Artillery companies on the Rock were to be relieved by others from England and Newfoundland. The Corsicans were to be disbanded; they were now reinforced by a further group of 26 who had been driven ashore in South Barbary in May 1782 and were newly arrived from captivity. One great difficulty was that most British soldiers had been engaged on three-year agreements, so that even to keep the regiments at a peace-time strength of 400 rank-and-file might be difficult. Men in the corps due to depart were offered a bounty of one-and-a-half guineas in cash to volunteer to remain. Eliott thought that even in peace-time a garrison of 4,000 effectives should be the aim of government. Not only was much rebuilding needed; he had no confidence in Spanish good faith, believing that the King of Spain would think any means justified to recover Gibraltar. The Government agreed to Eliott's figure of 4,000 men, and promised to send the 11th and 32nd regiments, then in Ireland, to reinforce him. The bounty succeeded in attracting over 800 men, who re-enlisted, said Eliott, 'with as much frolic and mirth as at a country fair'. One might have thought that these soldiers would have seen enough of the Rock to last them a lifetime; but cash in hand was always a potent force in engaging recruits. As for the Corsicans, Eliott gave a guinea to each private soldier, one-and-a-half guineas to corporals and drummers, two guineas to sergeants and to each officer a sum equal to six years' half-pay. Every Corsican also had carriage and food to any destination he chose. Eliott had other moneys to distribute. Payment was granted to all troops in the Gibraltar garrison for bat, baggage and forage, as in cases of regiments taking the field, for each year from 1779 onwards; these sums, usually about £550 each year for each regiment, were for officers' expenses, a kind of additional active service allowance. Prize-money amounts and rates also caused much correspondence: £16,000 was granted for the floating batteries, £14,000 for the *St Michael* (which had reached England safely and been added to the Royal Navy). Even Eliott's staff appointments, so long the subject of grudging comment from their original formation in June 1779, were approved; the total of this particular claim amounted to £2,465 10*s*. 0*d*. The settlement of this business was a great relief to Eliott, who excused his constant (and very necessary) reiteration of the case for payment by saying that he had 'always looked upon pecuniary considerations as too sordid for the mind of an officer in military command. It may be said that this is the language of affluence, but believe me, Sir, with this very same notion I first took up the profession of a soldier.' But claims for subordinates were fully justified. And in the event correspondence about these staff pay matters was still going on between Eliott and London well into 1785, when the money was still not paid to the Hanoverians and others.

Special pleas were made by Eliott on behalf of certain men: the surgeon of the 56th for instance, Thomas Chisholm, who had lost his right leg, had the other one broken and was still in great pain as late as November 1783; and for certain former soldiers, now retired on pensions of a shilling a day, who, 'worthy old men', were 'in certain distress'. Eliott, pressing these cases for urgent consideration, asked that government might pardon 'the frankness of a soldier's pleading for the worn-out veteran'. In welcoming a letter asking him to recommend 20 sergeants as out-pensioners of Chelsea Hospital, at a shilling a day extra bounty, he said, 'no men could be more worthy such provision from their country'. This particular despatch, sent from London on 18 July, had been detained in the Spanish Post Office, and was not received at Gibraltar until the end of October 1783. Such incidents, allied with arrests of Gibraltarian fishermen, confirmed Eliott's distrust of Spanish goodwill. It was also shown in his repeated statements that they were not pulling down their batteries and fortifications as agreed. Spilsbury and other officers had commented on the solidity of their magazines and guard-houses and their strongly built platforms and traverses. In the end the Government gave Eliott permission to go out and complete the levelling of the abandoned Spanish works himself, if wind and weather had made such action necessary.

By October 1783 the 12th, 39th, 56th and 58th were embarking for England; the others had gone. The 72nd, back in Manchester, were feasted on roast beef and plum pudding ('and a quart of strong beer') and held their last parade on 7 September 1783, when their colours were laid up in the Old Church.

The second battalion of the 73rd, less those who had re-enlisted on the Rock, sailed for home in May 1783, landed at Portsmouth and spent some time there in barracks before marching off towards Scotland in August. There they were disbanded at Stirling on 3 October; the men went off to their homes, after five adventurous years of military service; those officers who were senior in their rank to those of the first battalion in India were given the option of joining them there at their own expense. All accepted, including the lieutenant-colonel. The regiment, later renumbered the 71st Foot, known as the Highland Light Infantry, gathered a formidable list of well-known and well-deserved honours; among these was proudly carried that of 'Gibraltar, 1780–1783', inherited from the 2/73rd.

The 97th Foot disappeared without trace. Other regiments bearing the same number had no connection with this unit, whose 167 casualties formed an appreciable proportion of the total of 1,231 sustained by the whole garrison. One of its few surviving relics is a colour found in 1963 still preserved in the family of the first colonel; it was transferred from New Zealand, where it was discovered, to a regimental museum in Kent, where in 1881 a later 97th Foot was merged into the Queen's Own Royal West Kent Regiment.

To Eliott, long in British service, the departure of his companions in danger can have caused neither surprise nor sorrow. It is not surprising, in the conditions of disbandment and breaking of contracts seemingly inevitable in the British army when once a crisis is over, that two of the Hanoverian regiments were kept on the Rock after the peace, although the original suggestion of government had been that all three should be rapidly withdrawn. But with these German troops there were no tiresome complications with an elected Parliament; they were mercenaries and professional soldiers in a sense unknown in Britain.

The Gibraltar regiments which went home kept the memory of their part in the great siege as a proud heritage. The 12th became the Suffolk Regiment, the 39th the Dorsets; the 56th developed into the second battalion of the Essex Regiment, the 58th the second Northampton-shires. Each regiment bore the Castle and Key of Gibraltar, with the motto of the Rock, '*Montis Insignia Calpe*', among its badges and distinctions. Only the two last comers, the 25th (later the King's Own Scottish Borderers) and the 59th (later the second battalion East Lancashire Regiment), who had played no part in the more extended or spectacular phases of the siege, and who escaped reduction, were awarded no sign of their presence; but both had sufficient honours of their own not to worry. Even in the great organisational upheavals of the 1960s, when the painful process of forcing an old and unbeaten collection of infantry regiments into a more modern pattern was under-taken, the Castle of Gibraltar kept its place on the regimental badge of the 'Royal Anglian Regiment'. This formation included the remnants of no fewer than eight formerly independent bodies, among them the inheritors of the traditions of the 12th, 56th and 58th Foot. Other noble and well-earned honours and badges disappeared. But not 'Gibraltar'. And there are men alive proud to have served in what is still called 'the Gibraltar Battery' of the Royal Artillery, descended from the men who served there in 1779–83.

This pride of soldiers in participation in the great siege is evidenced in many ways. The first list of battle honours authorised to be borne on the colours of infantry regiments was issued in April 1784; and 'Gibraltar' was henceforward to be seen on the second colours of the 12th, 39th, 56th and 58th regiments, underneath the regimental num-ber. The Hanoverian Corps also preserved the distinction. A company of the London Scottish, as late as September 1916, capturing German soldiers in the River Somme area, were astonished to find them wearing an armlet on which was the word 'Gibraltar'; they belonged to units of the Imperial German Army which traced their pedigree, by a somewhat imperfect route, back to the three regiments of de la Motte, Hardenberg (later Sydow) and Reden; their standards carried the words '*Mit Eliot zu Ruhm und Sieg*' ('With Eliott to Glory and Victory').

Besides these official honours, there was a great outpouring of pic-tures, engravings, plans and sketches, widely dispersed and sold and still to be found in considerable numbers. Besides large paintings, like that by John Trumbull of the sortie of November 1781, and that by G. Carter, of Eliott on the King's Bastion during the assault by the battering-ships, there were many cheaper unofficial ventures, published for quick profit. There were even medals; unofficial because few royal awards were made in the eighteenth century for military and naval achievement, and none for British participants in either the Seven Years

War or the War of American Independence. But there still exist many
collectors' pieces, some in silver, some in copper, of a type known as the
'Red-Hot Shot Medal'; they usually bear on one side the representation
of the *Pastora* battering-ship (often with a name engraved; and these
names are often of men known to have been present in Gibraltar in
September 1782) and on the other a drawing of a furnace and the
inscription; 'Spaniards defeated by Red Hot Shot at Gibraltar, Sept.
13th, 1782'. Almost certainly these were struck by an enterprising
armourer or jeweller in Gibraltar itself, for private sale to members of
the garrison. There were other similar souvenirs, engraved buckles, and
other objects manufactured from the metal of captured guns or significant timbers. Many families connected with the great siege still possess
treasured relics of this nature, and some proudly handed down even the
names of ancestors present during those critical and honourable years
on the Rock of Gibraltar.

After the cessation of hostilities, Eliott had time to turn to relations
with the Moorish states on the opposite shore. One case concerned
John Podesta, a Genoese, to whom Eliott had given a pass for trading
with Gibraltar in return for security of £500. This man's vessel had been
arrested and confiscated at Algiers; and Podesta and his crew had been
made slaves after the open breach in September 1780. The British
Consul, Mr Collett, had sent Eliott the news and asked him to let Lord
Hillsborough know. Podesta had lived in Gibraltar for 24 years; but
although Eliott had protested on many occasions the Moors refused to
free him. Violence had also been shown to British consuls and traders,
while some of the Corsicans driven ashore in North Africa by storms
had been chained like dogs. In March 1783 Sir Roger Curtis was sent to
Morocco to reopen friendly relations. Long and highly elaborate letters
had at various times during the siege and immediately afterwards been
received from the Moors, usually beginning with such phrases as 'To
our friend and beloved General Eliott . . .', 'My friend and sir, I kiss
your hands' . . ., 'Peace to the true and faithful' . . ., 'I am the Servant
of God and of my Master . . .,' but nothing had been done. On his part,
Eliott was very formal, ending his letters 'I have the honour to be with
the truest sentiments of esteem and regard, your Excellency . . .', and,
when Curtis sailed, he took with him a present of four fine brass guns
from the battering-ships, mounted and with shot and 100 barrels of
powder, 'knowing it impossible an Ambassador should have a favourable reception, who did not bring with him a present for his immediate
introduction'. Curtis also carried instructions received from Lord
North, whom the extraordinary complications of British parliamentary

intrigues had brought back into office, in April 1783, as Secretary of State, alongside his old antagonist, Charles James Fox, under the nominal direction of the Duke of Portland. These instructions were that the immediate release of all captive British subjects should be demanded. The Emperor of Morocco sent seven brass mortars back to Eliott in September 1783 when peace was officially declared, when a further gift of £500 worth of coarse linen, surplus to Gibraltar's requirements, was delivered to him.

Eliott's own release from Gibraltar did not take place until shortly after 21 May 1787, when he penned his last letter home. At the time of his return, despite all efforts, four wrecks off the harbour were still a danger to shipping. Shortly after arriving home, a further honour was somewhat tardily bestowed upon him, when on 14 June 1787 he was raised to the peerage as Lord Heathfield, baron of Gibraltar; Heathfield was the name of the charming house and estate in Sussex which he had bought with his share of the Havana prize money over 20 years earlier.

George Augustus Eliott died in his seventy-third year on 6 July 1790, at Aix-la-Chapelle, of palsy, two days before he had intended to start for Gibraltar. He was buried in Heathfield Church; the plate of his coffin was made from a gun recovered from one of the sunken battering-ships. One of the most lasting of his rewards was the magnificent portrait painted by Sir Joshua Reynolds; in his hand he holds the key of Gibraltar and behind him can be seen one of the depress guns invented during the siege.

Robert Boyd, second-in-command, 'the storekeeper general', died on 13 May 1794 in Gibraltar itself; he had succeeded Eliott as Governor there, and like his master had been made a Knight of the Bath. He was by his own directions buried in a tomb in the King's Bastion, the powerful work of which he had laid the first stone in 1773 and which he had personally seen completed; a tablet marks the spot. By sheer longevity (he was 84 years old when he died) he had attained the rank of General.

William Green the engineer and the two naval officers prominent in the siege also prospered. Green became a baronet and a general; Curtis and Knowles full admirals. To Rodney and Howe their reliefs of Gibraltar were items in a long succession of honourable achievements.

On the enemy's side, the French armies and navies moved off into the awaiting turmoil of the Revolution, where the old régime vanished. Perhaps the oddest fate awaited that casual and bored spectator of the Grand Assault, the Comte d'Artois, younger brother of the French

King. When he died in 1836 he had survived not only the Revolution
itself but the July uprising in Paris of 1830, which possessed as its chief
aim his own expulsion from the Throne of France, where he had
reigned for six years as Charles X, the ultra-royalist, the most reaction-
ary French king who ever lived.

Of the lesser figures of the siege, John Drinkwater is probably the
most important. A Lancashire lad, born in June 1762, he was only 15
years old when he became an ensign in the new 72nd Foot, the Royal
Manchester Volunteers; sent at once to Gibraltar, he kept a careful day-
to-day diary of events, became a captain and returned home to publish
in 1785 his account of the siege. It became a popular favourite at once,
going through four editions in as many years. In 1787 Drinkwater
rejoined the army, buying a captaincy in the second battalion of the 1st
Foot, then stationed at Gibraltar; there he was personally welcomed by
Eliott; and there in 1793 he founded the Garrison Library, a model of
its kind and still greatly flourishing as one of Gibraltar's British-type
societies and clubs. He served at Toulon and in Corsica; and, becoming
a friend of Horatio Nelson, was present at the Battle off Cape St
Vincent, being chosen to take home news of the victory. He retired as a
colonel and lived a happy and busy life in various military capacities
until his death at Leatherhead in Surrey in 1844, at the age of 81; he
was then said to be the last survivor of the great siege.

Of John Spilsbury, the author of another siege diary, little is known.
From 1777 until retirement in 1795 he served as a captain in the 12th
Foot; he died in 1838. His daily journal of the siege was begun in June
1779, and finishes with the embarkation of the regiment, very early on a
wet and windy morning in November 1783. This diary, quite untouched
and never formally prepared for publication, was given to the Gibraltar
Garrison Library in 1866 and published by that body in 1908. Brief,
often caustic comments on events and people, and careful and well-
drawn sketches of buildings, cannon, batteries and entrenchments,
with plans and diagrams, give much information and important contemporary evidence. Of the other diarists even less is known, but their
existence is further proof of the popularity and widespread interest in
the siege. Samuel Ancell's account, for instance, ran through two editions by 1785; he was a soldier (not a commissioned officer) in the 58th
Foot (then known as the Rutlandshire Regiment), served with it
throughout the siege, and described events in what purports to be a
series of letters to his brother. Ancell lived in Liverpool and it was in
that town that most of his subscribers dwelt. Other diarists were anonymous, and some of their books may well have been compiled merely

from hearsay or have been written up from others by authors anxious to profit from a popular market.

Sergeant-Major Henry Ince was another soldier content to live, like his commander, on the Rock he had helped to hold. He retired in 1791, after 30 years' service, but was continued on the works as an overseer. Later he was commissioned in the Royal Garrison Battalion. He lived in a farm at the top of the Rock, still called by his name, and became a notable figure in Gibraltar, on familiar terms with all his superiors, even with that distant and slightly repugnant figure, the Duke of Kent, when he was Governor. Ince finally returned home to Penzance and died there in June 1809, aged 72.

'Shot' (John Brand) and 'Shell' (Thomas Richmond), those lads of keenest eyesight, when the siege was over, continued in the soldier-artificer company, one as a mason, the other as a carpenter, until discharged in 1789 and appointed assistant draughtsman; they were then employed in making scale models (25 feet to an inch) in polished stone of the King's Bastion and the North Front of Gibraltar. In 1793 each was appointed a second lieutenant in the Royal Engineers. Unfortunately both died in the same year, almost immediately after being stationed in the fever-haunted West Indies. Their models were sent home and were for long on show at Woolwich Arsenal.

As for Gibraltar itself, the town took many years to recover from its devastation. The civilians sent away at the worst time came flocking back, when they could find a passage. Many of them, carried away to England, sent in scores of desperate petitions to the British Government asking for help; some wanted passages, others compensation for shops and houses, burnt or looted. When the town was rebuilt, at first the old site was neglected, for houses and streets were almost obliterated. But as peaceful years followed the long siege so the population of this well-placed port and depot grew and the houses crept back along the shore and up the lower slopes. Never again was it so closely menaced, though its value as a naval base and fortress was demonstrated over and over again. It was in Gibraltar Bay that the British warships badly shattered at Trafalgar sheltered to refit; it was in what is still known as the Trafalgar Cemetery that the dead were interred. Here, throughout the nineteenth century, the subterranean galleries first driven by Ince were enlarged until whole regiments and very large numbers of guns were impregnably sheltered.

Eliott would still recognise much about the place, the vast rocky heights, seemingly sheer over the town huddled beneath the long, high skyline, shimmering in the hot weather, or wrapped in clammy mists when the levanter blows. The Convent is still His Excellency the Governor's residence; the pieces of furniture made from the battering-ships' timbers are still there. Important visitors land at the steps of the Ragged Staff, and welcoming salutes are fired from the King's Bastion. 'Gunfire' occurs every morning and evening and the ceremony of the Keys of Gibraltar is maintained.

Over a thousand miles from the nearest point of the United Kingdom, Gibraltar regards itself very much as an integral part of Great Britain.

# Principal Sources

*A. Manuscript Sources*

The following volumes in the Public Record Office contain documents, dispatches, letters, returns, drawings and plans of value:

W.O.1/286 (Gibraltar, 1755–1787); W.O.4/317; W.O.26/32; W.O.34/133; C.O. 91/25—1779; C.O. 91/26—1780 (Jan.–Nov.); C.O. 91/27—1780 (Dec.–1781); C.O. 91/28—1782 (Jan.–July); C.O. 91/29—1782 (July–Dec.); C.O. 91/30—1783 (Jan.–Nov.); H.O. 50/379

Naval affairs are found in various 'Admiralty' classes, of which the following logs are of special interest:

ADM/51/840, Captain's Log of H.M.S. *Sandwich* (1780)
ADM/51/139, Captain's Log of H.M.S. *Britannia* (1780–1781)
ADM/51/1036, Captain's Log of H.M.S. *Victory* (1782)

The War Office Library also contains certain manuscripts dealing with Gibraltar.

*B. Main Contemporary Printed Sources*

S. Ancell (of 58th Regiment), *A Circumstantial Journal of the long and tedious blockade and Siege of Gibraltar, from the twelfth of September, 1779 to the third day of February, 1783* (2nd ed., Liverpool, 1785): 'containing an authentic account of the most remarkable transactions, in which the enemy's motions, works, approaches, firings etc., are particularly described'

John Drinkwater (captain of the Royal Manchester Volunteers), *A History of the Late Siege of Gibraltar, with a description and account of the Garrison from the earliest periods* (London, 1785)

Mrs Green (wife of the Chief Engineer of Gibraltar), *A Lady's Experiences in the Great Siege of Gibraltar, 1779–1783* (From *The Royal Engineers Journal*, 1912)

Captain Spilsbury (of 12th Regiment), *A Journal of the Siege of Gibraltar, 1779–1783* (edit. H. T. Frere, Gibraltar, 1908)

*C. Other Printed Sources*

Allen Andrews, *Proud Fortress; the fighting story of Gibraltar* (London, 1958)

*Authentic and Accurate Journal of the Late Siege of Gibraltar* (London), being a circumstantial account of every material transaction relative to that memorable event, from the day on which the communication between that Garrison and Spain was shut up, to the arrival of the Thetis frigate with the preliminary articles of peace

W. Laird Clowes, *The Royal Navy: a History*, vols. 3 and 4 (London, 1898–9)

S. Conn, *Gibraltar in British Diplomacy in the Eighteenth Century* (Yale, 1942)

*Conseil de Guerre Privé* sur l'événement de Gibraltar en 1782 pour servir d'exercice sur l'art des sièges (1785)

Major-General J. C. Dalton, *The Rock and the Royal Artillery* (from *The Journal of the Royal Artillery*, 1924–5)

*A Description of Gibraltar* (1782)

J. W. Fortescue, *History of the British Army*, Vol. III (London, 1911)

G. T. Garratt, *Gibraltar and the Mediterranean* (London, 1939)

*Histoire du Siège de Gibraltar* (possibly by Michaud d'Arcon or Des Landes du Houdan) (1783)

H. W. Howes, *The Gibraltarian: the origin and development of the population of Gibraltar from 1704* (1951)

*Journal of the Society for Army Historical Research* (*passim*, especially Vols. 3 and 15, London, 1924 and 1936)

T. H. McGuffie, 'The Royal Manchester Volunteers', in *The Manchester Review* (Summer, 1955)

P. Mackesy, *The War for America, 1775–1783* (London, 1964)

G. J. Marcus, *A Naval History of England*, Vol. 1: 'The Formative Centuries' (London, 1961)

*Mémoire pour servir à l'histoire du siège de Gibraltar* (Cadiz, 1783)

Lieutenant-Colonel L. B. Oatts, *Proud Heritage: the story of the Highland Light Infantry*, Vol. 1 (London, 1952)

José Plá, *Gibraltar* (English ed., London, 1955)

Regimental Histories: various volumes of Richard Cannon's *Historical Records* of British regiments

Captain J. Sayer, *The History of Gibraltar: and of its political relation to the events in Europe; from the commencement of the Moorish Dynasty in Spain to the last Morocco War* (London, 1862)

Various Directories and Guide Books to Gibraltar, and information obtained from the Commonwealth Institute

J. S. Watson, *The Reign of George III, 1760–1815* (Oxford, 1960)

# Index

The numerals in **heavy type** refer to the *figure number* of the illustrations